Is That a Fact?

TEACHING NONFICTION
WRITING K-3

Tony Stead

Foreword by Tomie dePaola

Stenhouse Publishers
Portland, Maine

Stenhouse Publishers
www.stenhouse.com

Credits
Page 5: *Chickens* by Diane Snowball. Copyright © 1995. Reprinted by permission of Mondo Publishing.
Pages 41, 55: *Meet the Octopus* by Sylvia M. James. Copyright © 1996. Reprinted by permission of Mondo Publishing.
Page 53: *Spiders* by Esther Cullen. Copyright © 1996. Reprinted by permission of Mondo Publishing.
Page 56: *From Egg to Butterfly* by David Drew. Copyright © 1997. Reprinted by permission of David Drew.

Library of Congress Cataloging-in-Publication Data
Stead, Tony.
      Is that a fact? : teaching nonfiction writing K–3 / Tony Stead.
      p. cm.
      Includes bibliographical references.
      ISBN 1-57110-331-7
      1. English language—Composition and exercises—Study and teaching (Elementary) 2. Exposition (Rhetoric) I. Title.
LB1576.S786 2001
372.62'3044—dc21   2001042045

Cover design by Judith Arisman
Cover and interior photographs by Tony Stead

Manufactured in the United States of America on acid-free paper
06 05 04   9 8 7 6 5

To my wife, Jennifer, and my son, Fraser,
my guiding lights and continuing inspiration

Contents

Foreword

To borrow from the sentiment of a popular cliché, if Tony Stead didn't exist, we'd have to invent him, that is if we care about children and the importance that reading and writing will play in their lives as they become adolescents, young adults, mature persons, and then seniors.

Tony knows in his heart—and that's the key word here, heart—that the future of the planet is in enriching the lives of the youngest members of our "spaceship Earth."

The heart has long ago become the symbol of love and caring and this is Tony. Oh, he obviously has theories, statistics, professional skills, and so on, under his belt. But all you have to do is experience one of Tony's presentations to teachers, and you witness the love he has pouring out of him for the excitement of teaching young people about the thrills of reading and (again) writing. After all, we are all natural storytellers (or "liars" as some would say about tellers of tall tales), but when we are faced with the task of writing it all down, that's where, if we can manage it, the thrill comes in. I can "talk" a new book through with my editor, using voice inflection, gestures, and even a song and tap dance or two, but when the reality of writing it all down faces me, that's when the wheat and chaff are separated.

But enough of this. The book you are about to read is destined to be the first, middle, and maybe even the last word on nonfiction writing for young, young children. It is certainly a book that you will return to over and over again as you do with a beloved cookbook. Tony gives you "recipes" on how you can feed and nourish those young hearts and souls in your care, whether you are a teacher, a parent or caregiver, or just a person who looks at a young child and sees the world "about to be."

I'm glad Tony has put his "storytelling" onto the written page. After all, his genius has to be made available to a wider audience than those sitting in one of his presentations (although if you get a chance to see "Tony Live in Concert," don't miss him), and writing things down forces a writer to clarify all his or her thoughts.

Nonfiction. Why don't we just call it Life? And who ever said that five- and six-year-olds don't experience life? As Tony quotes Donald Graves, "the notion that someone can write about an idea and thereby affect the lives and thinking of others . . ." is the key here.

If you just *tell* a story, only your audience hears it at that moment. Writing it down is the sharing that can take the story to a different level. Now add nonfiction to this and the expansion that happens with children is truly miraculous. That's why this book is so important.

Just read and listen to Tony. He will guide you so gently and so convincingly to realize the importance of nonfiction writing for very young children.

I'm not asking you to believe me. I'm only asking you to experience this remarkable book. Then you'll be hard put not to believe what Tony Stead has to offer you.

A teacher said to me, "But I want to ask you . . ." I interrupted and said, "Don't ask me. Ask Tony!" Tony will tell you!

Tomie dePaola

Acknowledgments

No author writes alone. We all simply add to the wealth of thoughts and words of those before us. Indeed, it is a fact that writing this book was not a solo pursuit; although I recorded the ideas, it was the wisdom and support of many that made this book possible. I thank all these people, and specifically I would like to acknowledge the following.

Thanks to the wonderful Philippa Stratton and Brenda Power for their continued advice, and to Philippa for always picking up the phone even when she knew I was the one on the other end with yet another "I need help" plea. With the British, American, and Australian perspectives, we now have a book that would please the United Nations. Thanks also to Tom Seavey and Martha Drury of Stenhouse and to Donna Bouvier.

Many thanks to the principal Sal Romano and the amazing staff at P.S. 148 in District 30, New York, especially to the teachers I worked with over the past four years: Philamina Agostini, Judy Ballister, Pam Crawley, Linda La Porte, Jessica Mazzocco, Jeanine McCarthy, Maryanne Meza, Susan Mustac, Pat Nevins, and Sonia Radovich. You opened up your classrooms and minds to a world of possibilities, and we have all grown through the experience. Thanks also to the principal Robert Weinstein, staff developer Isobel Marcus, and the staff of P.S. 8 in District 10, New York, valued colleagues all.

Everyone has mentors, and a number of people have had a huge impact on my thinking and learning. First I would like to acknowledge my mother, Patricia. Thinking back to those early years when you were both mother and father, when you worked three jobs to put me through college and yet still had time always to smile, I know I am where I am because of you. Thanks to the incredible Marilyn Woolley, who first showed me the power and gratification that teaching can bring, and the importance of not building ivory towers but continually working with and learning from children, who are our most important teachers. Many thanks to Cheryl Semple, who walked into my classroom in 1985 and literally changed my life. You have been a constant friend, encourager, and mentor. I would also like to acknowledge Donald Graves, who although not a personal friend has been my most influential mentor when it comes to the writing process. His work continues to inspire me. The work of Brian Cambourne has also had a huge impact on my thinking and learning. Brian, when I had the opportunity to present with you ten years ago it was the highlight of my career. You are one of the masters.

I would also like to thank a number of special people in my life. To my dear friend Diane Snowball, who has continued to give me encouragement and support. My new life in the United States started because of your belief in my ability. To Mimi Aronson, who taught me "Jewish" as a second language and has become a loved member of my new American family. To my good friend Tomie dePaola, who not only inspires me through his beautiful books but also encourages me to strive onward and always put my best foot forward. We are honored that you are our son Fraser's godfather. To Bob Hechtel from White Bird, who like Tomie takes an active interest in my accomplishments and encourages me to put words into print. To Sara Scungio, who is such an important part our lives and a valued friend. To Mark Vineis, who has been a tower of support over the past five years. I thank Mark especially for many marathon discussions at airports and on planes across the United States. To Anne Hammond, for her support and keeping us connected with life and the thinking "down under." To Charlotte Montgomery, who has opened her home and her wealth of knowledge to me and my family. To Paul Molyneux, brother, friend, confidant, and mentor. You are such an important part of my journey through life.

I thank my ever-growing Mondo family, who make feel a valued member of their clan. You are all simply fantastic. Also to the wonderful team at Scholastic Canada, who treat me like a king each time I visit their beautiful country. I thank Sharon Taberski, who is not only one of the best teachers in the United States, but also a valued friend. I would also like to acknowledge Richard Gentry, Joetta Beaver, and Maureen Morriss for their valued advice. Peggy Sherman and William Hagood are two people I am indebted to for almost forcing me to put pen to paper. William, when you made me commit to writing this book in front of an audience in Alabama I could have killed you. It is only now, after sleepless nights and hours in front of a computer screen, with the book completed, that I have decided to thank you.

Thanks to the thousands of teachers who have attended my workshops over the past five years. Their questions helped me define and redefine my thinking about teaching children how to write nonfiction. Thanks also to all my Australian colleagues and friends, whom I miss dearly and am constantly thinking about. As I wrote this book you were always with me.

Finally I would like to thank the two most important people in my life. My six-year-old son, Fraser, constantly invites me to view life through the eyes of the child, a view that is full of imagination, creativity, wonder, and awe, where anything and everything is possible. And finally my wife, Jennifer. They say "Behind every good man there is a woman." You have shown that this saying is flawed. It should be "Next to every good man" and, at times, "In front of." Thank you for being my soul mate and for making this book possible.

PART 1

TEACHING NONFICTION WRITING

Opening Doors to a World of Possibilities

It is 3 P.M. and I am picking up my son, Fraser, from school. This is a rare occurrence for me. Normally I am away, my job as a consultant taking me to schools in parts of the United States I never knew existed. Waiting for Fraser, I am ready to ask him the usual question, "So what did you do at school today?" and expect the usual reply, "Nothing," even though I know his day has been packed full of exciting adventures that I will eventually hear about later that evening. Today, however, is different. Before I even have the opportunity to greet him, Fraser runs up to me with an enthusiasm akin to a child's first visit to Disneyland. "Papa," he shouts, "We're doing nonfiction writing, and I'm doing dogs, and Sharon lets me. I have to go and get some books and find out about them. I love dogs. Can you believe it? Dogs. My favorite!"

This kind of excitement over nonfiction research and writing around a topic of high interest I have seen many times before, with children in my own classroom. Fraser's teacher, Sharon Taberski, like many other teachers has opened up a whole new world of possibilities in the writing classroom. The children's excitement is infectious and stays with them long after a unit is completed. Fraser's friend Alexander, who was also fortunate enough to have had Sharon as his teacher the year before, still talks about his nonfiction report on cats and continues to compose nonfiction pieces at home. What is so refreshing is that these boys are in grades 1 and 2. We are talking about five- and six-year-olds who have already discovered the magic of nonfiction writing. Moreover, enthusiasm for nonfiction writing is not limited to boys (a common myth among many educators). In my many years of working with young children I have found girls become equally engaged in nonfiction writing when the subject matter is of interest to them personally. I believe that too often when we explore nonfiction writing in the early years, it usually focuses on topics such as frogs, spiders, bugs, and other creepy-crawlys that do little to turn girls on to nonfiction writing.

Tapping into the enthusiasm that writing nonfiction inspires in both girls and boys is something that I believe we educators do not do enough, especially in the early years of schooling. I am reminded of an observation made by Donald Graves back in 1994. He wrote, "Unfortunately, little nonfiction, beyond personal narrative, is practiced in classrooms. Children are content to tell their own stories, but the notion that someone can write about an idea and thereby affect the lives and thinking of others is rarely discussed" (1994, p. 306).

Like Graves, I believe many teachers even today have not opened their doors to the possibilities beyond narrative when it comes to their writing programs. I know that for many years in my own classroom, my writing program revolved around the world of narrative and, in particular, fantasy. I would give my students many demonstrations of how to make their writing better. These demonstrations usually consisted of showing them how to plan, compose, edit, and proofread their writing, as well as how to publish their work and how to improve their spelling and grammar.

My students were engaged in their daily writing rituals and produced some wonderful pieces. They loved writing each day and were eager to publish their pieces so they could get their hands on all the wonderful markers and glitter that were strictly reserved for publishing. They became masters in the art of process and at times didn't even appear to need me to assist them with their pieces. I had taught them well how to get help from my daily demonstrations, from charts in the classroom, or by conferring with a peer. They eagerly shared their pieces with each other and their parents and looked forward to writer's workshop each day. Many even chose to write during free activity time, something unheard of in my beginning years of teaching.

Writer's workshop had become the epicenter of my classroom, and visitors started arriving to look, learn, praise, and question. At times my children thought themselves celebrities and would eagerly and easily talk with visiting educators. I remember one year when Georgia, one of my first graders, told visitors from the University of New Hampshire who had traveled to Australia to see classrooms in action, "If you want to know how our writing program works, don't ask Tony, ask me or Renee because we know best." Our American visitors were stunned by the children's confidence and aptitude for learning. I was so proud of my children and of my own efforts in creating an environment that stimulated, supported, and engaged my children as writers.

However, something was missing. There was too little variety in what my students chose to write about. Typically my kindergartners would write, "I love my mom" every day or would tell what had happened at home last night—"I played with my toys." "I went to a party." The entries by my first and second graders varied little from those of the kindergartners. They usually concerned home or school experiences. Although it was only natural that the children's voices be governed by what was happening to them in their day-to-day lives, I knew that nonfiction should have been a key element of their writing experience, and sadly it was not. What I needed to do as their teacher was tap my students' experiences and create new ones so that they could discover different purposes and formats for writing.

I began by reading nonfiction material to my children as part of my daily read-aloud and shared reading routines. One book I read was *Chickens* by Diane Snowball (Figure 1.1). Before reading the book, I asked the children to

■ **Figure 1.1** Cover of *Chickens* (Snowball 1995)

look at the cover and make predictions about the book's content. They thought that the little chicken on the right was going to run away from home and all his friends were talking about how to stop him from doing so. It quickly became evident to me from such comments that they expected this book to be a story. After all, what I usually read to them was fiction.

I opened the cover and read them the first page: "This is a rooster." Then I asked them if they thought their prediction about the book's content was correct. "Yes," they answered in unison. "That's the father chicken," remarked Carlo, "and he is the one who told the baby chicken off and that's why the baby chicken is running away." I accepted this and moved on to the next page: "This is a hen." "That's the mother chicken and she told the baby chicken off too because he wouldn't eat his dinner!" exclaimed Renee. It was obvious from these comments that my children were going to hang on to their prediction about a runaway chicken for as long as they could. However, the next page— "Roosters and hens mate to have chickens"—threw all their predictions to the wind (and me with it as well: I had a lot of careful explaining to do regarding that page; but that's another story).

After the reading, we talked about how this text was a different kind of book because it told us true things about chickens. We discussed how authors write these types of books to tell people facts about certain animals. I also alerted them to the labels in the book, and we discussed the way writers of nonfiction often use tags to assist their readers. One week later one of my second-grade students, Laura, proudly produced a story she had been working on. Laura was an avid writer. We were only four months into the school year and she had already produced five stories, all of which revolved around her being a princess and her many adventures. I don't know how many times she'd been rescued by a prince in her many stories. I really thought this could be the next Danielle Steele or Barbara Cartland sitting in front of me. But Laura's new piece was different. I was both surprised and delighted when I read it. This piece was nonfiction and, like Diane Snowball's book, it centered around the topic of chickens.

Clearly the reading of *Chickens* and our subsequent discussions had inspired Laura to write her own piece of nonfiction. In fact, on her fourth page she used labels for her illustrations, just as the author of *Chickens* had (see Figure 1.2). Laura informed me, "Diane Snowball has good information about chickens; but Tony, I know more than she does." I told her I would pass this information on to Diane the next time I saw her.

Laura had discovered a new purpose for writing: to report facts about animals. She used some of the traditional ways authors relay their information, including diagrams, labels, and arrows to describe the cycle of chickens' losing and growing new feathers. Laura was very excited about her latest piece of writing and informed me that she wanted to write more about all the other animals she had information about.

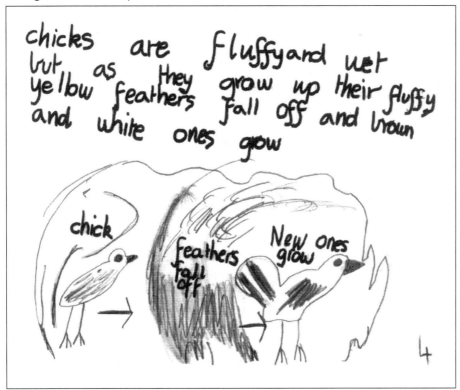

I realized then that for too long I had kept my students in a world of personal narrative and fantasy by providing demonstrations of these writing forms almost exclusively. When I looked through my classroom library I found that 90 percent of the books were fiction stories. My read-alouds and shared readings were limited to the world of make-believe or personal narrative. No wonder my children wrote the same things every day and had become masters of these few forms. While I still believed that fiction and personal narrative were important, I realized they were only part of the bigger picture.

Defining Nonfiction Writing: A Bigger Picture

I believe that when teachers—myself included—have introduced children to nonfiction writing we have used the word *nonfiction* far too restrictively. We have thought that by teaching children how to write signs, recipes, and rules for a game we were teaching them how to write nonfiction, when what we were really doing was teaching them specific forms of instructional text. Signs, game rules, and recipes, while all important forms of nonfiction, only tell the reader how to follow a set procedure.

This notion of defining nonfiction too restrictively includes report writing—in particular, animal reports, a favorite of thousands of teachers around the country. Countless times I have heard teachers tell me that they always do a unit on nonfiction writing each year by having their students write scientific reports on animals. It is true that these teachers are studying nonfiction with their children, but this type of report is only one way to describe or relate facts about something; and while it is important, it is still only a fraction of what nonfiction texts are all about.

Attempting to list the different purposes of nonfiction is not an easy task. As Lucy Calkins so clearly states, "There is no magical list" (1994, p. 364). There are, however, a number of key purposes for writing nonfiction that we need to be aware of and certainly need to introduce to children in the primary grades. Instructing and persuading are powerful purposes for writing, and children should be introduced to these types of writing in their primary years. Table 1.1 lists some of the key purposes for writing nonfiction with the corresponding forms. While this is certainly not a "magical list," it does highlight some of the different purposes for writing nonfiction. As can be seen in Table 1.1, nonfiction writing involves far more than just report writing about animals. The table includes texts for persuasion, explanation, retelling, and instruction.

As shown in Table 1.1, several writing forms, such as letters, are used for many purposes. Yet too often we simply teach children only a single purpose for a given form. When I first read Graves's book on nonfiction (1989) I was amazed at his examples of how letters can be written for so many purposes. Letters are a quintessential form of nonfiction writing, which should be explored in the beginning years of schooling. Reports are another example of a form of nonfiction writing that can be written for many different purposes. A science report, for example, is usually written to describe and explain, whereas a book report is often composed to retell and persuade.

When composing nonfiction, writers often have more than one purpose in a given text. For example, while a piece like Laura's about chickens may describe their physical appearance and habitat, it may also instruct the reader on how to care for chickens and perhaps also explain how they are able to fly. What young writers always need to be aware of is who their audience is and what information they are trying to convey. Keeping these things in mind will enable them to make wise decisions about what information they should include and help them avoid simply writing down everything that comes to mind.

Behold the Power of Nonfiction

From a look at Table 1.1 it becomes clear that fictional narrative alone will not be enough to help us through life's journey. Recently I was talking with Joyce,

■ **Table 1.1** Purpose and Types of Nonfiction Writing (based on Martin 1985)

Purpose	Common Forms Relevant to Elementary Schoolchildren	
To describe	Personal descriptions (wanted posters, missing posters, etc.) Poetry Scientific reports about animals, plants, and machines	Reports about countries Definitions Letters Illustrations Captions Labels
To explain	Scientific explanations of how and why a phenomenon occurs Personal narratives that explain how and why something happens	Elaborations Reports Letters Illustrations Captions Labels
To instruct	Recipes Rules Directions Experiments Games Lists	Maps Letters Illustrations Captions Labels
To persuade	Debates Reviews Advertisements Evaluations Book reports	Letters Posters Poetry Cartoons Illustrations
To retell information about a person or past event (nonfiction narrative)	Reports Autobiographies/ biographies Letters	Poetry Journals Scripts Historical retellings
To explore and maintain relationships with others	Cards Letters Questionnaires	Interviews Poetry

the math staff developer at one of the schools where I work in the Bronx. The fifth-grade students had just taken a citywide math exam. When I asked Joyce how it went, she replied that the children would do well if they knew how to follow instructions. She reported that the math itself was not too complex, but she feared that many of the students found the instructions difficult to understand. Clearly these children would be disempowered if they lacked the knowledge of how instructional texts work.

The language demands on all of us are escalating as we begin this new century. As technology increases, our ability to understand and use a wide range of different text types also must increase. Without this ability we become powerless to attain our immediate goals and future needs.

This point was clearly demonstrated to me when my wife and I inquired about green cards. We wanted to find out how we might continue to live and work in the United States. We were told that one possibility was to enter a lottery whereby a certain number of green cards were issued to nonresidents each year. When we inquired further, we found out that over one million people apply for green cards each year, but over half of the applicants are automatically disqualified because they fail to complete the application form correctly. I wonder how many people complete their tax returns correctly or know the appropriate method for writing a letter of complaint to a company or firm in order to get adequate compensation for faulty goods or services. "Read the fine print" is a common saying. I wonder how many people don't understand what the fine print is telling them.

Some time ago I recorded all the types of reading, writing, listening, and speaking I was engaged in over the course of a day as an adult. I did the same for my five-year-old son, Fraser. I wanted to see just how important it was for both of us to engage in language forms apart from narrative and fiction.

I was surprised to find that over 80 percent of my engagements with language fell outside of narrative. During the day I became constantly aware of how many times I had to follow instructions in order to survive. Just getting to work required me to interpret over a hundred signs or other forms of instruction. Within the classroom where I was consulting that day, I needed to provide countless demonstrations and explanations dealing with everything from where the bathrooms were for a new child entering the classroom to how to tie shoelaces. I filled in forms, completed an assessment report, wrote letters, notes, and messages for purposes of explanation, instruction, and persuasion, and got home only to find a leaky dishwasher, which required another barrage of explanations and instructions to workmen over the telephone. Even as I watched television that night I was surprised to find that my viewing consisted mainly of nonfiction programs. The news, biographies, and quiz shows exposed me to the world of persuasion, explanation, description, and instruction. I finally got to the narrative form when I tucked into bed and read part of a mystery novel before falling asleep.

What was more surprising was my son's engagements with language when I observed him one Saturday. Almost 90 percent of his world was nonfiction. From trying to figure out how to win the game on his Game Boy to instructing me on which clothes he needed to wear and why it was so important for him to wear his Pokémon sweater even though the temperature had just hit 90 degrees. His questions were constant: How? When? Where? and of course the one that haunts us all as teachers and parents—Why? Why? Why? It became evident to me that this little boy, like millions of other children, wanted to know how this big, wide, wonderful world works and what he could get out of it. He was also eager to teach me what he had already learned and was adamant that the rules for a particular game were as he told me, not as I tried to instruct him, because he had played this once before and what would I know about it anyway, even if I did have the rules in hand. He certainly had the oral language to explain, instruct, and persuade; what he needed was the ability to translate this knowledge into written form.

When I think about my years as a teacher, although fairy tales and fantasy always engaged my students, it was when rain or snow was pelting down on the classroom windowpanes or a bug happened to walk across one of the children's tables that excitement and engagement were at their peak. I think of Sylvia Ashton Warner's timeless classic *Teacher* (1963) and Albert Cullum's *The Geranium on the Window Sill Just Died, but Teacher You Went Right On* (1971). These books remind us to seize the moment and harness children's natural curiosity about themselves and their world to classroom instruction. What we need to do as teachers is tap this excitement, seize upon it, and help children discover that when they write they can do far more than simply record what they did last night. They can write for the purpose of instruction in the form of rules of a game to let novices such as myself learn how to play. They can write for the purpose of scientific explanation, to let readers know why it snows, or simply to describe chickens and dogs, or in Dorothy's words from the Wizard of Oz "lions and tigers and bears."

What we as teachers must do is help children discover what the types of nonfiction writing look like and the structures and features that competent writers use when writing for specific purposes. Children write personal narratives and stories not because this is the limit of their experiences but because they don't know how to write outside of these forms. Their writing demonstrations, expectations, and engagements are limited by us, their teachers. Yet in considering the writing process in general (Figure 1.3), nonfiction writing clearly has an important place.

Children need to be introduced to the different purposes of writing. They need to know how to plan, compose, revise, and publish text types apart from narrative. We teachers are not unlike our students when it comes to an overemphasis on narrative. We, like they, feel comfortable with the structure and associated language forms of story. Our own limited knowledge of different writing genres and how they work has made us poor models and guides for our children. We need to do more of what Sharon Taberski has done for Fraser and the other children in his class: open the door to a wide world of possibilities.

The Why: Purpose (Social Process)

The purpose is determined both by the writer's need to record thoughts and ideas about a topic (the what) to oneself or others and by interests and experiences both internal and external.

 The purpose in turn determines

The How: Text Type

Once the purpose is known, the writer must decide what form will best relay the intended message.

 This in turn determines

The Composition

Actually writing the piece involves several steps:

- Planning
  The writer makes decisions about what is to be included and how the text is to be organized based on the writing form selected.

- Composing
  The writer needs to research, select ideas, and expand on these to convey the message with the intended audience and the selected text type in mind.

- Recording
  As the writer selects and expands on ideas, he or she uses knowledge of the surface features or conventions of language such as spelling, grammar, punctuation, and handwriting.

- Revising
  The writer makes revisions on both the content and the form of the writing, ensuring that the piece includes what is needed for the intended result and the surface features of the writing are correct.

- Publishing
  The writer makes decisions on the style and layout of the piece based on purpose and audience.

An Approach to Teaching Nonfiction Writing

When I was developing the genre study for writing workshop, I took a hard look at how nonfiction writing was taught and viewed in the past. I realized that I had laughed like everyone else at cartoon strips and family comedy television plots about the child forced to write a dreaded report and the teacher who demanded a perfect performance. But this situation is not a laughing matter for the child overwhelmed by the task, nor does it encourage a positive attitude towards nonfiction.

Christine Duthie

Like many researchers, Christine Duthie (1996) has acknowledged the importance of encouraging a positive attitude toward nonfiction writing. Over the past thirty years much research has been done on how children acquire language. Research by Don Holdaway (1979), Brian Cambourne (1988), Frank Smith (1982, 1986, 1988), Don Graves (1981, 1983), and Ken Goodman (1986), and others has helped us gain insight into language learning and has affected our approaches to teaching. This research has had an enormous impact on teaching generally and on the teaching and learning of nonfiction writing specifically. Table 2.1 is a synthesis of these findings, which form the basis of my approach to teaching nonfiction writing. The aim is to develop in all children a positive attitude toward writing nonfiction and make the writing of such texts enjoyable yet challenging and achievable.

Taking Beliefs into Practice: A Framework for Teaching Nonfiction Writing

Lucy Calkins (1994) talks about children living like nonfiction writers and working together as a team to explore specific genres over a period of time. This common-sense approach to teaching and learning allows children to go deep with their understanding of how specific text types work. Such deep understanding, unfortunately, is difficult to achieve in many classrooms. I believe one of the biggest concerns for teachers today is attempting to get through a dense curriculum, which often results in the teacher's bombarding the children with a sea of knowledge in order to cover content. We end up doing what I call "surfing the curriculum" in order to achieve as much as we can in the shortest period of time. Consequently, our students end up with surface understanding. If we want children to become able writers for many different purposes, we need to dive deep and give our children comprehensive learning engagements so that they can develop deeper understanding about how different text types work. A nonfiction study of anything less than a week's duration will do little to foster such understanding. Most of the teachers I have worked with have found that nonfiction explorations in their classrooms usually average three to four weeks.

The framework for teaching nonfiction writing described in the following pages is one I have worked with over the past ten years and is based on the principles outlined in Table 2.1. It takes into account the research of many scholars and my experience working in both my own classes in Australia and with countless teachers and children across the United States in a variety of school settings. This framework is by no means the only way nonfiction writing should be taught in the early years of schooling, but it does highlight key elements that encourage children to become more able writers of nonfiction. Included as a specific example is a unit of a study using the text format of recipes. This particular unit of study lasted approximately four weeks for 60 minutes each day as part of writer's workshop in a second-grade classroom. An overview of this four-week unit is presented as Table 2.2 at the end of this chapter.

Children Best Learn How to Write Nonfiction When They:	Implications for Practice
See a purpose for the writing and have an audience in mind.	Children need to be given authentic purposes for writing nonfiction and be aware of why authors write different types of nonfiction.
See many models of different types of nonfiction writing for a variety of purposes.	Teachers need to provide children with an abundance of nonfiction texts as part of both shared reading and read-alouds as well as books in the classroom library for children's independent reading.
See demonstrations of how to write different text types for different purposes.	Teachers need to provide demonstrations on author's craft, research skills, and language mechanics to make explicit what writers do when they are working with specific genres. These demonstrations need to be in individual, small-group, and whole-class settings according to identified needs.
Are given time and opportunity to engage in working with nonfiction texts.	Schedules need to allow adequate time for children to engage in the process of writing nonfiction pieces. These engagements should not be one-day wonders but rather comprehensive units of study that will help the children learn from ongoing engagements.
Are allowed to take on responsibility for their learning.	Children need to be part of the decision-making process when selecting the content of what they wish to write about independently.
Are given opportunities to learn from each other.	The classroom must be structured to allow frequent opportunities for children to discuss and share their writing pieces with each other.
Are expected to learn.	Clear expectations that all children can succeed must be made evident to all learners through positive feedback and constructive demonstrations.
Feel comfortable in having a try.	Teachers need to accept and praise children's efforts while giving added support to help them make their writing better.

Step 1: Selecting the Writing Purpose (Specific Genre) and Relevant Form

The first thing the teacher must do is decide which of the social processes or purposes for nonfiction writing would be most beneficial for the children to engage in and select a relevant form or text type. This can be determined by units of study currently being implemented in the classroom in other curriculum areas, such as science, social studies, or health, together with the particular interests of the children. Also important in the selection process is the children's prior knowledge of the writing form being considered. It would be pointless to do an in-depth study of how to write descriptions through scientific reports if the children had been working with reports extensively in past years and were competent in writing in this form. What would be more suitable is to explore a new writing purpose and relevant form in order to extend the children's understanding of nonfiction writing.

In Helen's second-grade classroom where I had been working and researching, the children were studying food in a unit on nutrition. Helen decided that a perfect link to this unit would be for her students to make a book of favorite recipes. Helen had also noticed that none of her children actively chose to write any form of instructional text in writer's workshop. This was an important factor in her decision to create a recipe book. The unit on nutrition presented Helen with many other possibilities for nonfiction writing, such as informational reports about food or persuasive texts on why children should not eat too much junk food. Her selection of an instructional text as the focus was based on her children's needs as writers. Although Helen and I viewed the children's abilities to explore how instructional texts worked as important, we knew it was imperative that the children themselves saw the value of such writing and were suitably engaged in this specific type of text.

Step 2: Immersing the Children into a Content Area to Create a Real Context for Their Learning the Purpose of the Writing and Its Relevant Form

For Helen and me to have simply said to the children "Let's write a recipe book on how to prepare our favorite foods" would not have been effective. The children would most likely have agreed simply because they were obedient, without any real understanding of purpose and audience. Jim Earley, a publisher's representative from Florida, once told me that even though the saying "You can lead a horse to water but you can't make him drink" was true, Jim believed that "if you walk the horse around long enough he'd get so thirsty he'd want to drink." This made a lot of sense to me when I thought about getting children involved in things I know to be beneficial for them but that I also know they see no immediate purpose for. It is a fine art to get the children to see the value of drinking that water. We can demand that they do so, which is certainly not constructive when it comes to good teaching practices based on solid beliefs on how children learn; or we can simply lead and encourage them to think that drinking that water is so wonderful that they would be missing out big time if they didn't at least try a few drops. We need to lead them to what Bobbi Fisher (1991) describes as "joyful learning." I don't know how many times I have applied this understanding when rearing my own son. He, like many other children, always hated bath time. Simply buying green coloring for the bath water and telling him that this was crocodile water and he was the crocodile did the trick. (Unfortunately, this presented us with a new dilemma: getting him out of the bath!)

Is That a Fact?

What was needed in Helen's classroom was the children's seeing a purpose for writing a recipe book and becoming eager to do it. Helen accomplished this by reading Shelley Harwayne's book *What's Cooking?* and then engaging her students in a discussion on their favorite foods.

Helen: So what did you think about the book?

Jeremy: I liked the part when they made pizza. I love pizza.

Maryanne: So do I. My mom makes great pizza. It's got lots of cheese.

Helen: So who here likes pizza? [*A sea of hands waves eagerly.*] Mmm, looks like you all do. Why don't we try and make some ourselves?

Children [*in unison*]: Yeah!

Alex: And then can we eat it?

Helen: Of course, Alex. Then if you like we can write about how we made it and share it with the other second-grade children so they can make their own. Who'd like to do that?

Children [*in unison*]: Yeah!

Mario: But we don't know how to make it. I don't know how.

Helen: Don't worry about that, Mario. I'm sure I can help you find out, and I'm certain we can find out how from a recipe book or from Maryanne's mom.

Jose: My mom can help too.

Helen: That's great, Jose. I wonder if there are any other foods we know how to make. We could also write out ways to make them and include it with how to make the pizza.

Gustavo: I know how to make chocolate milk.

Maria: I know how to make chocolate cookies.

Jose: Me too.

At this stage twenty-five children were eagerly waving their hands, wanting to tell Helen of the many foods they knew how to make. The waiting was too much for many of them; they started calling out their responses. Within twenty seconds the classroom has become a hub of excited talk. It took some time to calm everyone down.

Helen: So it looks like we all have things to tell and write about when it comes to making foods. So why don't I starting writing down some of these things you know how to make and then you can choose one and write down how to make it and we can include it in our recipe book. Then when you're all finished, we can come back and start thinking about making that delicious pizza we talked about earlier.

This example shows how easy it is to immerse children into a real context for writing an instructional piece. Helen's students were all eager to start drinking that water Jim Earley had talked about earlier. In fact, trying to stop them from consuming it would have been impossible.

Now that the context had been set, Helen next needed to determine her students' prior knowledge of how to write in the specific form chosen—in this case, recipes.

Step 3: Assessing Each Child's Skills and Understanding in Writing in the Specific Form Selected

The next step is one I believe we rarely do as teachers. How easy it would have been for Helen and her children to begin making pizza and then write up the procedure for doing so. But instead, if we are to truly assist children in their quest to become better writers for many purposes, we need to acknowledge what they already know as writers and base our demonstrations around what they need.

Over recent years we have seen the benefits of assessment informing instruction especially when it comes to reading workshop and in particular guided reading. Research by notable educators such as Marie Clay (1991, 1992, 1993) and Irene Fountas and Gay Su Pinnell (1996) has shown us the value of using children's prior knowledge to build new learning. Unfortunately, when it comes to writing, we do most of our assessments at the end of implementation, not before it, and in so doing we provide children with demonstrations and engagements into language processes we *think* they need, not what we *know* they need. What is needed is an assessment rubric that identifies the key skills and understanding that children need when writing a specific piece of nonfiction writing—in Helen's case, instructional writing. Key factors to consider include children's understanding of the purpose of the writing; their skills in research; knowledge of craft, including elements of structure, language features, voice, and mechanics.

Helen and I had many discussions on this point and finally decided to assess each child's knowledge of writing instructions through recipes both prior to and at the conclusion of the unit's implementation. As part of their earlier discussion, Helen had brainstormed with the children all the things they knew how to make and made a list on the chalkboard. These included Gustavo's suggestion on how to make chocolate milk, Maria's idea on how to make chocolate cookies, and suggestions by other members of the class: how to make a sandwich, breakfast, and a hot dog. Helen and I then asked each child to select one item from the list they felt confident about and to tell us through writing and pictures how to prepare it.

Once completed, we used the assessment rubric for instructional texts that I had designed. (See Figure 2.1 for an example of a completed form.) We filled this out for each child after carefully examining each individual's written piece. The children's writing samples served as wonderful springboards into the types of demonstrations they needed in order to be effective communicators when instructing others. Typically, most of the children wrote just one or two sentences, which gave the reader little guidance in how to complete the selected task. Dario's piece on how to make a peanut butter sandwich, for example, simply stated, "Get some bread and peanut butter." Maryanne wrote, "Sandwiches are good to eat. Make them at home."

None of the children, with the exception of Franco and Elizabeth, included diagrams to help the reader follow their instructions. We realized that Franco and Elizabeth's knowledge of using diagrams would be beneficial to tap into later during whole-class discussions.

Helen and I made a list of all the demonstrations needed based on what the children had not included in their own written recipes and our own knowledge of what is required for writing recipes. They were as follows:

Structure
Including the name of the food to be cooked
Including the ingredients and utensils needed
Including the method in a logical order

Language Features
Using action verbs
Using adjectives and adverbs
Providing clear and detailed instructions
Using diagrams and labels to demonstrate procedures
Using linking words such as then, first, and after

Voice
Engaging the reader in an interesting way
Using words that paint pictures for the reader
Including an inviting beginning

Research
Using books to locate information
Using nonbook resources to locate information

Mechanics
Knowing correct spelling of words
Using legible handwriting

Equipped with this knowledge, we were now ready to make the pizza and have the children discover the way authors successfully instruct others on completing a given task by means of a recipe. We would then have the children go back and look at their own written recipes and revise them based on their newfound understanding of how instructional texts work.

Step 4: Implementing a Whole-Class Exploration of the Selected Text

Over the next week the children, Helen, and I made the pizza with the assistance of cookbooks. The children talked with their parents and shared their knowledge with each other. Helen and I provided numerous demonstrations using modeled writing, shared readings, read-alouds, and follow-up discussions on recipes. Topics included the choice of an appropriate text structure, language features, voice, and conventions of writing such as spelling, handwriting, grammar, and publishing. We based these demonstrations on the skills and understanding not evident in the children's own written recipes. Some of the demonstrations were conducted by the children themselves—for example, we asked Franco and Elizabeth to tell us how their use of pictures in their recipes helped the reader know what to do.

On the language features of recipes and the children's sense of voice, many of our discussions focused on the importance of using words that describe things as clearly as possible to the reader, such as using appropriate verbs, nouns, adjectives, and adverbs. Yet we rarely used these terms with the children. Instead, we referred to "doing" words (verbs), "seeing" words (nouns), "how to do something" words (adverbs), and "what it looks like" words (adjectives). This terminology seemed to be far more supportive in helping children visualize the types of words needed to make recipes more engaging and easier for readers to understand. We also showed the children how authors use a good opening to engage their readers.

At the conclusion of each demonstration or discussion, we asked the children to tell us what authors used when writing a good recipe for others to follow. These we recorded onto a chart. The children came up with the following:

A Good Recipe:
Tells the reader what is going to be made.
Has information from books and from talking to people.
Lists all the ingredients and what you need to make it.
Makes sense.
Has pictures and labels to help the reader see what to do.
Lists things to do in the right order.
Uses good words to help the reader understand what to do (doing words, seeing words, how to do something words, what it looks like words).
Has no spelling mistakes.
Sometimes has a picture of what is going to be made at the start.
Has good writing.
Looks good.

Is That a Fact?

The children then used this chart to help Helen write on the chalkboard their own recipe for making pizza. This shared writing creation proved successful; the children were eager to tell Helen and me exactly what should be included in the recipe.

What was noteworthy about this writing of the recipe was that the children were able to tell us explicitly what the purpose, appropriate text structure, and language features for writing recipes were. The information they had obtained had taught them the importance of research and that good writers of recipes are also good researchers of recipes. They also noted the importance of the surface features, or mechanics, of writing, such as spelling, handwriting, and grammar, but only as part of what made a good recipe. Helen's students were able to see that writing was far more than just correct spelling and neat handwriting. Their understanding of recipes they had discovered for themselves, through our demonstrations, questioning techniques, and shared reading. They had not simply been told how to write a recipe; they had *discovered* how to write one through a whole-class investigation with Helen and me as their guides.

I believe that as teachers we often demonstrate to children expecting them to grasp the idea instantly. We give too little consideration to the extra support they require in order to fully internalize the demonstrations provided. It is as if we were to expect children to jump into the pool and swim after just a few demonstrations from us. Children require not only numerous demonstrations and models; they also need us as teachers to share some of the responsibility for their learning by giving them added support. We need to jump into the swimming pool with them and hold them up until they feel confident enough to let go and swim for themselves. Vygotsky's concept of the zone of proximal development (1978) and Bruner's notion of scaffolding (1986) highlight the importance of providing support for the learner through joint construction and ownership of the learning by both teacher and student.

Once Helen had recorded her students' recipe, she divided the class into groups of four and gave each group one part of the recipe to illustrate and publish on large sheets of paper. These were then collated and bound to form a big book entitled *How to Make Fabulous Pizza*. The book was then shared with the class next door and of course there was a waiting list for the book to be taken home each night by individual children, for them to share it with families and friends. Sammy, one of the more confident and outspoken members of the class, managed to jump to the head of the waiting list when he explained, "My mom has to see this book now. She has to—she cooks really bad."

Step 5: Encouraging Independent Explorations of the Text Type Being Explored

At this point, the implementation process in my own writing classroom would often falter. Often I would provide countless demonstrations for my students but never follow through with the expectation that they take up the learning themselves. Encouraging students' independent construction of something newly learned is imperative if the teacher is to see what they have learned through the demonstrations provided to the whole class. Simply showing children how a thing is done without letting them independently practice it is not a good model for learning. Children need to try writing in the selected form with the teacher providing ongoing demonstrations and support.

Helen encouraged her students to go back and rewrite their original recipes using their newfound knowledge of how authors write such texts as a guide. At this stage of the process, Helen and I also gave the children the option of composing a recipe different from their original if they so chose. This gave our learners ongoing choice of content, which followed from our belief that children best learn to write nonfiction when they are allowed to take on responsibility for their learning. We reminded the children that the recipes would be compiled into a class recipe book that others would read. With their audience in mind, the children decided that their original pieces needed a lot of work. This gave way to many discussions on how to improve their original pieces. One child, Catherine, reminded us of the chart the class had created on what makes a good recipe and suggested that reviewing that chart would be helpful.

Here we see the power of Helen's having had the children articulate what they had learned through the whole-class investigation and recording their understanding. They could use this record to assist them with their own independent construction of a written recipe. Helen and I also took the process one step further. We asked the children to tell us exactly what steps we took when we wrote our joint recipe for pizza. We explained that remembering these steps would help them when rewriting their own recipes. With careful questioning and clarification we came up with the following:

How to Write a Recipe
First you find something you know how to make or something you want to know how to make.
Write down what you already know.
Look at recipe books or ask people to help you find out how to really make it.
Write it down, but don't copy.
Go back and put things in the right order. Use the chart on what makes a good recipe to help you.
Put in all the pictures to help the reader.
Fix up all your spelling mistakes or get someone to help you do this.
Publish it. Make sure your handwriting is fantastic.
Share it with someone.

In examining the two charts we can see how they gave the children the necessary tools for them either to revise their original pieces or to begin a new recipe. These charts recorded the children's understanding of both an author's craft in writing a recipe and the process necessary to construct such a text. They not only allowed the children to understand how and what they learned, but they also helped Helen and me know what future demonstrations might be necessary to extend the children's understanding.

During the next two weeks the children reworked their original pieces or constructed new ones. Helen and I provided the necessary demonstrations and positive feedback in individual, small-group, and whole-class settings. The ongoing support for the children during this time was critical, as some of the children needed further demonstrations to help them with their independent writing pieces. Helen and I began to organize guided writing groups to give the children this added support, as not all of them were ready yet to swim alone. When the pieces were complete we collected them into a whole-class recipe book; then we celebrated our accomplishment and shared it with others. It would have been easy at this stage to have thought the unit of study complete. But now the need for Helen to assess each child's growth in understanding how instructional texts work came to the fore.

Step 6: Conducting Follow-Up Assessments to Determine Each Child's Writing Skills and Understanding of the Specific Form

Comparing a child's written piece with prior pieces is one of the greatest assessment tools we can utilize as teachers. For example, compare Dario's first piece of writing on how to make a peanut butter sandwich with his piece at the conclusion of the unit, on how to make a ham sandwich.

Here is Dario's first piece, how to make a peanut butter sandwich:

Get some bread and peanut butter.

And here is his later piece, on how to make a ham sandwich, which he wrote during independent exploration:

How You Make a Ham Sandwich that people want to eat
You need. Some bread, ham and a good knife
What You Do.
Get the bread you like. I like white.
Get some good ham from the supermarket.
Put the ham on the bread.
Put some more bread on top of the ham.

Cut it with a knife. Be careful because the knife could cut you and it will
   hurt.
Eat it.

Clearly Helen's immersion of the class, and subsequent demonstrations, on how to write a recipe had an enormous impact on Dario's ability to write this type of text. Dario continued to write recipes long after the unit was completed. Evidently he had not only discovered a new purpose for writing but had also chosen to take up this form of writing as an enjoyable activity. This was true of the vast majority of Helen's children. They didn't simply revert back to writing personal narratives and fantasy stories when the unit was over; they actively engaged in nonfiction writing—specifically recipes.

If we look closely at the assessment rubric that Helen and I completed for both Dario's first piece (dated February 24) and the one he wrote at the conclusion of the unit (March 15), as shown in Figure 2.1, it is easy to see his increased understanding of, and skills in, writing recipes. (The form also evaluates a third, later, piece of Dario's from March 26. More on that third piece below.) By March 15, Dario is starting to use his knowledge of specific language features, such as verbs, adverbs, adjectives, and appropriate headings. His increased knowledge of the linguistic structure of recipes is also obvious as he identifies his goal, the materials needed, and the method to follow. This he had not done in his initial piece. What was also pleasing to see was Dario's strong sense of voice. His inclusion of the fact that he preferred white bread and that if you are not careful with the knife it will cut you adds personal depth to the piece. Developing children's sense of voice, especially in nonfiction writing, is crucial. (Refer to Chapter 4 for further information on voice.) We can also see that Dario is developing his skills as a researcher by locating information from both book and nonbook sources.

In regards to the surface features of the text, our assessment was based not just on the two recipes we had in front of us, but also on prior written pieces by Dario in both draft and published forms, such as past journal entries and other written tasks. While it was easy to assess his increased knowledge of the text structure and language features of writing recipes, when it came to the surface features of writing, we needed to take into account more than just the recipes. After all, the surface features of writing, such as spelling, grammar, presentation, and handwriting are present in all forms of writing, not just recipes. (See Chapter 5 for more information about helping children become more confident and competent with the surface features of writing.)

Using the Assessment Rubric

The assessment rubric shown in Figure 2.1 is just one format that can be used to assess children's skills and understanding in writing a specific nonfiction text type. Assessment rubrics dealing with other types are shown in Part Two,

■ Figure 2.1 Assessment rubric for Dario

Assessment Rubric for Instructional Writing

Key: N: Not in evidence   S: Showing signs of   C: Consolidating   M: Mostly   N/A: Not applicable

Name: *Dario* **Grade:** *2* **Date:** **Text Type or Title:**	2/24 *recipe*	3/15 *recipe*	3/26 *recipe*
Purpose			
Understands why instructional texts are used	*Unsure*	*M*	*M*
Recognizes different types of instructional texts	*Unsure*	*Unsure*	*Unsure*
Craft (Structure, features, voice)			
Linguistic or Text Structure Selects appropriate text type based on purpose	*S*	*S*	*S*
Aim or Goal Tells reader what is to be achieved	*N*	*S*	*M*
Materials or Equipment Lists items and quantities needed to perform task	*N*	*C*	*M*
Method Uses a logical sequence of steps	*N*	*C*	*M*
Includes all essential steps	*N*	*S*	*M*
Uses diagrams, labels, and pictures	*N*	*S*	*S*
Text/Language Features Uses linking words to do with time (first, then, after, when)	*N*	*N*	*S*
Uses present tense (you cut, you serve, you open)	*C*	*C*	*M*
Uses action verbs (take, proceed, open, wash)	*N*	*S*	*S*
Uses adverbs (*carefully* open, *gently* turn, *slowly* push)	*N*	*S*	*S*
Uses adjectives (open the *red* packet, get a *large* bowl)	*N*	*S*	*S*
Includes appropriate headings based on the text structure chosen	*S*	*C*	*M*
Voice Uses an enticing title and/or setting to engage the reader	*N*	*S*	*C*
Is able to express ideas using own language as opposed to copying down what others say or information from books they read	*N*	*S*	*S*
Uses descriptive language that paints pictures for the reader	*N*	*S*	*S*
Is able to state information in a unique or surprising manner	*N*	*N*	*S*
Research Skills			
Is able to locate information from books	*N*	*S*	*C*
Is able to locate information from nonbook sources	*N*	*S*	*S*
Is able to interpret and talk about information located	*S*	*S*	*C*
Surface Features (Mechanics)			
Handwriting neat and legible	*S*	*S*	*C*
Shows improvement in attempts at spelling words	*S*	*S*	*S*
Uses grammatically correct language	*S*	*S*	*S*
Shows improvement in use of punctuation	*N*	*S*	*S*
Uses an appropriate publishing format	*N*	*S*	*N/A*
Work generally well presented	*S*	*S*	*C*

where other nonfiction units are explored. These rubrics are by no means the only form of assessment teachers can use; they are simply one way for teachers to track individual children's progress. Many of the key indicators outlined on the assessment rubric given here are generic and can apply to any form of writing, even personal narrative and fantasy; but some of the key indicators, especially those dealing with text structure, are specific to the text type being explored. In using this or other rubrics, it is helpful to keep a portfolio for each child and pass it on to the teacher the following year. In this way teachers can build on past assessments by their colleagues to help them design future units of study and the necessary demonstrations and engagements for their learners. Chapter 14 of Stephanie Harvey's book *Nonfiction Matters* (1998) is a wonderful reference for teachers and those in school systems who are considering designing their own assessment rubrics for nonfiction writing.

I call this form of assessment a "rubric" rather than a "checklist" for an important reason. I have always found it difficult to assess children's work by using a series of check marks; often children display degrees of understanding of specific skills and strategies. One cannot always simply say "yes, this child definitely understands this" or "no, they don't." By having a rubric that allows notation of a gradient of understanding and skills a child possesses, we are better able to scaffold each child's learning during whole-class, small-group, and independent demonstrations and learning engagements.

Another point about rubrics is that, as was the case with Dario, a final piece usually is done at the conclusion of the unit, after the child has received much support in both small-group and whole-class encounters. It is, in essence, an assessment of what the child could achieve with support, unlike the initial piece, which may be done with no support. To truly gauge what Dario, for example, could achieve independently Helen would have to assess Dario's skills in writing an instructional piece after the unit had been completed to see what he had truly learned. This is exactly what Helen did, recording on Dario's assessment rubric a third instructional piece, which he wrote after the conclusion of the unit. We can see by the entries on the assessment rubric for that March 26 piece that Dario had internalized some of the key features he used in his second piece, the one he wrote with support.

This idea of internalization is important, and I discussed the subject with Joetta Beaver, the author of the Developmental Reading Assessment (DRA). Joetta and I agreed that there were two types of assessments that we need to be aware of as teachers. The first is concerned with what the child is able to do without assistance—in other words, the child's independent skills and understanding. The second has to do with skills Vygotsky (1978) described as being in the child's zone of proximal development—those the child can use with support. As teachers, we need to be aware of both of these types of assessment and ensure that when we track children's progress we consider what they can do both with and without teacher support.

Assessment Through Interviewing

Although using an assessment rubric to track individual children's growth in working with a specific writing form can yield much useful information, interviewing is also a powerful assessment tool. To really know what a child has understood it is necessary to find out what is going on in their minds to gauge their cognitive development. In Dario's case, for example, it was difficult for Helen to gauge his understanding of purpose simply by looking at his written pieces. To ascertain what Dario had learned, we decided to talk with him (and the other children).

After the completion of the unit we called each child up for a brief interview about their written pieces and what they had learned about writing an instructional piece. My interview with Dario went like this:

Tony: Hey, Dario, this is a fantastic recipe on how to make a ham sandwich. It's making me hungry just reading it.

Dario: Yeah, it's good. I love ham sandwiches.

Tony: So, Dario, who did you write this for?

Dario: It's for our recipe book. It's for other kids so they can know how to make 'em. I bet they can't make 'em like me.

Tony: I'll bet not. So, Dario, if you had to write another recipe, say on how to make chocolate milk, how would you do it?

Dario: Chocolate milk! I don't like chocolate milk. I like orange juice.

Tony: Okay, then. If you had to write about how to make orange juice, what would you write?

Dario: You have to say what you need, like oranges and something to get the juice out of it. You need a glass, too, to drink it out of.

Tony: Is there anything else you would write about?

Dario: Yeah, but don't you know, Tony? [*He laughs.*] Can't you make orange juice?

Tony: Sure I can, but I want to know how you make it to see if we make it the same way.

Dario [*looking at me skeptically—I don't think he believes I can really make orange juice*]: Well, you have to tell people what to do first, like get the orange and cut it. [*He looks away to locate the process chart in the classroom on the features of good recipes.*] Oh yeah, then you put some pictures in to show what to do.

Tony: Why would you put in pictures?

Dario: 'Cause some kids can't read. The pictures show you what to do. You know I can read real good.

Tony: I know you can. Is there anything else you would include in the recipe?

Dario [*thinks for a moment*]: Nah. You know I like oranges a lot. My mom buys a lot of them.

Tony: Would you tell me about your mom buying lots of oranges in your recipe?

Dario [*looking at me, puzzled*]: Nah.

Tony: Why not?

Dario: 'Cause you don't put stuff like that in.

Tony: Why not?

Dario: I don't know, you just don't. It doesn't help kids make juice.

Tony: So, Dario, what are you going to write about next?

Dario: Mmm. [*Thinks for a moment.*] I think I'm gonna write how to make orange juice for you. [*Laughs.*]

Tony: You really don't believe I know how to make orange juice, do you? Well, how lucky I am to have a recipe written just for me.

As you can see by reading my interview with Dario, this interview in conjunction with his assessment rubric gives us valuable insight into Dario's understanding of writing recipes. He has clearly articulated that he is aware of the purpose for writing recipes (to instruct), and he has also identified some of the text structure and language features necessary to write a recipe. He has not simply followed a set of rules but has internalized the process.

Apart from interviewing children, having them complete a self-assessment questionnaire is another method a teacher can utilize to gauge understanding. This allows learners to take an active role in the assessment process and lets them see their own growth as writers. Appendix A is a sample self-assessment questionnaire that can be given to children at the completion of a nonfiction exploration. This questionnaire is particularly relevant for second and third graders, who would probably not find filling out such a questionnaire too difficult. For younger children, the interview is probably more appropriate.

Step 7: Future Considerations for Teaching and Learning

We could add one more step to the process: considering future teaching and learning. Helen had to decide whether to continue exploring instructional texts with her students, this time perhaps with a different form, such as signs or game rules; or whether to launch into an exploration of a whole new type of nonfiction writing, with a different purpose and form. She told me she would make that decision soon, but for now she was content to let her children continue writing recipes, which was what most of them wanted to continue doing. Others chose to turn to personal narratives in the form of journals, which Helen had introduced at the beginning of the school year.

Later, Helen told me that instructional writing was something she would most likely revisit at some point in the future, as she had noticed improvement in all of her students and wanted to consolidate some of this understanding at a later stage. Helen also told me that if she were to do the unit again she would make changes to her implementation practices. She wanted to allow even more time for small-group instruction to assist her less able learners at their point of need.

Helen's reflection at the end of the unit strengthened her ability as a teacher in implementing future units of study. So often we teachers spend all our time reflecting on our children's learning outcomes and never reflect on our own. If a child doesn't understand something it is not necessarily the child's fault. It is more likely that our teaching has not been focused or explicit enough to help the child become successful with new learning. Only through ongoing reflection of our existing practices can we become better able to help all our children learn. My motto has always been "When a teacher ceases to be a learner, a teacher ceases to be a teacher." Helen's reflecting on her experience in the classroom meant she was continuing to be a learner herself, and this in turn would have an enormous impact on her children's capacity to learn how to be successful writers of nonfiction.

As a summary of the framework for teaching nonfiction writing detailed in this chapter, Table 2.2 lists the steps involved and how best to implement them, using Helen's experience as an example.

■ **Table 2.2** A Framework for Nonfiction Exploration: Helen's Four-Week Unit on Recipes

Implementation Steps	Considerations for Implementation	Description of Activities
1. Selecting the writing purpose (specific genre) and relevant form.	The teacher needs to take into account: • Children's prior knowledge of and engagements in writing in different forms of nonfiction. • Children's interests. • Other units of study being implemented that could be linked to a nonfiction study.	Prior to commencement of unit, Helen decides to explore writing recipes as part of a health unit on nutrition. This decision is also based on her observation that none of her children have engaged in writing instructional texts during writer's workshop.
2. Immersing the children into a content area to create a real context for their learning the purpose of the writing and its relevant form.	The teacher must provide children with relevant: • Reading-to experiences. • Shared readings. • Common experiences such as field trips, videos, books, etc.	Helen gets the children into the idea of writing recipes by reading Shelley Harwayne's book *What's Cooking?* and suggesting that the class make pizza. She also brainstorms with the children recipes that they know how to make for a whole-class recipe book.

Implementation Steps	Considerations for Implementation	Description of Activities
3. Assessing each child's skills and understanding in writing in the specific form selected.	The teacher must suitably immerse the children so that they will want to write in the selected form.	Helen's students each write a recipe from the list they have brainstormed together.
	The teacher must use a comprehensive assessment rubric to identify each child's prior knowledge of writing in the selected form.	Helen analyzes each child's written piece using the assessment rubric to assess each child's understanding of how to write an instructional piece.
	The teacher must use the assessment rubric to identify demonstrations needed to help children become effective writers in the selected form.	She identifies the necessary demonstrations that her children need in order to deepen their understanding of how to write an instructional piece.
4. Implementing a whole-class exploration of the selected text.	Children need appropriate models of the selected form to assist them with their research.	Helen and the children make pizza using books and interviews with family members to assist with the process.
	The teacher needs to provide children with shared reading and writing encounters to discover the author's craft of constructing the selected text.	Helen provides the children with demonstrations of how to write a recipe through read-alouds, shared reading, and modeled writing.
	Children need to be given the opportunity to articulate their findings about author's craft to both the teacher and each other.	Children articulate their understanding; Helen charts their contributions.
	Children's findings need to be charted by the teacher as a point of reference.	
	The children, with the teacher, need to construct a text using the process charts as a guide.	The children, with Helen, research, compose, revise, and publish their recipe on how to make pizza.

Implementation Steps	Considerations for Implementation	Description of Activities
5. Encouraging independent explorations of the text type being explored.	The teacher must demonstrate to the children how to do research.	Helen brainstorms with the children the process they went through in writing the pizza recipe. The points are recorded on a chart.
	Children need an opportunity to construct or make revisions to past pieces independently.	The children go back to their original recipes and begin revisions using the process charts and appropriate resources as guides. Some children decide to write new recipes.
	The teacher needs to provide children with ongoing demonstrations and support at a whole-class, small-group, and individual level.	Helen continues to provide ongoing support through whole-class, small-group, and individual encounters.
	The teacher needs to provide children with appropriate resources.	
	Children need an opportunity to publish and share their pieces with an audience.	The children's recipes are published, collated, celebrated, and shared with an audience.
6. Conducting follow-up assessments to determine each child's writing skills and understanding of the specific form.	Using each child's individual piece, the teacher needs to reexamine the assessment rubric used in Step 3 to identify children's individual progress.	Helen compares the children's original recipes with their revised pieces to determine each student's growth. She records her findings on the assessment rubric.
	The teacher may decide to have each child reflect on his or her learning. This could be in the form of an interview or a self-assessment task.	Helen calls each child up for a brief interview to better determine their understanding about writing an instructional piece.
7. Considering future teaching and learning.	The teacher needs to continue utilizing the assessment rubric selected in Step 3 to further record individual children's progress on future pieces.	Helen continues to monitor children's understanding whenever they choose to write another instructional piece.
	The teacher needs to reflect on the unit of study to make decisions on future explorations and changes in future practice.	Helen reflects on her practice and decides to include more time for small-group instruction in future explorations.

Helping Children Locate Information

What does this say, Tony? I can't read it. Should I copy it?
                                        Johnathon, grade 1

When children are given a research project, usually they simply record everything they know about a topic, regardless of its accuracy or validity; add a few illustrations; then believe their job is done. In many cases, like Johnathon, children will simply copy large slabs of text, giving little thought to the validity and relevance of the information they laboriously copy. Independent research is not for the most part in our students' comfort zone. If we are to help them learn to become researchers, we must take four major considerations into account:

1. How to help children locate information for their research.
2. How to help them interpret the information they gather.
3. How to help them discover different ways to represent the information.
4. How to help them publish and share their research.

In this chapter we examine the first consideration; later chapters explain how to handle the others.

Helping children locate information for their research involves more than just giving them books to use. Not only must we consider a myriad of nonbook resources; we must also consider ways to help children search out these resources themselves and not rely solely on us, their teachers, to be the main provider.

Identifying Available Resources

Pam's first graders had been doing a unit of study on writing reports and had chosen the topic Ants as the whole-class investigation. The class had written everything they knew about ants, but they needed more information to add to the report. Pam and I brainstormed with the children all the possible sources for finding additional information. We recorded the children's suggestions onto a chart entitled "How to Find Out About Something"; it read as follows:

How to Find Out About Something
From:

Books, magazines, and cassette tapes
—Classroom library
—School library
—Local library

Home
—Family members and friends
—Television

The Internet
The experts

Research
—Observations
—Field trips

This chart became a valuable resource for the children, not just for this exploration but throughout the year, whenever they were doing research on any topic, whatever the genre. Pam and I made sure that they referred to the chart whenever they needed to locate additional information during whole-class and individual explorations.

Books, Magazines, and Cassette Tapes

Shelley Harwayne writes, "No matter the grade level, when I walk in and out of classrooms, I expect to see classroom libraries brimming with nonfiction texts" (1999, p. 24). Her expectations are well founded. If we want young children to become able writers of nonfiction, we need to provide them with a multitude of resources.

One of the most common questions teachers ask me is "How do I stop my children from copying large sections of text from books when they try to do research?" In order to effectively answer this question we need to ask a different question: Why do children copy in the first place? The answer is obvious when we think about it from a child's perspective. Children copy because they are unable to read, comprehend, and articulate what is in front of them, because most of the time the texts they have selected or have been given are too hard for them.

This point was demonstrated to me when I visited a kindergarten classroom in Massachusetts and watched as a group of enthusiastic learners showed me what they had found out about bears. One girl proudly showed me a page she had written, which I proceeded to read: "Bears, like humans, are mammals. There are many different types of bears, including the polar bear, brown bear, grizzly bear, and black bear." I was amazed to think that a kindergarten child could produce such sophisticated language and have such an in-depth knowledge of bears. I asked her to read it to me. With great enthusiasm she snatched the paper from my hands and read, "Bears are beautiful. They look nice. I love bears." It was evident that the information on her paper she had simply directly copied from the book about bears sitting on the table in front of her. When I looked around the room I saw that the majority of children in the class had also produced pages of information about bears, all copied from books on their tables. Clearly what the children in this class needed were materials at appropriate reading levels and for the classroom library to be organized to give them easy access to the books they required.

The Classroom Library

In many classrooms across the country, I have seen books in classroom libraries organized in a way that combines level and topic to enable children to select appropriate reading material. The nonfiction materials in these classroom libraries are usually grouped together in one basket or container and simply labeled "Nonfiction." While this can be a good way to initially help children access information based on interest and appropriate reading level, two points need to be considered.

First, as discussed in Chapter 1, the category "nonfiction" is very broad and needs to broken down to help children find what they need for their specific purpose. Having one or two baskets to store all the nonfiction material is not adequate. If children are engaged in writing reports on animals, they need to be able to easily find informational texts on the animal they are researching without having to look through baskets of books on countless topics. Similarly, if they are working with instructional texts they should have books on recipes and procedures in a specific location in the classroom library.

An easy way to organize the classroom library is to break down the nonfiction baskets in the classroom into specific content areas that relate to a specific genre of nonfiction. Andrea, for example, achieved this in her second-grade classroom by having several baskets of books on each of the following topics. In the column across from each topic is the type of nonfiction the basket held.

Title of Basket	Type of Nonfiction
Animals	Description
Space	Description
The Ocean	Description
Dinosaurs	Description
Countries	Description
Sports	Description
People and Their Jobs	Description/nonfiction narrative
Celebrations	Description/nonfiction narrative
Recipes	Instructions
How to Make	Instructions
How to Care For	Instructions
How to Do	Instructions
Atlases and Maps	Instructions
How and Why	Scientific explanation
Experiments	Scientific explanation
Autobiographies and Biographies	Nonfiction narrative
Past Events	Nonfiction narrative
What Do You Think	Persuasion

With this arrangement, when Andrea was implementing a unit of study on writing procedural texts, she and her students could easily access the books in the classroom library that would aid them in their research. Organizing the nonfiction material this way also enabled Andrea to see what additional resources were needed. For example, if the baskets of "How to . . ." books only contained a few books each, Andrea knew she would need to borrow many more from the school and local library if the children were to have good examples of procedural texts and become successful researchers and writers in this form.

Andrea placed books and magazines on how to care for specific pets, such as dogs, cats, and birds, in the "How to Care For" basket and not the "Animals" basket. She did this because although these books dealt with animals, they were instructional texts, and the children knew if they needed to find instructions on caring for pets, the "How to Care For" basket would be their best option.

The second point to consider in organizing the classroom library is the need to have a variety of different levels of books within each nonfiction basket so that all children are able to select material at a level they can read and comprehend. In Andrea's classroom, this was achieved by simply color-coding many of the books in each of the nonfiction baskets. For example, in the "Space" basket were books with blue, yellow, red, or pink stickers. The children knew from discussions and demonstrations that if they selected a space book with a pink sticker and found it a little too hard, they might find the books with a red or yellow sticker a better choice.

Another advantage of color-coding some of the books is that it gives the teacher an idea of the number of different levels of texts that are available. This idea was powerfully demonstrated to me some years ago when I was working with a group of teachers in Connecticut. Margo, one of the teachers, informed me that she had over 3,000 books in her classroom library. The task of organizing the nonfiction material into specific content areas linked to genre seemed to her both sensible and achievable, but the task of then trying to color-code these books according to level was daunting. I agreed that it would be a slow process and assured her that it was not necessary to have everything organized within a month.

Six months later Margo contacted me to say that she had completed the task of color-coding and had been shocked to find that she needed to acquire more books in each of her nonfiction baskets. I too was shocked. After all, 3,000 books is a lot of material for one classroom. Why would she need even more? Margo told me that when she sorted her books she found that only 20 percent of them were nonfiction, and most of these were descriptive books about animals, only one aspect of nonfiction. What was more surprising was that of the relatively few nonfiction books she had, about 80 percent were at reading levels way above where the majority of her children were reading. Margo's children, like many children, probably had found copying the only achievable means of recording information when they were trying to work with the nonfiction in the classroom. Margo needed not only to purchase more nonfiction material but also to ensure that the texts chosen were matched to the needs and abilities of her children.

Using Cassette Tapes

I am constantly amazed by the number of cassette tapes that are now being recorded to accompany nonfiction books, yet perpetually depressed when I see how few of these tapes make their way into our classrooms. Many schools when purchasing nonfiction materials never even bother to buy the tapes that accompany the books. This means that many of our young learners who are pre-emergent or early emergent readers are missing out on a great opportunity to locate information for research because of their inability to read more complex texts. Emergent and fluent readers are also missing out on valuable information from texts too complex for them to read independently. Having cassette tapes to accompany books makes so much sense, especially when we consider Margaret Mooney's (1990) notion of reading to, with, and by children. When we read to children we are greatly supporting them as readers, for we are doing the hard part for them by reading the selected text. This gives them an opportunity to listen and to learn the language and concepts in the book without having to worry about decoding the words in front of them. The research on the value of reading to children from birth is extensive, especially on its strengthening children's abilities as both readers and writers. It is well documented that listening comprehension precedes reading comprehension; without listening comprehension children may be able to learn to decode the words in a book but will have no notion of what these words are telling them. By purchasing audio tapes that accompany the nonfiction books we buy and letting children have access to a listening post during research time, we open up a whole new world of possibilities for developing our students' listening comprehension and gathering information for research.

The School Library

Often the school library to a young child is a labyrinth of books, many of which are either out of reach or, as my colleague Diane Snowball puts it, a "sea of spines." To inquisitive children eager to search for information on a given topic, the minute they walk through the library door they are overwhelmed with the daunting task of locating appropriate resources.

One way to assist children with this quest is to let the school librarian know ahead of time exactly what the children are researching so that appropriate books and magazines can be placed in baskets or tubs for the children's to access. Pat Nevins, the librarian at P.S. 148 in Queens, provides a prime example of how librarians can help children locate appropriate resources in the school library. When Pat was informed that the first graders were doing a whole-class investigation on report writing with ants as the topic, she collected books and magazines on ants in the classroom library and placed them in three baskets according to text difficulty. When the children went to the library they were able to easily find the books they needed and begin looking through them to gather information. The children's time was not wasted in endlessly searching through the thousands of books on the library shelves. Pat did leave some of the books on ants on the shelves and directed some of the more competent young researchers to the appropriate section of the school library for additional resources.

The Local Library

As teachers we should utilize our community resources as much as possible. The local library is a terrific starting point. When I was a primary-grade teacher one of my first missions was always to take my students on a field trip to the local library and encourage parents to join their children in obtaining library cards. Most parents want to be of assistance to their children in school, and the simple task of having them join the local library and take their child on a regular basis is a great start.

Local libraries are also a valuable source of materials not available in the school library. Most local libraries allow teachers to borrow many books for classroom use. When I was teaching a unit on explanatory texts, for example, I needed good examples to present as models for my students; but I found that our school library was short of such texts. Fortunately, I was able to borrow many examples of explanatory texts from the local library. It is wise to inform the local librarian of topics you are exploring in your class. Like school librarians, they can be a great help to you when it comes to finding useful sources of information.

Using a Table of Contents and Index

When assisting children in locating information from books and magazines, show them how to use the table of contents and the index. I am constantly amazed at how many of our young learners are ignorant of these aids when they attempt to locate information in printed materials. While it understandable that beginning learners, such as kindergartners and first graders, may find this task too difficult, it is surprising to see how many children in grades 2 and 3 are unable to use these pages to help them find specific information. Children tend to read nonfiction as they would fiction. They simply start reading on the first page in the hope that they will come across information relevant to their research. What these children have not yet learned is that when reading nonfiction it is not always necessary to begin on the first page.

I recall a second-grade classroom where I had been working. The children were doing independent research with the aim of writing a report on an animal or thing of their choice. Only two children in the class were turning to the contents page in books to locate specific information. The rest were becoming frustrated by having to wade through page after page in order to locate the information they required. I brought the children together and showed them a big book called *Meet the Octopus* by Sylvia M. James (1996). I opened it to the contents page and asked the children what this page was called and why the author included it. The children all knew it was called a contents page, and many were able to discuss its use. Then I asked how such a page could help them with locating information in their own research. All of a sudden, all the lights went on at once. They immediately understood how much time this single page could save them in their search for information for their reports. Apparently, although their teacher had in the past discussed what a contents page was, it was done in the abstract, isolated from purpose and never in the context of how it could help the children locate information as writers.

Next, I showed them the index at the end of the book (Figure 3.1) and asked how such a page could help them with their research. They found this a difficult question to answer and were a little confused by all the numbers on the page. Finally one little girl, Roberta, pointed to the word *arms* at the top of the page and said, "I think it means that if you want to buy a book on octopus arms it will cost you $4." This was an interesting theory, so I asked her why the numbers 13 and 16 were also next to the word *arms* to which she replied, "You know, Tony, it's more expensive in some bookstores than others. This tells you how much you might have to spend if you want to buy the book." I congratulated Roberta on her interesting idea and then informed the children of the true meaning of the page. When the children went back to their research, not only did they begin using the contents and the index pages to locate information, but many of them went on to include a contents page in their own reports.

Information from Home: Family Members and Friends

When we think about how information is acquired in general, we find that word of mouth is one of the most common sources. Knowledge from the home environment is something we need to tap into when helping students with research. For many children who find print daunting, families are an excellent means of information. After all, before children enter school, most of the information they gain about the world around them is through family members. My own son's inquisitive nature drove my wife and me crazy. I thought if I heard him ask the question "Why?" one more time I would go crazy. Yet it was my answers to his questions that gave him his perspective on life. That all changed when he started school; then it was his teacher, Isabel, who had all the answers. The fact that I too was a teacher was irrelevant to him. As far as he was concerned his teacher was the holder of all knowledge, and what she

■ **Figure 3.1** The index from *Meet the Octopus* (James 1996)

Index

arms   4, 13, 16
baby octopus   20-21
beak   18
body   4, 6, 12, 22
common octopus   5, 16
den   14, 15
dwarf octopus   5
eggs   19-20
enemies   11, 13, 20
escaping   10-12
food   15, 18
funnel   12
giant octopus   5, 19
hiding   7-9
hunting   15-18
ink cloud   10-11
moray eel   11, 13
mouth   4
size   5
suction cups   4, 16

said was golden. I can't thank Isabel enough for impressing on her students the importance of listening to their family members and neighbors.

In one of my own classrooms I recall a unit on writing explanatory texts on the topic of why it rains. The students and I began by talking about what we already knew, and I had produced with the children a process chart on how we could find out more. One of the options was to ask our family members and friends at home. Maria, one the first graders, remarked, "It's no good me asking my family. They're all dumb. They're not smart like you and me, Tony." I told her to ask anyway, and the following day she came tearing into the classroom, eager to share. "Guess what, Tony?" she said. "My mom and I went outside last night and looked at the clouds. She showed me which ones were ready to throw

water on us because their tummies were full, and she was right. We got so wet."
I reminded her of her comment the day before about having a dumb family and
she replied, "Well, yeah, they're sort of smart—but still not like you and me."

A Letter to Parents

Another way of encouraging children to use home resources for research is to
send a letter to their parents prior to the commencement of a unit of study.
This way you can alert parents to the topic being studied and how they can
help. I believe it is important for us as teachers to directly communicate with
parents and not leave it to chance that the child will inform the parents of
what is going on inside the classroom and how the parents might be of assistance. (I know that whenever I asked my son what he did at school that day,
the reply was usually "Nothing" or "We played.") Here is the letter Pam and I
sent home to parents when we were having the class write reports about ants.
(A generic letter to parents is given in Appendix B.)

> Dear Parents,
>
> Over the next three weeks grade 1 Room 213 will be doing a whole-
> class investigation on ants, and then your child will be doing his or her
> own investigation on an animal of his or her choice. The children will
> have lots of questions they want answered, and you can be of assistance
> to them. Below are some ways to help.
>
> Talk to your child about ants. Ask what he or she already knows and
> tell what you know. Write or draw this information together, and have
> your child bring it to school.
>
> Join your child as a member of the local library and see if you can find
> books about ants for you to read together.
>
> With your child, collect ants in a jar and study them. Talk about what
> you see, draw what you see, write about what you see.
>
> If you have an Internet connection, see what you can find out about
> ants. You will probably discover a lot of information, much of it with sci-
> entific terms unfamiliar to your child, so don't overload him or her with
> facts. Just put into your own words some interesting information. *We
> don't want the children to come into the classroom with pages of scientific facts
> that you have simply printed from the Internet.* It is far more valuable for
> them to come into the classroom with a few facts they can talk about in
> their own words.
>
> When your child has selected an animal for investigation after the ant
> study, he or she will need your help again.
>
> Thank you so much for your help.
>
> Yours sincerely,
>
> Pam and Tony

Is That a Fact?

As you can see, we emphasized the fact that we did not want the children to come in with printed matter full of technical and scientific terminology that they could not read. Our emphasis was on oral language, a very important factor when there are many children in the class who are beginning readers.

Friends at School

Children's learning from each other is a valuable resource we can utilize to help them extend their understanding of a given topic. This is especially true when the children are engaged in individual investigations. During the writing workshop, children need to feel comfortable asking each other for specific information, and the teacher needs to set these routines in motion from the beginning. I always encouraged my students to help each other with their research. This stemmed from my belief that children can and do learn from each other and that I, the teacher, am not the sole holder of information. I recently saw an example of this in a kindergarten classroom where I had been working. Carla, a motivated and confident little learner, was struggling with a report on cats that she had been working on. She had reached the point where she could think of nothing else to write about. I questioned her carefully in order to get her to extend her ideas and think more deeply about what she was writing. Carla became frustrated with my attempts and simply stated, "Tony, you're not helping me much. I think I'll talk to Andrea. She's got a cat. She'll help me." Sure enough, after her discussion with her friend Andrea, Carla produced a mountain of information. Children seem to have their own unique way of communicating with each other, which we as adults are often unable to tap into. I call this "kid talk" and have found it to be a very effective component of my writing program.

One way to encourage kid talk is to make a chart listing all the individual investigations children are engaged in to display in the classroom. An example of this can be seen in a unit of study I did on procedural texts. We had completed our whole-class investigation on how to grow carrots, and the children had all selected a topic they were going to explore individually. I listed these on a chart, as follows:

Our Investigations
How we get to school: Melissa, Maryanne, and Henry
How to make a sandwich: Christopher, Peter, Lucy, Pedro, and Marsia
How to play soccer: William, John G, John R, Franco, and Alex
How to make a cake: Sara, Joanna, Jay, Petra, and Alexis
How to make your mom happy: Jason
How to look after dogs: Wanda, Richie, Christian, Jeff, and Melinda

I then discussed with the children ways they could help each other with their investigations by telling each other information they had about each other's topics. In the beginning I orchestrated this by pairing children up and giving them five minutes to talk with each other about their topics. This was an enlightening experience for me, as I soon realized that although my students often drove me crazy with their constant chatter, when I asked them to talk to each other on a given topic they were silent. I couldn't believe it: here I was, telling them to talk, and they didn't know how. I proceeded to provide a whole-class demonstration by having Lucy stand in front of her peers and ask them to tell her as much as they could about making sandwiches. This proved to be an effective strategy, so each day during individual explorations I made sure to allow time for whole-class discussion on one of the topics selected. It was not long before the children were able to assist each other on their own and talk together in pairs. They had learned ways to share specific information.

Oral language is a powerful medium that all writers need to engage in before putting pen to paper. However, we need to demonstrate specific kinds of talk, as children often are engaged in limited forms of oral language, usually revolving around playground matters.

Television

Television—that dreaded word! How we love to blame it for all evils. Yes, it does contribute to many problems with our children, but it can also be one of our greatest assets when it comes to research as long as it is used appropriately. I have all but given up on asking children to go home and see if there is anything on television about the topic we are studying because chances are there is not. If by some miracle there is, the child has to contend with convincing family members that it is more important for them to watch the documentary on ants than the latest game show or sitcom. It rarely works. Television is far more powerful in a controlled environment—namely, the classroom, when you, the teacher, can guide children through viewing with careful questioning.

In the unit on ants, for example, I brought a documentary into the classroom for the children to see. We watched the first five minutes of the documentary; I then stopped the tape. I asked the children to tell me what they had found out so far and recorded this onto chart paper as information we could use for our report. I then asked them to look closely at the next five minutes to see if there was information that we didn't already have that could be added to our report. Occasionally I would also freeze the screen so that the children could concentrate on a certain visual to notice, for example, what specific ants looked liked.

This approach worked well. It broke up the documentary into small, manageable chunks and allowed children to process and talk about these small chunks of information. If I had simply let them watch all of the documentary in one sitting, chances are that many of them would have become restless and the information they gave me at the end of the watching would have been confined to a few isolated facts they had remembered. These facts would most likely have come from the end of the documentary, because the last pieces of information presented would be the ones they would remember.

Over the years I have built up a collection of television programs and documentaries that I can use in class when we explore a specific genre and related topic. Segments from the Cooking Channel, for example, are great to show children when they are exploring recipes.

The Internet

Technology is increasing at such a rapid rate that it is difficult for most us to keep up. The Internet is a prime example of the vast amount of information available to us, with new web sites expanding at an enormous rate. This poses problems when we ask children to use the Internet to locate information, as they are faced with massive amounts of information often at reading levels far beyond their abilities.

One way to assist our learners is to have them locate information on the Internet with their parents and family members at home as described earlier. If Internet access is available in the classroom, the teaching assistants or classroom helpers can be of help. They can work with the children to locate information on the Internet, then read the relevant information to the children and ask them to talk about it in their own words. In this way children will be able to record information confidently, in their own words, and not just copy or print out slabs of information from the web. Having an assistant work with the children on the Internet also alleviates the problem of you, the teacher, spending too much time with one child when there are twenty-five others who also need your help.

Letting the children work on the computer in pairs without assistance is another option, but I have rarely had success with this method. Unless the children are experts at surfing the net they will spend copious amounts of time just trying to find relevant web pages, let alone getting any real research done. Young learners need guidance. They need to be shown how to locate information on the Internet. Adult supervision is essential to achieve this.

Sally's third-grade classroom had what I called "the Internet moms." Each day one of these wonderful helpers would come into Sally's classroom to work with a pair of children on the Internet to assist them with locating information for their research. We are still trying to form a group of "Internet dads," but unfortunately they are at the moment a rare species in the classroom.

The Experts

Depending on what is being explored, writing letters with the children to experts is another potentially useful source of information. I recall a second-grade classroom where we were writing a whole-class investigation on spiders as part of our unit on report writing. As a class I modeled to the children what a letter looked like; then together we wrote a letter to the local zoo for information on spiders. Two weeks later the children were delighted to receive a large package from the zoo with lots of information about spiders, which was added to our whole-class report. By writing the letter with the children I was demonstrating how one form of writing—namely, letters—could assist us in the creation of another—namely, reports. So often we demonstrate letter writing to children with no real context for engagement. I remember a story my friend and colleague Faye Bolton told me. A teacher had told Faye that when she did letter writing she had her students write to the ducklings in a story she read to them. Faye asked the teacher, "Did the ducklings write back?" Faye's implied point is a good one: too often we engage our students in purposeless activities. In this scenario it would have been far more relevant if the children had written to the author of the book with their opinions and questions about the story. That way there was a chance that the children might receive a reply.

When writing to experts it is best to do it early in the investigation, it can take a while to get a response. It would be a shame to get a reply only after the whole-class investigation is over.

Direct Experience: Observations and Field Trips

Of all the ways for children to gather information, direct experience—the hands-on approach—is one of the most powerful. Much, however, depends on what is actually being investigated. For example, if the children were exploring how to write explanatory texts with the question "Why there is night and day?" as the whole-class investigation, apart from a possible field trip to the planetarium their information gathering would be limited to printed materials and discussions. But if the children were studying how to write reports and insects was the whole-class topic, the teacher could bring in jars containing insects for the children to study firsthand.

In my third-grade classroom this was exactly what I did. The children were divided into groups of four, and each group was given a jar containing a small number of insects. I also gave each group a number of magnifiers. (These flat magnifying sheets can be purchased inexpensively, often from bookstores, as they are often used to assist people with poor eyesight when reading.) I also set up an ant farm for the children to study. I gave each child a name tag, which had under each name the words "Researcher on Insects." I told the children that they were scientists and that each day, as part of our whole-class investigation, we were going to study insects to add to our report. The children took to this concept of being researchers with enthusiasm. Many of them bought in their father's old white shirts to use as lab coats. One child, Renee, also brought in a pair of glasses with the lenses removed. With her lab coat, name tag, glasses, and pencil behind her ear she looked quite the part.

Field trips are another excellent means of giving children a direct experience with research. However, a field trip should have a clear focus and not simply be just an outing. Often when engaging children in research through field trips the parameters are too broad, and consequently the children have little idea of what information they are supposed to be gathering. I recall one year when we were studying explanatory texts, with airports as the topic. I arranged an outing to the airport. The children and I had been talking about what goes on at airports, and I thought the field trip would do much to add to our investigation. Unfortunately, however, I gave the children and the parent helpers no idea of just what we should be looking for during our visit. Consequently, when we returned to school after our visit the only things the children could describe were the shops they had seen and the bus ride home.

I learned my lesson. The following year, when I repeated the unit of investigation with a different group of children, I was far better prepared. This time, prior to the field trip I brainstormed with the children all the relevant information we needed to collect to complete our investigation on airports. I then wrote this information on a sheet of paper, with notes on specific things the children should look for while they were there:

We are going to the airport.
Can you find out:
What happens to people's bags?
Where people check in?
How many different airplanes you saw?
Where people can eat if they get hungry?
Where people collect their bags when they get off the plane?
Where people get onto the plane?
Where people go if they need information?
How people know what gate to go to?
How people know if their plane is late?

I gave my parent helpers a copy of the sheet and asked them to ensure that they discussed the information with the group of children they were working with on the field trip. When we returned to school and began our in-class discussions I was amazed at how much specific information the children had gathered for our study of airports. Although these children, like the previous year's group, had tales to tell about the bus ride home, they had also gathered enough information for us to complete our study.

Interpreting, Recording, Publishing, and Sharing Information

Look, Tony, I drawed a picture—mmm, I mean a dye-dye-gram. It tells you how to play tennis.

Maria, kindergarten

In Chapter 3 we examined ways to help children locate information for research. Once children have completed this task, they need to know how to interpret, record, publish, and share the information they have gathered. Children need to be aware that in writing nonfiction there are a variety of ways to do this. As teachers, we need to help our young researchers make sense of what they read so they are able to interpret not just print but other visual information as well, such as illustrations, diagrams, labels, and maps. The ability to interpret such information will have an enormous impact on the ways they represent and share their research and will help them realize that writers of nonfiction use a variety of features to inform their readers.

Interpreting Information: Fact Versus Opinion

Being able to discern fact from opinion can be difficult not just for young readers and writers, but for everyone. In the past several years when I have conducted workshops for teachers on how to help children write nonfiction, I often invite them to write a piece of nonfiction of their own at the beginning of the workshop. I then ask them to identify which statements they have written are facts and which are opinions. It is amazing to see how many teachers find, to their surprise, that at least one of their statements is not, as they had assumed, a fact, but an opinion. With this in mind we have to ask ourselves a serious question. If we as teachers find it hard to distinguish between fact and opinion, how can we expect young children always to be able to?

While I certainly believe it is important to help students distinguish between fact and opinion, I recognize that this is a complex concept to grasp and do not expect them to experience immediate success. Many years ago I was working with a group of third graders who informed me that sharks eat people. I asked them if they thought all sharks ate people and they replied, "Yes." Nothing I read to them could convince them otherwise, so I simply gave up. (I'm sure the screening of *Jaws* on television earlier that week did little to help.) I believe we need to lead our children gradually to understanding what a fact is and how it differs from an opinion. We also need to demonstrate to children that personal experiences and opinions can have a place in nonfiction writing, as long as they do not dominate the piece. (Refer to the section "The Importance of Voice" later in this chapter for more on the role of opinion and point of view.)

One effective way to help children understand the difference between fact and opinion was demonstrated in Pam Crawley's first-grade classroom. The children had been researching the seashore as part of learning how to write informational reports and had visited the seashore to gather information. When the children returned to school, Pam brainstormed with them some of the information they had discovered and put it on a chart.

Pam discussed with the children the fact that authors not only gather information but also interpret it. She raised the issue of fact versus opinion. The children, with Pam, came up with the following definitions: a *fact* is something you know to be true, something you have read or seen with your own eyes; an *opinion* is something you think or feel. Pam then turned to each of the statements on the chart and asked the children if it was definitely a fact. If the response was yes, she wrote the letter "F" next to the statement. If the children doubted that the statement was factual, Pam wrote the letter "O" next to it.

Some of the statements caused a little confusion, as they were not entirely true. One such statement was "Shells have holes." Pam's questioning techniques were crucial at this point. Asking "Do shells have holes?" would not have sufficed, as most of the children would have simply answered yes. Pam handed out some shells and asked the children to look at them. She asked if anyone had a shell without holes. A number of children replied yes. She then asked if anyone had a shell with holes, to which some children also answered yes. Pam then drew them to the statement "Shells have holes" and asked if this was true for all shells. At this point the children were ready to eliminate the statement altogether but Pam asked the children how they could make this statement true. The words *some* and *most* were thus introduced to the children as words authors use to make certain statements factual. The children then alerted Pam to the statement "Coral has holes" and suggested that the word *some* would also make this statement factual. Pam and the children referred to books about the seashore to verify the validity of certain statements.

Pam discussed with the children how sometimes authors use their own experiences to add weight to particular facts. For example, the statement "Shells smell horrible" was not one that would necessarily have to be eliminated as fact. Given the information that tiny animals live in shells and that many of them die and get washed up on shore, it is certainly reasonable to state that some shells do smell horrible. Pam didn't want the children to lose their voice when writing nonfiction, as that would make their pieces dry and lifeless. At the conclusion of the discussion Pam displayed the finished chart in the classroom, to serve as a reminder of the process researchers go through not only in gathering information but in interpreting it and sorting fact from opinion:

Nonfiction contains lots of facts.

Ways researchers find facts:
1. Observe—take notes.
2. Read what other researchers wrote.
3. Interview—take notes.
Facts: Something you know to be true. Something you have read or seen with your own eyes. (F)
Opinions: Something you think or feel. (O)

What we learned about the seashore from our field trip, looking at books and interviewing people:
There are little rocks like pebbles. (F)
There is lots of sand that was made by water hitting rocks. (F)
You can find shells on the shore. (F)
The seashore is scary and smells. (O)
Shells have holes. (Some)
Coral is hard. (Some)

Coral is gray and blue. (Some)
Coral is made up of millions of animal skeletons. (F)
Coral lives in warm water. (Some)
You can find shells on the seashore. (F)
Shells are the homes to little animals. (F)
Shells smell horrible. (O)
The water is cold. (Sometimes)
Crabs live at the seashore. (Some)
Crabs don't like people. They bite them. (O)
The seashore is smelly. (O)

When it came time for the children to engage in their own independent explorations, Pam reminded them to refer to the chart and check their information to see how much of it was factual. She also reminded them to use the words *most* and *some* if they were unsure and to look through books as a means of verifying their statements. Many of the children did begin to use the words *most* and *some* in their reports. Others, however, did not, which suggested to Pam that she would have to go over the information on fact versus opinion in both whole-class and small-group settings. As teachers we need to acknowledge that one-off demonstrations are not enough. Many children require numerous demonstrations before they internalize new learning.

Interpreting Information from Illustrations

Teaching children to understand what an illustration is telling them is not a practice we have traditionally spent time on in our daily routines. More often than not we are focused on getting our learners to concentrate on the print; yet illustrations, diagrams, and labels are equally informative. This is especially true for nonfiction material, where illustrations represent information not always included in the text. In this way, nonfiction differs from fiction. In fiction, illustrations usually support the text rather than add new information. Young learners need to learn how to read and interpret illustrations found in nonfiction material in order to access new information. I believe that in kindergarten especially it is imperative that we show children how to access information from pictures, as the majority of kindergartners are unable to read print.

One example of how to help children read illustrations is from a K–1 split classroom I had in New York. I used a big book entitled *Spiders* (Cullen 1996) as part of a whole-class investigation on report writing and showed the children page 4 from that book (see Figure 4.1), which contained many illustrations. I covered up the print at the bottom of the page before showing them the page. I asked the children to look carefully at the page and tell me what

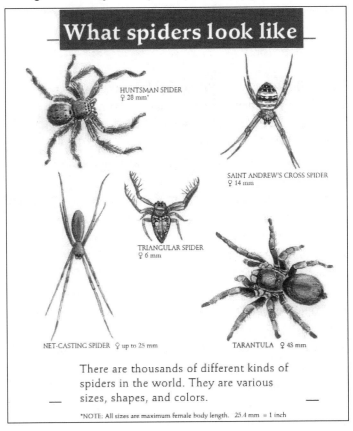

There are thousands of different kinds of spiders in the world. They are various sizes, shapes, and colors.

*NOTE: All sizes are maximum female body length. 25.4 mm = 1 inch

they saw; then I charted their findings on the chalkboard. They came up with the following:

Spiders have long legs.
Some spiders are big.
Some spiders are small.
Spiders are scary.
Spiders bite people.
Some spiders are hairy.
Some spiders are fat and some are skinny.
Spiders have eyes.
Spiders have eight legs.
Some spiders are brown and some are black.

After charting the children's findings I drew their attention to specific aspects of the illustrations, such as the body of the tarantula, and asked them to look closely and tell me what else they saw. They came up with the following:

The tarantula's body is like two circles.
The tarantula has hairs on its legs.
The tarantula looks mean.
The tarantula can bite you.

At this stage I needed to go back with the children and discuss the statements they had made, for some of them were personal opinions, not fact. I drew their attention to the statement "Spiders bite people" and asked them if the picture showed spiders biting. They told me that it did not, so we decided to eliminate this statement. I then went through each statement to get them to confirm their findings with the illustrations. This was an important step in helping the children stick to interpreting what was actually in front of them, as they were extremely eager to share their own personal experiences and anecdotes and as a result had a hard time sticking to the facts presented in the illustration.

After confirming and deleting specific statements I uncovered the print at the bottom of the page and read it to them. We discussed how the illustrations had given us so much more information than the print on that page and that it was a good idea to look very closely at the pictures on a page to find out more. I then divided the children into pairs and gave each pair a picture of an animal and asked them to tell each other what the picture told them, reminding them that what they mentioned had to be something they could actually see in the picture. This was an enlightening experience for them, and the level of conversation was high. The children came up with many interesting facts and were eager to share them with me.

When it came time for the children to research their own animal of choice during individual investigations, I alerted them to the pictures in the books they had borrowed and encouraged them to look closely for information. Many of my beginning readers used these pictures as their main source of information and produced informative reports without ever having read a word on a page. The use of pictures, together with asking friends and family members, gave these beginning readers an option for research and ensured that they didn't simply copy slabs of text from a book. This was also true for the children who were fluent readers. These children also needed to know that doing research was not strictly limited to reading about a topic from a book but included reading pictures, diagrams, and graphs. How very true is the saying "A picture is worth a thousand words." We just need to teach our children how to read the picture.

Representing Information

Just as illustrations are useful in children's researching information, they are also a fine way to show what they have learned.

Illustrations, Diagrams, and Labels

For most children, illustrations are a simple means to represent thought. Young children represent their thoughts in pictorial form long before they begin to experiment with print. Once they begin using print, their pictures begin simply to reflect their written ideas. What we need to demonstrate to children is the power of using pictures not only to support their writing but also to give additional information. One example of how to do this can be seen from the experience of a group of first and second graders.

We had been working on a unit of study on how to write animal reports, and the children and I were ready to add illustrations to our whole-class report on dogs. I began the session by showing and reading to the children page 15 from the big book *Meet the Octopus* by Sylvia M. James (1996), as shown in Figure 4.2.

I asked them if they could find something on the page, apart from the words, that told them what the octopus eats. Many of the children looked blankly at the page, but a few were eager to draw my attention to the diagram and point out that there were pictures of crabs and a lobster and a scallop. I then asked them what they thought the words with the red lines coming from them were. They told me that these were the words *crab*, *lobster*, and *shrimp*,

■ **Figure 4.2** Page 15 of *Meet the Octopus* (James 1996)

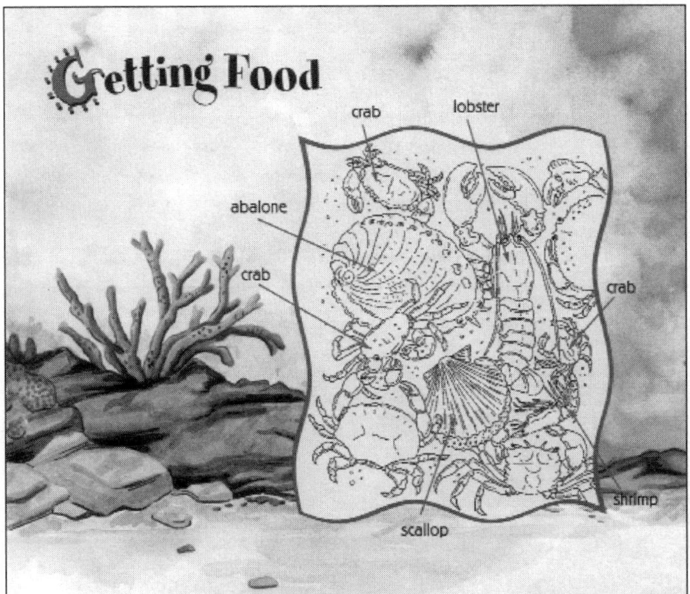

but they also alerted me to the fact that there also were words they couldn't read. I read them the word *abalone,* then informed them that all these words were called "labels" or "tags" and that the author had used a diagram with labels to tell the reader additional information about what the octopus ate.

The following day I gave out copies of *From Egg to Butterfly* (Drew 1997) and alerted the children to the diagram on page 5 of that book, on the life cycle of the butterfly (Figure 4.3). I asked them to tell me what the diagram told them. After much discussion they realized that the author had used one diagram to represent all the information contained in the book. The children thought this was terrific (or, in their words, "cool").

We then turned to our report on dogs and decided to use diagrams and labels in many different places throughout the report. In some instances we decided to get rid of some of the text and let the diagrams do the talking. When it came time for the children to write their own reports, I reminded them to use diagrams and labels to add more information for their readers. It was satisfying to see how many used illustrations and labels to represent the information in their individual reports.

Jose, a first grader who had in the past struggled with writing and usually spent most of his time during writer's workshop recording the same entries with little enthusiasm, surprised me the most with his piece on cats (see Figure 4.4). Jose's piece thrilled me. It was evident that he had processed two important pieces of information: first, he had understood the organizational structure of reports; and second, he had used diagrams to inform his readers. His use of lines to connect his headings, together with his information and diagrams, was certainly innovative. After sharing his piece with the class he told me, "This is fun writing. I want to do more like this."

■ **Figure 4.3** Page 5 of *From Egg to Butterfly* (Drew 1997)

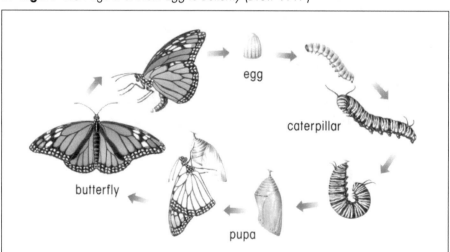

Is That a Fact?

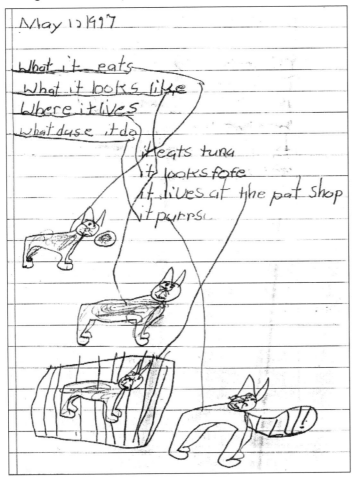

May 12 1997

What it eats
What it looks like
Where it lives
what duse it do

it eats tuna
it looks fofe
it lives at the pat shop
it purrse

This newly discovered technique of using diagrams was not restricted to writing workshop. During math workshop some days later, as the children were working on making up their own addition and subtraction problems, I saw Kevin, a first grader, in deep conversation with Elizabeth, a second grader. When I went over to see what they were talking about I was delighted to discover that they were comparing their use of diagrams to represent their mathematical information. Kevin informed me that his picture (Figure 4.5) was like the butterfly picture that David Drew had used in his book. He explained to me that the picture showed him going to the zoo hoping to see lions, his favorite animal. He told me to follow the arrows because this was a picture of him seeing one lion, then two more, then three. The final arrow led to a picture of him smiling because he had seen six lions, which made him very happy.

Elizabeth explained to me that her picture (Figure 4.6) showed her catching two butterflies and then four more, then another, but one flew away.

■ **Figure 4.5** Kevin's illustration of a math problem

■ **Figure 4.6** Elizabeth's illustration of a math problem

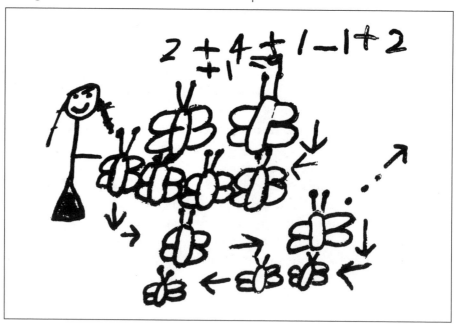

She told me that this didn't matter, because she then caught two more and then another one, so she now had nine. Elizabeth's use of repeated dots with an arrow to signify the butterfly that flew away was truly ingenious.

Another excellent means for children to represent the information they have researched is the Venn diagram. In many classrooms across the country I have seen outstanding examples of these. In my own classroom during a whole-class investigation on writing instructional texts, I demonstrated to my students how they could use Venn diagrams to present information. We had selected rules for playing basketball and soccer as our topic. After listing all the rules for each game I asked the children to look closely at what rules were similar for each sport and what rules were different. I wrote their responses onto a Venn diagram to show them how such an illustration might be used to show overlapping information (see Figure 4.7).

The children became excited with this new form of representation. Some of them, especially the second graders, began to use Venn diagrams to represent their information when doing their individual investigations.

Maps and Keys

How many times have you had to follow written directions in order to get to a destination you've never been to before? It can be frustrating, especially when the directions are not clear or a vital piece of information has been omitted. We have all had that sinking feeling of being lost, and in the case of tourists visiting another country where language is a barrier the situation can quickly turn into a nightmare. I remember clearly when I was visiting Venice and

■ **Figure 4.7** A Venn diagram

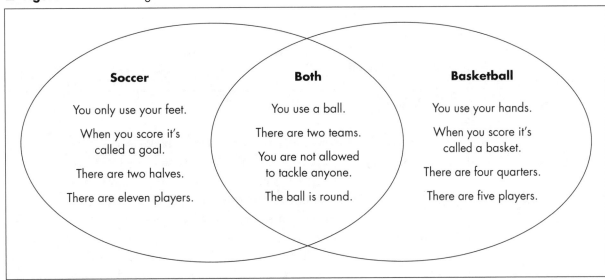

attempting to follow a set of instructions from a travel guide to the hotel where we were going to stay. The directions certainly appeared explicit enough before we actually had to follow them. My wife, son, and I ended up on a three-hour tour of the labyrinth of narrow streets and alleys that make up Venice. Asking the locals for directions proved more frustrating than attempting to follow the guidebook. Finally, by pure chance, we happened upon a tourist information office and bought a detailed map of this beautiful city, which was not looking so pretty to us at the time. With map in hand we were able to find the hotel in less than ten minutes. What was most frustrating was that when we got there we realized that the hotel was only minutes from our initial point of arrival. I now always make it a rule to have a detailed map before embarking on any journey to a new destination.

Maps and keys are important parts of nonfiction writing and are specifically relevant to instructional texts. Children need to learn not only how to interpret a map but how to construct one. One example of how I engaged children in maps was during a unit of study on instructional texts with a second-grade class. I had linked this study with a social studies unit on our school and neighborhood. The children and I discussed the way maps helped readers follow directions, and I showed them many examples from various books I had collected. One terrific resource was *The Key to Maps* by Harley Chan (2001). This book consists of a simple text full of maps with keys, which show children how to locate specific places of interest using the maps and keys as a reference.

I divided the class into small groups and gave each group a copy of the book. We then discussed how maps and keys helped the reader find specific information and what elements a good map needed to contain. I charted their responses, as seen below:

A Good Map:
Has pictures to help the reader.
Has a key to show the reader different things to look for.
Shows you the distance you have to walk.
Is easy to follow.
Has roads and streets to show you which way to go.
Is not too small to read.

I then gave the children a sheet of paper and asked them if they could try to construct a map to show people what our classroom looked like so that we could give it to visitors and new children to help them know where to find different things in our classroom. They came up with many different ways of representing the layout of the classroom, but what was common to all the maps was that each child had attempted to use a key with illustrations to represent their information. Later in our investigation we went on a walk through our neighborhood, and I gave each child a clipboard with paper and pencil to record illustrations of shops, houses, buildings, and trees so that later we could use the pictures to construct a map of our neighborhood. I noticed that the more examples of maps I showed the children and the more they tried to design their own, the better they got at it. They started to include details readers would need and began to take a top-down perspective. Over the course of our study I came to realize that children need many demonstrations and engagements for them adequately to understand and use new information. But by the end of the unit we had compiled a wonderful book entitled *Our Book of Maps*, which included maps of our school, homes, and neighborhood. Appendix C provides some forms that can be used as a starting point for children designing their own book of maps.

The Importance of Voice

Stephanie Harvey (1998) describes the importance of voice, in her words "Showing not telling: How not to sound like an encyclopedia" (p. 157). In her book *Nonfiction Matters*, she raises many issues of particular relevance to the writing of nonfiction in the early years of school. Young children can easily fall into a clinical, repetitious, and monotonous way of representing the facts they have found. Their sense of voice can be easily lost, making their piece indistinguishable from all the others. It is what I call the "Orwell 1984" approach to recording research. An example of this was Kathy's report on flowers:

Flowers by Kathy
Flowers are pretty.
Flowers can be red.
Flowers can be yellow.
Flowers can smell nice.
Flowers have a stalk.
Flowers have leaves.
Flowers can be small.
Flowers can be big.
Flowers grow in the garden.
Flowers like rain.

Here is a prime example of the "Orwell 1984" approach. What was so depressing about reading this piece was when one compared it to her initial piece on flowers, which she wrote before she began her research:

Flowers by Kathy
I love flowers they look good. The yellow ones make me happy.
Flowers live in the garden. The bees live with them. They like rain. They love the sun.

Kathy had collected a wealth of good information for her research project; she just need guidance in representing it in a way that would be engaging for her audience.

One suggestion to help Kathy and other children who simply record their information as a list is through modeled writing encounters. In Kathy's classroom I had noticed that she was not the only learner generating uninteresting streams of information; there were at least five others. I brought them together for a small-group modeled writing session. I showed the group a list of all the information I had collected about bees, then demonstrated how I kept my sense of voice by using words that engage the reader. First, I wrote the words "Bees give us honey," then crossed it out and wrote "Do you like honey? Do you know that without bees we wouldn't have any?" While doing this I thought aloud so that the children could hear my thought process. I used questions such as "Now, what words could I use to make my information sound really interesting?" At the conclusion of the demonstration I asked the children to go back and look at their information to see if they could make it sound interesting. I noticed that Kathy proceeded to cross out her first statement, "Flowers are pretty, and replaced it with "Flowers are very pretty. Lots of people love them." Clearly my brief demonstration had already had an impact on her understanding that good writers of nonfiction engage their readers with interesting language. This demonstration I constantly repeated, both in small-group and whole-class settings.

Although nonfiction writing is based on factual information, children need to understand that their own personal experiences can be called into play to give depth and voice to the information they have gathered. Ralph Fletcher (1993) and Stephanie Harvey (1998) both talk about the importance of voice in writing nonfiction. Here is a different example, Brendan's piece about dogs:

Dogs by Brendan
Dogs can bark.
Dogs have got big teeth.
The dog near my house tries to chase me when I go home.
I've got a dog. His name is Ralph.
Dogs hate cats.

In this piece Brendan includes personal experiences about both his dog and the dog near his house. This information, however, is not directly linked to factual information about dogs in general, which was to have been the purpose of his piece. What Brendan needed to understand was how the information about the dog near his house was valuable information when it was used to support factual information about dogs in general—for example, he could add the sentence "Sometimes dogs chase things that move" before "The dog near my house tries to chase me when I go home." Similarly, the information about Ralph could be extended to tell us what Ralph ate to support factual information about what dogs eat in general—for example, "Dogs eat bones. I've got a dog called Ralph. He likes to eat bones." Brendan, like many learners, certainly needs to be encouraged to tap his own personal experiences; however, he also needs to realize that nonfiction writing includes facts and differs from personal narrative in both purpose and structure.

Here are some other topics for which valuable demonstrations can be made to help children give life to their nonfiction pieces:

Using adjectives.
Using adverbs.
Using similes.
Making interesting beginnings.
Composing great conclusions.
Asking your readers a question to capture their interest.
Trying to say things in different ways.
Including only the most amazing facts.

Publishing Research: A Sea of Possibilities

Once children have gathered their information they are usually eager to publish their research and share it with an audience. Traditionally in many classrooms children's publications usually take the form of books or charts. Nonfiction in particular, however, presents a sea of opportunities when it comes to publishing. Our young writers need to be exposed to the range of possibilities when presenting their research. In Table 1.1 I outlined some of the key purposes and relevant forms of nonfiction. Table 4.1 takes those purposes and outlines the many ways children can publish and share their research.

Many young writers like to see a project completed quickly, and the thought of continually revising and adding information to their pieces before finally publishing them can be frustrating. There's no problem letting these early learners publish as they go in order to maintain their interest and give them a sense of accomplishment. Kelly, a kindergartner, is a prime example. Kelly was working on a persuasive piece as part of her individual investigation entitled "Should children have to go to school?" She had told me that she wanted to write that school was fun, so kids should go. After she had finished representing her idea through picture and scribble I asked her if she could tell me another reason why children should go to school. She replied that school made you learn stuff. I asked her if she would like to write and draw about this. Her reply was forthright: "No. I'll do that tomorrow. I want to make this one look better." It was evident that Kelly had had enough of the composing process and was eager to present today's argument in a polished

■ **Table 4.1** Nonfiction Publishing Possibilities

Purpose	Ways to Publish Research
To describe	Wanted posters Scientific reports in the form of books, charts, and posters Audio cassette tapes Videos, either of children talking about their research or mini-documentaries
To explain	Demonstrations of experiments Scientific explanations in the form of books, charts, and posters Audio cassette tapes Videos (documentaries)
To instruct	A book of favorite recipes Rule books or posters A book of maps Letters that give instructions Board games, complete with instructions
To persuade	Debates Letters to newspapers Reviews Posters to be displayed around the school or in the local community Interviews
To retell information about a person or past event (nonfiction narrative)	Biographies Letters to people in the community Diaries or journals Theatrical performances Movies Scripts
To explore and maintain relationships with others	Cards Letters Questionnaires Interviews

form, so I let her. Within five days Kelly had completed her piece by doing a little bit of composing and publishing each day. To have demanded that she do all her composing first before taking her piece to publication would not have been advisable, as it would have taken the decision-making process away from her and made the composing a chore that she would only com-

64

plete because I, the teacher, told her to. The joy of being a writer would have been lost—something I never want to have happen to my students. Eventually in later pieces Kelly began to do far more composing before taking her pieces to publication. She had begun to build up a stamina for composing. Some pieces she decided didn't need to be published but were suitable to share in draft form.

For learners who have built up a stamina for composing, I always encourage them to work on their drafts, continually adding new information and making revisions. They are aware that not all their pieces need to be published; they select carefully those pieces they want to work on more closely with an eye toward publication.

In assisting children with the publishing process we must provide them with appropriate materials. In my own classroom I always had a publishing cart full of colored markers, colored pencils, letter stencils, cardboard, various types of paper, glue, scissors, and magazines for cutting out pictures. I assigned monitors to care for the cart and to ensure that supplies were kept tidy. Many of my students brought in items from home to add to the cart, and we also asked for donations. It was not long before our cart was full of wonderful materials for the children to use. Some of their favorite reading material became stationers' catalogues. They would plot and plan all the materials they thought we needed to buy with whatever funds we had.

I also had a copyright and date stamp to use on completed pieces so that the children could see themselves as real writers who produced "copyrighted works" for their audience. I remember when I introduced them to the concept of the copyright stamp and explained to them that writers used this symbol to stop other writers from copying their words. The children thought this was a great idea. Todd, a first grader, surprised me with his next piece, on explanations. He had chosen the topic "why planes fly" and had written:

Plans © fli © coz © thay © hav © wings ©.

When I asked Todd why he had included all the copyright signs he told me that all the words were his and that he wanted to make sure no one copied any of them.

Linda La Porte, a kindergarten teacher whom I worked with at P.S. 148 in New York, had what she called an author's box for her students to utilize as writers (see Figure 4.8). This box contained a variety of materials—crayons, pencils, an assortment of papers, and markers—for children to use when composing and publishing their research. The author's box went home each night with a different child and included a letter to parents explaining ways they could help their children at home with the writing process. (An example of such a letter is shown in Appendix D.) The author's box became so popular that soon Linda had to construct another ten to meet the growing demand!

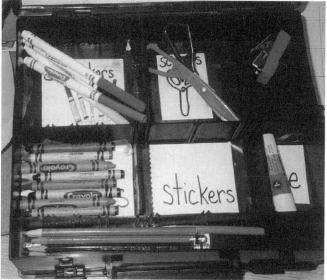

The author's box is just one way to encourage the home-school connection in assisting children as writers of nonfiction. As teachers we place an enormous emphasis on children's reading at home with their parents and spend large amounts of money on take-home books to encourage literacy in the home. Unfortunately, however, when it comes to writing things are different. Writing at home is usually viewed as a solo activity with the parents' role seen as supervisor rather than helper. We need to place an equal emphasis on children's writing at home with their parents if we want them to develop a positive attitude toward writing and the necessary skills as researchers and writers of nonfiction.

Sharing Research

When children have completed their publications, it is important for the teacher to establish ways for the children to share their research or, in the words of Shelley Harwayne (1999), help them in "Going Public." After all, writers write for a purpose and that purpose usually involves an audience of readers. Sharing is important because it develops in our children a sense of pride in their work. This sharing should not be confined to children's published pieces but should include opportunities for children to discuss their research and findings during the composing process. It needs to be an integral part of the daily writing workshop. In my own classroom I always ensured that there was ample time allowed each day for at least one child to share a piece of research they were working on so as to get feedback and advice from their peers. To that end, I displayed a "sharetime chart," which listed all the children's names (Figure 4.9). When a child had had a chance to share his or her research, whether in a polished or a draft format, I colored in a square on the

■ **Figure 4.9** Sharetime chart

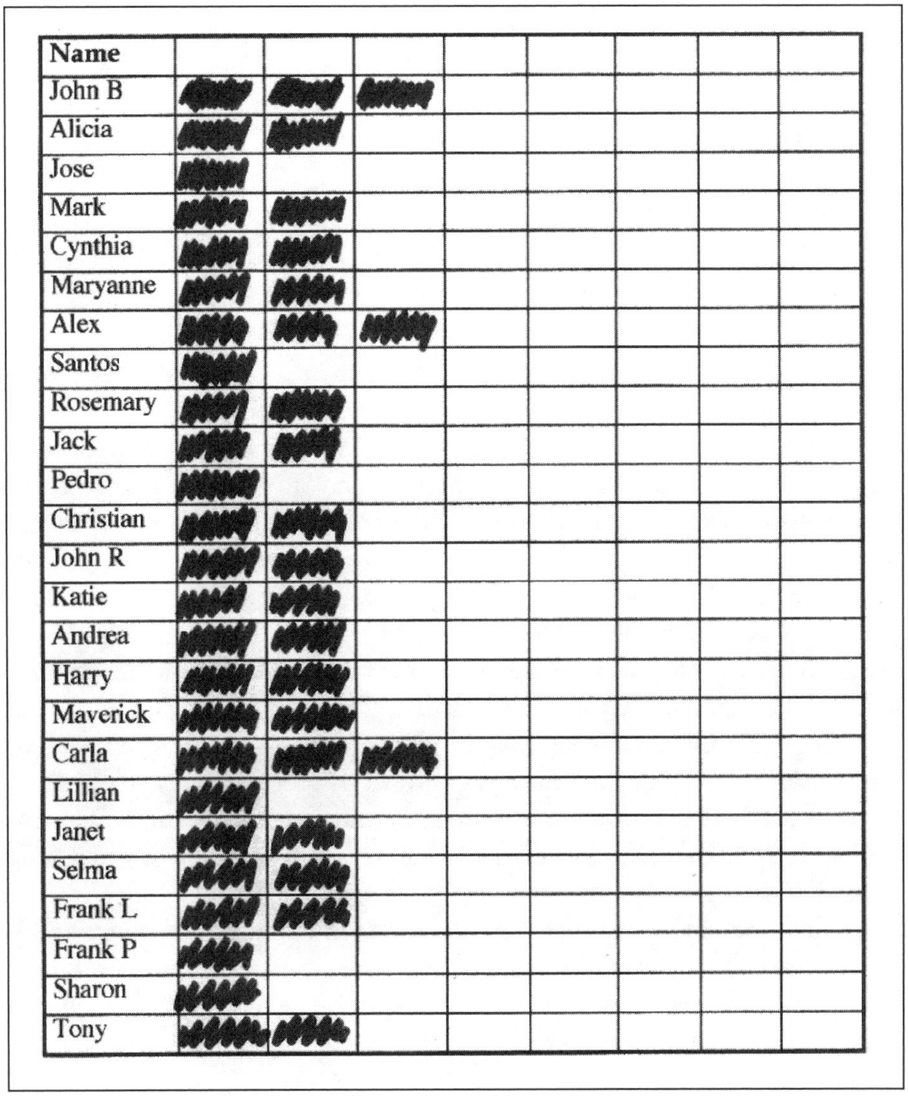

Name								
John B	▨	▨	▨					
Alicia	▨	▨						
Jose	▨							
Mark	▨	▨						
Cynthia	▨	▨						
Maryanne	▨	▨						
Alex	▨	▨	▨					
Santos	▨							
Rosemary	▨	▨						
Jack	▨	▨						
Pedro	▨							
Christian	▨	▨						
John R	▨	▨						
Katie	▨	▨						
Andrea	▨	▨						
Harry	▨	▨						
Maverick	▨	▨						
Carla	▨	▨	▨					
Lillian	▨							
Janet	▨	▨						
Selma	▨	▨						
Frank L	▨	▨						
Frank P	▨							
Sharon	▨							
Tony	▨	▨						

chart next to the child's name to signify that that individual had shared a piece with the class. This became an important evaluative tool for me as it allowed me to see which children had in fact shared pieces of writing with their peers. Often as teachers we simply select children at random to share pieces, and it is usually the children with the loudest requests that continually share, leaving some of our more introverted learners always in the position of audience. As you can see by the chart in Figure 4.9, Jose, Santos, Pedro, Lillian, Frank P, and Sharon had shared only once and needed further opportunities to share their research with their peers. I also included my own name on the chart and shared pieces of my writing to demonstrate the kinds of things to talk about when it was time to share. Teachers with limited display space in their classroom can keep a record of sharing encounters in their planning book and show it to the children as needed. Appendix E presents a sample sharetime sheet.

When a child is sharing in front of their peers, it is important that everyone can see and hear him or her. Many young learners speak softly when talking in front of the class and consequently only the children at the front can hear what they are saying. This quickly leads to problems, as the children in the rear become bored and usually start talking to each other. Before long, the child sharing at the front is drowned out by the noise of the children in the rear. One way I overcome this dilemma is by having the child who is sharing use a karaoke machine or other device that projects sound. (Thanks to Chuck Murfitt, a teacher from the Eliot School in Boston, for this idea.) This ensures that every child can always hear the person who is sharing work.

One good idea for having children share their published explorations is to set a deadline for their individual investigations to be completed so that a class party or author's launch can be arranged. One year my students had studied procedural texts and had written their own favorite recipes. I arranged an official launch of their recipes. The children and I composed a letter to family and friends and invited them to the launch. We prepared food and served our visitors lemonade in plastic champagne glasses. Together we toasted our wonderful authors. Then the children read their publications to the eager audience. The principal, one of our guests, declared that our classroom had become a publishing house that rivaled the very best.

Organizing sharing sessions with other classes is another good way for children to share their publications or works in progress. This is especially effective if a number of classes are working on the same unit of study. One year we had four different classes working on persuasive texts. Each day as part of writer's workshop we would send small groups of children to different classes to share their individual investigations. At the Manhattan New School, which my son attends, his kindergarten teacher, together with the third-grade teacher, had the two classes pair up and work together on a piece. Fraser and Itimar, his third-grade writing buddy, produced a wonderful procedural text on how to plan a birthday party.

Children's published individual investigations together with published whole-class investigations can be housed in the classroom library for other children to read or in a separate section of the classroom reserved exclusively for published works. I have also found it advantageous to house these publications in topic baskets (discussed at the beginning of Chapter 3). At the end of the school year I always allowed my children to take their publications home, but I also encouraged them to donate some to the classroom library for the children of future years to read and utilize as a resource when researching. I gave the children who had donated their publications a label to stick on their pieces to signify that they had donated this piece (for example, "This publication was kindly donated by Joanne Marcus in 1998. Thank you, Joanne.").

Many of the children were eager to donate their pieces. Within three years I had accumulated over 150 publications, including some cassette recordings, which had been placed in the various nonfiction topic baskets. These donations proved very valuable: they allowed me to build up a bank of nonfiction resources at readability levels my students could cope with. It also allowed the children to see models of what other children had produced and gave them guidance in writing their own pieces. In short, this was a perfect example of the reading-writing connection: my learners were reading the writing of their peers in order to become better writers for future audiences of their own.

One year one of my students, Josie, was doing a recipe as part of her individual investigation on procedural texts. She went over to the "recipes" basket to locate information. She grabbed one of the publications with the accompanying cassette tape from the basket with delight and hugged it tightly. "My brother wrote this when he was in grade two!" she exclaimed delightedly. "I can't wait to show him his book and listen to him on this," referring to the cassette tape. "I'm going to make my recipe just as good as his!"

Helping with Spelling

Tony, I got lots of stuff to write. Can you help me write it? I can't spell the words.

Joseph, grade 2

In Chapters 3 and 4 we examined ways to help children become better researchers and composers of nonfiction. Specifically, we explored ways to help them locate, interpret, represent, and share their information. Most of the information children gather and will want to share with an audience is represented through print. Given this fact, we need to be able to help them with the surface features of writing, specifically spelling.

Of all the writing skills, spelling is the one that frustrates many teachers. It also frustrates many children. For some, spelling words correctly becomes the focus of their writing, and getting across the information they have discovered becomes secondary. This was clearly demonstrated to me by Lucy, a third grader. I watched her as she attempted to write an explanation of how planes fly. Lucy was a very articulate learner and was extremely competent at research, but her spelling often gave her problems. I watched as she began writing the sentence "Planes need fuel to give them thrust so they can go high speeds and lift off the ground." It was evident that when she came to the word fuel she was unsure how to spell the word. She made several attempts, then crossed the word out and replaced it with the word gas. Lucy was restricting her choice of words because of her inability to spell. To Lucy, getting the correct spelling was more important than using the words that would best convey her message. This is common with many children. Usually the problem is at its peak in the beginning years of school, especially in kindergarten and first grade, where children have a limited number of words they feel comfortable spelling. It is no wonder these children record the same things every day in writing workshop. The usual daily record of "I love my mom" or "I went to the park" reflects words the children feel comfortable spelling and so form the basis of their message.

As teachers we need to find effective methods to encourage children to approximate—to try spelling words they want to use—so that their message becomes paramount in their writing, and is not governed solely by spelling. Research by Richard Gentry (1987), Richard Gentry and Jean Gillet (1993), and Faye Bolton and Diane Snowball (1993) has identified the various stages children go through on their way to becoming conventional spellers. By recognizing these stages of development we can better come up with strategies to support our learners, encouraging them to take risks when they write. Richard Gentry (1987) identifies these stages as the following:

> Scribbling and/or drawing (prior to invented spelling).
> The precommunicative stage.
> The semiphonetic stage.
> The phonetic stage.
> The transitional stage.
> The conventional stage.

Scribbling/Drawing

Before children use symbols to represent thought they often scribble or draw. This is commonly seen in children just starting kindergarten. They usually begin by drawing their thoughts (see Figure 5.1). Children at this stage do not yet understand that the alphabet can represent thought through various combinations based on sounds.

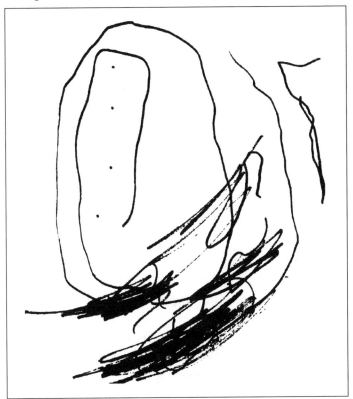

Figure 5.1 was part of kindergartner Jennifer's individual report on snakes. Jennifer told me that this was a picture of the snake and that it was eating some food. Jennifer also informed me that the marks under the picture were the writing. She told me it said, "The snake is black and yellow, and it likes to live in the jungle." Clearly Jennifer had valuable information to share with her audience and used both an illustration and her early concept of print, which was at this stage scribbling, to represent her thoughts.

When children are at this stage of literacy, I ask them what they have recorded or drawn. I write this down so I have a record to refer back to and read it back to them if they forget. If the child wants to publish the piece, then I write it down clearly for him or her to copy. I always give these children encouragement and tell them how wonderful their recordings are.

In order for these youngsters to move on to the next stages and begin using invented spelling, they need to learn the alphabet and become aware of phonemes and the relationship between sounds and letters. Much of this can be demonstrated during shared reading, shared and modeled writing, performing chants, singing songs, and doing other activities at literacy centers.

The Precommunicative Stage

At the precommunicative stage of development, children begin to become aware that thought can be represented by symbols. They may use both conventional and nonconventional symbols. They use letters they have seen around them, and may use strings of the same letters. They frequently mix upper- and lowercase letters, and their writing is usually not readable by others (see Figure 5.2).

Children at this stage do not understand letter-sound relationships, and this usually frustrates them. Many children at this stage are aware that what they are writing is spelled incorrectly, and they constantly ask the teacher for help. Their constant cries of "How do you spell———?" lead many teachers to despair. Children at this stage of development need to feel comfortable taking risks in using whatever symbols they feel are valid to record their research. They also need to use pictures and sketches to record their message. Their most obvious need is to develop their ability to hear specific sounds in words. As with children at the scribbling/drawing stage they need to learn letter-sound relationships through demonstrations during shared reading and writing encounters, along with chant rhymes and songs. But the question remains: What should we do as teachers to help these children up to the point at which they develop a basic understanding of letter-sound relationships?

Recently in one of the schools where I consult weekly, a teacher named Mary asked for ways to help her children record their findings during an investigation into instructional texts. Many of her children were at the precommunicative stage of writing, and when it came time for them to record their findings, many just sat staring blankly at the page. Others recorded page after page of letters and nonconventional symbols. Some of these children, such as Marian (see Figure 5.2), could tell Mary lots of information, while others looked at their marks on the paper oblivious that they were trying to convey a message. Some simply copied lists of words from around the room. Mary

■ **Figure 5.2** Marian: "You make the Jell-o with water. You mix it. The Jell-o is red. It tastes good. It is cold."

was frustrated and asked me for ideas on how to help her children become better writers and in particular better spellers.

The first step was to make sure that all the learners in Mary's class clearly knew the message they wished to convey before they began the recording process. (This is true for all writers, whatever their stage of development.) Mary and I began brainstorming as a class all the things the children were planning to write about. They had just finished making Jell-o and were going to record their findings for a book on favorite recipes. We ensured that each child knew exactly what he or she wanted to say before they went back to their places to write. The children were given time to talk to partners about what they were going to do so that they all had at least one idea to get them started.

Mary and I knew that even though all the children were now clear on what they were going to write, many, because of their lack of knowledge of letter-sound relationships, would find the recording process difficult. We encouraged these children to sketch their thoughts and use whatever letters they liked to convey their message. We kept records of their approximations so that their messages would not be lost. Some of the children would not write at all, so we encouraged them to do a drawing first and then we did the writing for them after they told us the message they wanted recorded. As we wrote for them we thought out loud to demonstrate our thought process—for example:

Tony: So what is your picture about?
Linda: This is me. I am making Jell-o.
Tony: Would you like to write about it?
Linda: No.
Tony: How about if I do the writing for you today?
Linda: [*Nods*].
Tony: Okay. [*As I write each word I say it. When I come to the word me I stop and say, "'Me'—I can hear an /m/ sound in that word. So I'm going to write the letter m." I do the same with the first letter of each word for the remainder of the sentence. When I am finished I look at Linda.*]
Tomorrow you might like to think of letters you want to use for the words you want to write.

I then asked Linda if she wanted to tell me more about making the Jell-o or if she wanted to publish this first piece. Linda informed me that she wanted to make a nice copy to share with her peers, so I gave her a clean sheet of paper for her to try recording her message, which I had written. At this stage children will usually do one of two things: they will either copy the print you have written for them or ask you to write it again. I usually encourage them to try copying the print, but if they refuse I gladly write it for them in pencil, as long as they agree to trace over the writing with marker or colored pencil and then complete their illustration.

Some children at the scribbling and precommunicative stages of development need a lot of support. We teachers need to provide them with appropriate scaffolding while encouraging them to take risks with their writing, so that eventually they will feel confident writing on their own. My entire engagement with Linda was brief, no longer than three minutes. It had to be brief, because I had to assist the other children in the class who needed help. I told the children to stay in their seats and while they were waiting for me they could draw their message, talk to their peers at their table about what they were writing, or turn to other assigned work. The one thing I didn't want happening is what I call "the snake"—a long line of children lined up to see me. Some children get very good at forming lines and can spend much of their time in writer's workshop standing in a line.

For the children in Mary's classroom who were comfortable at recording symbols to express thought, I would ask what they had written; then, as I had done with Linda, I gave them the option of either telling me more or taking the first part of their message to publication. It is not always necessary to write for the child at this stage of development, especially for a piece they are not going to take to publication. Some teachers find it useful to use Post-it notes to keep a record of the child's message so that they have a reference the following day to remind the child what he or she had written in case it was forgotten. It is important to give these children positive feedback and encourage them to continue to use symbols to represent their thoughts. However, I also periodically stop these children and ask them specific questions to see if they have developed enough knowledge of letter-sound relationships to begin spelling words semiphonetically.

There was one boy in Mary's classroom, named Jason, who had recorded many symbols, both conventional and nonconventional. When I asked him what his writing said he told me it read, "This is me. I made Jell-o with all my friends. I put water in." I asked him which word said "friends" and he pointed to the letters "Bbr" on the page. I then asked him to shut his eyes and say the word friends and tell me what sound he heard first. He told me that he could hear the sound /f/, so I asked him to write it. I then got him to repeat this process and tell me the next sound he heard. He told me /n/. We repeated this process until he had written *fnds* for *friends*. I congratulated Jason on his efforts. He beamed with pride and said "Oh, is *that* what you have to do." Evidently Jason had an awareness of letter-sound relationships. He had just not made the connection on how this could help him as a writer and make his message readable to others. I believe it is imperative always to be alert with children who are at a precommunicative stage of invented spelling so that as soon as they begin to develop letter-sound relationships I can show them how to use this knowledge to better convey their message through conventional spelling.

The Semiphonetic Stage

Children at the next stage of development, the semiphonetic stage, attempt letter-sound correspondence and make abbreviated attempts at recording words. They usually get the first sound represented correctly but have trouble with vowels. They may also use spaces between words. Their writing can sometimes be read by others, especially if the reader has a context for what is being written about. I am constantly amazed at how good some teachers get at being able to clearly read writing by children who are at this stage of development.

Solomon, whose writing about polar bears is shown in Figure 5.3, is clearly at the semiphonetic stage of development. He has copied the words "polar bears" from the cover of a book and then used his early knowledge of letter-sound relationships to write "are white." Children like Solomon need to learn to stretch out words and say them slowly so that they can begin to make more informed representations. To encourage this, in addition to shared and modeled writing experiences, interactive writing, especially in a small-group setting, is an effective strategy for these learners. The book *Interactive Writing* (Pinnell and Fountas 1999) is a useful reference for teachers who wish to help children develop as spellers through interactive writing engagements. For the children in Mary's classroom who were at this stage of development, as I moved around the classroom I constantly celebrated their attempts to record their thoughts and encouraged them to stretch out the words they were attempting to record to include all the sounds they could hear.

Joanne was one such learner. She had recorded the following:

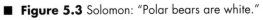

I MD Jl. Ya p Wt. Ya M. Ya P in DU RF.
(I made Jell-o. You put [in] water. You mix [it]. You put in the refrigerator.)

■ **Figure 5.3** Solomon: "Polar bears are white."

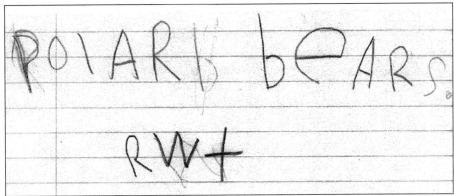

After asking her to read her writing to me, I asked her to close her eyes and say the word *made* slowly, then tell me all the sounds she heard and try to write this word again. She then wrote *mad*. I celebrated her attempt and then asked her to try to write her whole sentence again, only this time to stretch out each word, writing as many sounds as possible. Her final recording was as follows:

I MD Jlo. Y pt Wt. Y MS. Y Pt in DU RFJJ.

Joanne had indeed begun to stretch out the words and had made a giant leap with just one attempt. Children at this stage of development also benefit from using a word wall (see the last section of this chapter) as a reference for high-frequency words.

The Phonetic Stage

Learners at the phonetic stage of development assign letters on the basis of the sounds they hear in words. They represent all the sounds they hear in words, and they are aware of word segmentation and spatial orientation. Their writing can usually be read by others, and they are beginning to accumulate a small bank of known words, usually high-frequency words. An example of this stage is shown in Figure 5.4.

■ **Figure 5.4** Fraser: "What things float? Plastic can float. Wood can float. A feather can float."

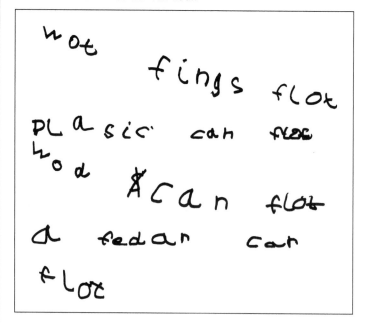

Is That a Fact?

Children at this stage of development need to experiment with alternative representations of the sounds they hear in words. They need to utilize word walls, early dictionaries, or personal word lists and refer to lists of word families and spelling patterns generated in the classroom through shared reading and writing encounters. These children need to know how onset and rime can help them become better spellers.

Several of the learners in Mary's classroom were at this stage of development. As I roved around the classroom I noticed Christian, who had written the following:

> Mkig Jelo. Pot in the wotr. Pot in the jelo. Mcs it togvr. Pot in the Refrigtr. Tak it owt.
>
> (Making Jell-o. Put in the water. Put in the Jell-o. Mix it together. Put [it] in the refrigerator. Take it out.)

I asked Christian what else he was going to tell me about making Jell-o. I did not at first mention his spelling, as I believed it was essential for him to continue to record his message. Too often as teachers we focus on children's spelling prior to getting them to focus on recording what they want to say. Doing this produces learners who see spelling as the most important aspect of writing, with the message secondary. Such learners will then begin to record only words they can spell.

When Christian had completed his composition I drew his attention to several words on his page. I asked him if there was anything in the classroom that could help him spell the word *put*. Mark, one of Christian's peers at the table, couldn't help overhearing, and he said, "The word wall." Together Mark and Christian went to the word wall and located the word. Christian then went through his piece and corrected all of his spellings of the word *put*.

I also alerted Christian to the word *take*, as this was a word that the children had explored when considering onset and rime during a recent shared reading encounter. I directed his attention to the classroom word-family lists that we had made. Christian found these lists to be of help and used them to correct many of his spelling errors.

The Transitional Stage

Children at the transitional stage of invented spelling are able to represent all essential sounds and have learned how to spell many words. They may reverse letter combinations for certain sounds—for example, *shuot* for *shout*, *bouhgt* for *bought*, or as is the case with Lisa in Figure 5.5, *hathc* for *hatch*.

Learners at the transitional stage may remain at this stage for a long period of time (Gentry and Gillet 1993). This fact helps to explain the frustration felt the Chicks haThc WITh ther beks and I DiDiT No That and when they haThc they are guwe and They look cut.

by many teachers who have an abundance of children at this developmental level. The children in Joanne's second-grade classroom were a prime example. Joanne was frustrated at what she saw as a lack of progress by many of her students. Many of them constantly misspelled words that had been brought to their attention several times, on the word wall and lists of word families, and during discussions. I believe that by this stage of development many children feel comfortable with spelling and have developed solid recording habits. For the most part many of these children have recorded the same spelling error so many times in their compositions that the misspellings look right to them. What is really problematic is when these misspellings start to look right to *us* because we have seen the words recorded incorrectly so many times. I remember once I had to stop and really think about how the word *they* was spelled. I had seen it recorded as *thay* by my students for so long that this spelling of the word had started to look correct to me.

Joanne needed to get her second graders out of their old habits and move them into becoming conventional spellers. Often the task of finding words on the word wall or word-family lists in another part of the classroom can become tedious for these children and interrupt their flow as they write. We decided to try giving these learners their own word books, which were simply blank pages with a letter of the alphabet on each page. This, together with personal word lists of words they often misspelled, allowed us to challenge them on spelling errors as we moved around the classroom. As with all learners, we stressed the importance of their getting their message down first; but we also told them to constantly refer to their word books and lists at their table when attempting to record their findings. In a way, we had to break old habits. One learner, Louise, who repeatedly misspelled the words *because*, *which*, and *there* finally broke the cycle after repeated challenges. "I know," she would say as I roved the classroom. "Look at our word books. You don't have to tell me. I can do it."

80

The Conventional Stage

Children who are conventional spellers spell most words correctly and have accumulated a large bank of learned words. These children experiment with alternative spellings and usually recognize when they have spelled a word incorrectly (see Figure 5.6 for an example).

As we can see in Frank's piece, his first draft of a report on animals of the ocean (shown in Figure 5.6), he has misspelled only those words that are content-specific to his investigation. He has also succeeded in underlining almost all his spelling errors (the exceptions being his rendition of *dolphins* and *killer* for *kill* in the second to last line). Although children at this stage of development can usually locate misspellings, getting them to do this once they have written their piece can sometimes be a daunting task, especially if they have

■ **Figure 5.6** Frank's piece

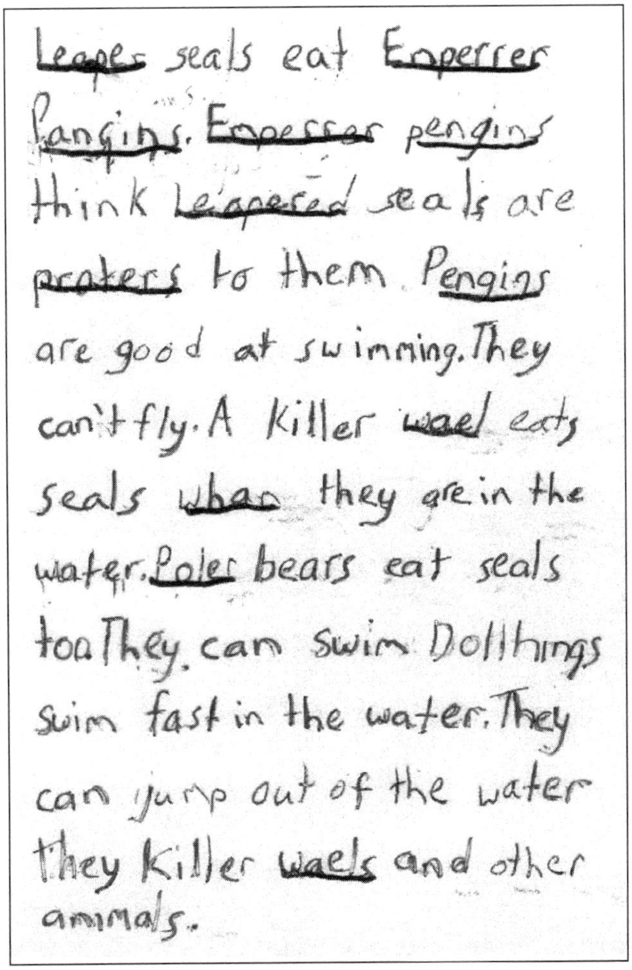
Leaper seals eat Enperrer
Pangins. Enperrer pengins
think Leapered seals are
prakers to them. Pengins
are good at swimming. They
can't fly. A Killer wael eats
seals whan they are in the
water. Poler bears eat seals
toa They can swim Dollthings
swim fast in the water. They
can jump out of the water
they Killer waels and other
animals.

large compositions to review. They often tire of trying to locate spelling errors and end up missing many of them. I often encourage these learners to underline words they are unsure of as they write. When these children begin to write words they are unsure of, they usually get a feeling that alerts them to the fact that they are not quite sure of the correct spelling. I encourage these children to be aware of this feeling of uncertainty, try spelling the word anyway, then underline it and continue with their composition. In this way they will have a list of words to check as soon as they have finished writing and will not have to go back and laboriously check for spelling errors.

Once children have a list of the words they need to check, they need to be shown how to use dictionaries and word lists to locate the correct spelling. If they are using the computer to record their research, they need to know how to use the spell check features of the word processing program they are utilizing.

Learners at both the transitional and the conventional stage of development need to learn ways not only to locate and fix incorrect spellings, but also to learn specific words they constantly misspell so that they don't repeatedly make the same spelling errors. This can be achieved through look-cover-write-check activities, personalized spelling tests, spelling games, spelling investigations, and personal word books and dictionaries. (For further information, see the professional books on spelling listed in the bibliography.)

Ideas for Helping Children Become Better Spellers

As teachers, we need to know exactly what each of our learners is doing when attempting to record research and their stage of development in order to assist them as we rove the classroom. Apart from just giving them assistance, we need to set in motion a variety of strategies students can utilize independently so that they do not have to rely solely on us, their teachers.

Pam Crawley, a first-grade teacher in Queens, New York, accomplished this by brainstorming with her children ways they could find out how to spell words. The chart read as follows:

Stuck on Spelling?
Tips from Grade 1 Room 301
1. Stretch it out. Listen closely.
2. Look at the alphabet chart.
3. Can you picture it in a book?
4. Look at the word wall and around the room.
5. Ask a friend.
6. Get a dictionary.
7. Do the best you can. Just try!

Is That a Fact?

As Pam roved the classroom she would always alert the children to this chart when they were encountering difficulties with spelling.

Word Walls

Word walls—a list of words displayed on a wall of the classroom—are an effective means to help children with spelling, especially spelling of high-frequency words. Word walls have a dual purpose in the classroom: one is to help children learn a bank of high-frequency words for reading; the other is as a reference for spelling words when writing. It is important to ensure that the words on the word wall have been introduced as part of either a shared reading encounter or a writing demonstration. Simply putting up the words without adequate discussion will mean that the children will not know why these words were displayed in the first place and how the word wall can assist them when they write. The words must be printed neatly and be large enough for children to see clearly. Record only high-frequency words. Other words that individual children need can be recorded into personal word books or on individual lists.

Theme Words

Creating a theme word list can assist children during a specific unit of study. This list can be especially useful for children who have a bank of known words but who struggle to spell specific content words associated with a specific writing task. (This was the case with Frank, an example of whose writing was shown in Figure 5.6.) When working on instructional texts with my students, for example, I brainstormed with them all the words we might need to use when writing recipes. I listed these on cards and displayed them under the title "Recipe Words":

make
take
stir
ingredients
shake
slice
flour
carefully
bake

At the conclusion of the unit the cards were taken down and stored in an envelope labeled "Recipe Words." We put the envelope in a box under the word wall for the children to use as a future reference.

EXPLORATIONS IN ACTION

PART 2

Instructional Writing

There is great excitement in the air in Susan Mustac's first-grade classroom. All the children have been replaced by scientists—and not your normal run-of-the-mill scientists. They are six- and seven-year-old scientists who are out to investigate, experiment, and record a multitude of findings. The excitement began one morning when Susan read the book *What Is a Scientist?* by Barbara Lehn (1988). After the reading the children were eager to tell Susan all about the things that scientists explored. They had stories to tell about Dr. Frankenstein and how he was a mad scientist locked away in his laboratory. Susan asked the children if they too would be like to be scientists and conduct experiments and the response was a unanimous yes. "I am going to find out lots of stuff," remarked Robin excitedly. "I'm going to be a mad scientist," said Luckney, which provoked great laughter from his classmates.

Susan had hoped to generate this type of excitement as a way of immersing her children in instructional writing. When Susan and I met to plan out the unit we decided to explore instructional texts through experiments as part of a science unit. Susan had commented to me that although she had done science experiments before, she had never considered linking it with her writing program as a way of getting her children to understand how instructional texts worked. In the past she had always focused on getting her children to understand the scientific phenomena of selected experiments, such as why things float or sink, or why ice melts. Her focus was always on achieving understanding as set out in her science course guides for first graders. What Susan hadn't realized was how easily she could link these scientific studies with her writing goals—in this case, developing her students' understanding of how instructional texts worked. Before we could set the unit in motion, however, Susan had to find out more about this kind of nonfiction writing so that she could provide appropriate demonstrations and learning engagements for her students. Here is the overview I gave.

Overview of Instructional Texts

To help get Susan started, I gave her an overview of instructional texts—their purpose, the forms they take, typical language features, and an analysis of an example of such a text.

Purpose/Social Function

The goal of instructional texts is to tell the reader how to achieve a particular goal or how to follow a set of procedures.

Types or Forms

Instructional texts can take many forms:

> Recipes
> Instructions on how to operate something
> Instructions on how to assemble or build something
> Instructions on how to care for something
> Game rules
> Protocols for experiments
> Directions
> Signs
> Maps
> Shopping lists

Text Structure

An instructional text is usually organized into three distinct parts:

1. What is to be achieved (title, goal, purpose, or aim).
2. The materials, ingredients, or equipment needed.
3. The procedure or steps the reader needs to follow in order to achieve the designated goal or aim. (These steps may be numbered; and sometimes illustrations, diagrams, and labels are used to assist the reader in following the steps.)

Sometimes there is a fourth part, on how to evaluate whether the procedure was successful. (For example, if the procedure selected was how to make cookies, the writer might add at the end, "Taste the cookies. If they are not sweet enough, add more sugar next time.")

Language Features

Instructional texts commonly have the following features:

Action words (examples: *put, let, stir, shake, kick, hold*).

Detailed information on amount, color, size, time (examples: put in *one* cup; take the *red* square; go through the *big* door; the first quarter goes for *20* minutes).

Detailed information on how, when, and where (examples: cut *carefully*; *after* going through the door; *one foot* from the center).

Usually either written in the second person (example: *you* take a ball) or the reader is not referred to at all (example: fold the paper). *Note:* Many young learners write instructional texts in the first person. This is natural for them and should not be discouraged.

An Example

Here is an analysis of an instructional text—in this case, a recipe. Language features are highlighted in bold.

How to make fruit salad for a class of 25 children.	Part 1: Title/aim
Things you need: required	Part 2: Materials/ingredients
8 **big** apples	Information on size
4 containers of strawberries	
2 melons	
8 oranges	
5 cups of raisins	Information on amounts
8 bananas	

2 lemons
A sharp knife
A mixing bowl
A large spoon

What to do:	Part 3: Procedure
Cut the apples, strawberries, melon and oranges into **small** pieces.	Action verb Information on size
Be careful with the knife.	Information on how
Put into a mixing bowl with the raisins and mix carefully with the spoon.	
You can then slice the banana and put it into the mixing bowl.	Second person
Squeeze the lemon juice into the mixing bowl and mix.	
The lemon juice should keep the apples and bananas from turning brown.	
Eat and enjoy.	
If you find the fruit salad too sour, mix in some sugar.	Part 4: Evaluation/testing

A Unit in Action

After reading the book *What Is a Scientist?* (Lehn 1988) and getting the children into the idea of being scientists, Susan set out on each table buckets with water and various objects—pins, pencils, erasers, paper squares, and so on. She then divided the children into small groups and asked them to find out which objects floated and which ones did not and then discuss why they thought specific objects stayed on the surface of the water while others sank to the bottom. The children were then to write up their experiments for the class next door so that that class could try to repeat the same experiment and see if they got the same results. Susan had the children write up their experiments prior to giving them any explicit instruction on how to write such instructional texts because she wanted to use these initial pieces to assess the children's individual understanding of writing instructions. These assessments would help her make her instructional decisions. In addition, by having the children write up their pieces for the class next door she was giving them an authentic purpose for writing.

Assessing the Children's Understandings

Susan used the indicators on the assessment rubric (see Figure 6.1) to determine each child's understanding. (See Chapter 2 for an example of a com-

Assessment Rubric for Instructional Writing

Key: N: Not in evidence   S: Showing signs of   C: Consolidating   M: Mostly   N/A: Not applicable

Name: Grade: Date: Text Type or Title:			
Purpose			
Understands why instructional texts are used			
Recognizes different types of instructional texts			
Craft (Structure, features, voice)			
Linguistic or Text Structure Selects appropriate text type based on purpose			
Aim or Goal Tells reader what is to be achieved			
Materials or Equipment Lists items and quantities needed to perform task			
Method Uses a logical sequence of steps			
Includes all essential steps			
Uses diagrams, labels, and pictures			
Text/Language Features Uses linking words to do with time (*first, then, after, when*)			
Uses present tense (you cut, you serve, you open)			
Uses action verbs (*take, proceed, open, wash*)			
Uses adverbs (*carefully* open, *gently* turn, *slowly* push)			
Uses adjectives (open the *red* packet, get a *large* bowl)			
Includes appropriate headings based on the text structure chosen			
Voice Uses an enticing title and/or setting to engage the reader			
Is able to express ideas using own language as opposed to copying down what others say or information from books they read			
Uses descriptive language that paints pictures for the reader			
Is able to state information in a unique or surprising manner			
Research Skills			
Is able to locate information from books			
Is able to locate information from nonbook sources			
Is able to interpret and talk about information located			
Surface Features (Mechanics)			
Handwriting neat and legible			
Shows improvement in attempts at spelling words			
Uses grammatically correct language			
Shows improvement in use of punctuation			
Uses an appropriate publishing format			
Work generally well presented			

pleted rubric for instructional texts.) She told me that she was amazed at the range of understanding the children seemed to have when it came to writing procedures. Some had no idea where to begin, while others displayed a wealth of knowledge. This was important for Susan to find out. The assessments suggested that while she would need to provide many basic demonstrations during whole-class and individual investigations, she would also need to provide more advanced demonstrations for some of her learners.

The students' range of knowledge can clearly be seen by comparing Julia's piece with Danny's.

Julia's piece

We put things in the water. I put in the wood and it floated.

Danny's piece

Sink/Float
Step 1. Put a bucket of water on the table.
Step 2. Put a pencil in the bucket.
Step 3. Put in a milk cap in the bucket of water.
Step 4. Put a penny in the bucket of water.
The penny sank. The cap floated. The button sank. The pencil floated.

Julia has written a simple retelling of her experiment. She has not demonstrated an understanding that her piece was supposed to instruct others on how to follow her set of procedures. This is common when children initially write instructions. They usually personalize the actions and simply tell the reader what they have done, making the piece not an instructional text at all but rather a personal narrative. Susan had many children at this early stage of development, which meant that she would have to provide many demonstrations on how writers of instructional texts need to tell their readers the steps that have to be followed to achieve an identified goal, and not simply recount their own experiences. Susan would also have to demonstrate how writers of instructional texts identify what is to be achieved, the materials needed, and how to perform the task step by step.

Danny was at the other end of the spectrum from Julia. His piece displayed an excellent understanding of writing instructional texts, especially for such a young writer. Danny had opened his piece with the beginnings of a stated goal to be achieved and had proceeded to list a logical set of steps and the outcome. Danny wrote the piece in an implied second person rather than as a personal narrative and used an action word (the verb "put") throughout the piece. Susan found that a number of children had written their procedures like Danny. This meant that her demonstrations should not be confined to just the basics. This was an important realization. In Susan's words, "I never thought I would have children with this level of understanding in my first-grade classroom. When I had done instructional texts in the past I always just provided demonstrations based on what I thought the children needed. I had never considered assessing them first to find out what they in fact already knew. If I had launched into this investigation without first assessing my kids, many of them, like Danny, would not have learned anything new because of the low level of demonstrations I would have provided." Susan also commented that the assessment rubric had helped her focus on the important elements of an instructional text as well as what to look for when assessing and teaching her students.

The Start of the Whole-Class Investigation

Armed with the knowledge of what each of her students knew about writing instructions, Susan was now ready to begin her whole-class investigation. The topic was finding out about liquids, gases, and solids. The children were asked what science experiments would be fun to do; Susan wrote their responses on a chart. She then asked them where they could find information on how scientists conduct experiments. The children replied that they could find books from the classroom library, the school library, and home. Susan had already obtained many books on how to conduct experiments and had placed them in a container labeled "How-to Books" in the classroom library for the children to use as a resource.

The children returned the next day with many books on experiments and were eager to share. Susan divided the children into small groups and asked each group to look through the books to see if they could find out how scientists write up their experiments. She later brought the children together to discuss their findings, which she wrote on a chart:

Steps in an Experiment
Name of the experiment
Guess—What do you think might happen?
Materials—What are the things you are using?
Steps—How did you do this experiment?
Observations—What did you see happening?
Results—What happened?

Susan informed me that developing this chart was an important step in helping her children understand how experiments were written up, specifically the importance of the writer's informing the audience of the steps needed. Susan had in the past presented these steps to her children in the hope of their taking them up in their writing. She had never in the past allowed them to discover these steps themselves. Doing so now, she felt, would help them internalize the information.

Researchers at Work

During the next five sessions Susan and the children conducted many experiments, which they had selected from their brainstormed list. At the conclusion of each experiment, Susan wrote up the procedures they had followed, using the structure from the chart "Steps in an Experiment." One such experiment was finding out that ice was frozen water and that it melted if it was not kept at a very cold temperature (see Figure 6.2).

It was always made clear to the children that the purpose of their experiments was to find out about gases, liquids, and solids, and the purpose of writing their experiments step by step was to instruct the class next door on how to repeat the process to see if they came up with the same findings. This was important for the children to understand, as it set up an authentic purpose for their writing and conveyed to them the idea that writers write for many different purposes.

After each experiment was written up, Susan gave it to the class next door to see if they could follow the procedures. The class next door were help-

■ **Figure 6.2** An experiment: ice and water

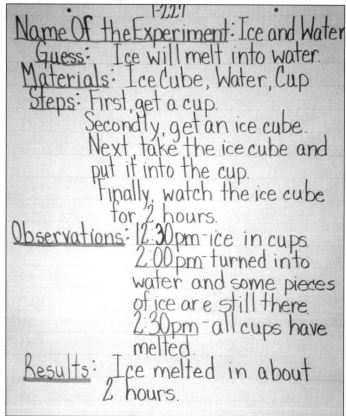

Is That a Fact?

ful for the feedback they provided. When they told Susan's class that they couldn't understand a particular instruction, Susan would take it back to her class for discussion and refinement. Susan commented that her classroom became alive with talk and that writer's workshop was no longer just a time for independent writing in a dome of silence but also included many opportunities for small-group and whole-class discussions. She could see that her writer's workshop was changing and that she was reaching a deeper understanding that good writers are first good talkers who are able to articulate their purpose, thoughts, and ideas.

Demonstrations

As the children continued to write up experiments with Susan, they became more articulate and aware of what makes a good instructional text and why it is important for writers to be clear with their instructions. They were internalizing the author's craft of writing instructions for others to follow. During the whole-class investigation Susan provided her children with many demonstrations based on her initial assessments of the children's understanding of writing procedures. These included demonstrations in both craft and mechanics:

Demonstrations in Craft

The importance of naming the experiment
Including all the equipment you need
Breaking down the procedure into small steps
Using diagrams and labels to help the reader
Using words such as *she*, *he*, *you*, *we*, and *they*
Using headings

Demonstrations in Mechanics

How to spell words
Using the word wall
Handwriting
Grammar
Using capital letters and periods

One demonstration the children picked up very quickly had to do with words scientists use when writing up experiments. Susan read the children many books on experiments. One such book was the big book *Today's Weather Is . . .: A Book of Experiments* by Lorraine Jean Hopping (2000). As Susan read the book aloud, she asked the children to notice the words the author was constantly using to help instruct her readers on how to conduct experiments. The children came up with many words from the book, which Susan wrote down and displayed in the classroom (see Figure 6.3). Susan constantly encouraged

■ **Figure 6.3** Words scientists use

the children to refer to this chart and to the other charts they had constructed together as they continued to conduct and write up experiments for the class next door.

Independent Investigations

Once the whole-class investigation had been completed, Susan reflected with the children on what features of the written experiments had made them easy for readers to understand. She referred the children back to the charts outlining the steps in an experiment, as well as the sample experiment (Figure 6.2) and the list of words scientists use (Figure 6.3). Then she gave them the opportunity to select and perform one of the following experiments from the list they had brainstormed at the beginning of the unit.

1. What makes ice melt the fastest?
2. What happens when you mix flour with water?
3. Does liquid change shape?
4. What things have liquid in them?

For the next two sessions the children worked in small groups while Susan provided support for each group as they conducted their chosen experi-

Is That a Fact?

ment. Susan gave each child in the group a role to perform and instructed them step by step on how to conduct the experiment. As an example, for one of the groups conducting the experiment "What happens when you mix flour with water?" Susan provided the following guide.

1. Tatiana and Luckney: get a cup of water and pour it into the container.
2. Robin and Julia: add the flour to the water.
3. Kalia and Andrea: mix them carefully together.
4. The group discusses what happened.
5. Each person writes up the experiment.

Susan found that she had to have only a few groups working at one time in order for her to give a sufficient level of support. Children not working in groups would continue with their personal writing, such as journals and letters, until it was their time to experiment. Susan was wise not to attempt to have all the children doing experiments at once, for unless there are classroom helpers to assist, chaos can set in very quickly.

Writing the Experiments

After each group finished, Susan asked each child to write up their group's experiment. Before the children began writing, however, Susan alerted them to the charts they had constructed during their whole-class investigation and reminded them that these charts would help them as they wrote. She also told the children that they could ask each other for help if they were encountering difficulties. As a result of this advice, Andrea, an early emergent reader, approached Robin, one of her classmates who was a fluent reader, and asked Robin to read to her the chart "Words Scientists Use." Robin happily obliged, and Andrea later told Susan, "I just gave Robin one of my stickers because she helped me a lot." It was delightful to see the children helping each other and relying on many resources in the classroom besides the teacher.

Whole-Class, Small-Group, and Individual Support

While her students were engaged in individual investigations, Susan always began the writer's workshop with a whole-class demonstration and then asked the children to go back to their pieces to make appropriate revisions based on what they had learned in the demonstrations. Like the ones conducted during the whole-class investigation, these demonstrations focused on both the craft and the mechanics of writing an instructional piece. It was evident that Susan was an astute observer of children; she was what Yetta Goodman (1982) calls "a kidwatcher." Each day during writer's workshop she would rove the classroom, assisting her learners as needed. When she observed that most of her children were encountering a similar problem she would stop the class and provide a brief whole-class demonstration.

As the children wrote their experiments, Susan often found it necessary to call small groups together to give added support. Beginning writers, such as Julia, were especially likely to need help. Many found the task of writing up their experiments a little daunting, so Susan showed them how to break it down section by section. She gave these some forms to use in writing their instructional texts (see Appendix F). The children were asked to think first only about the name of the experiment and write it down, and then to discuss and record the equipment they had used. Even as they were recording their experiments, Susan provided opportunities for these small groups first to talk about what they were going to write on the section of the form they were working on. This valuable time for discussion at the beginning of each workshop allowed the children to formulate, synthesize, and explain their thoughts before recording them. These young learners were far more successful as writers because they were encouraged to talk through their thoughts first.

The children were not expected to complete the recording of their experiments in one sitting but were allowed to concentrate on one section at a time and continue the following day as needed. One child, Jason, found it hard to concentrate for long periods of time and needed short breaks after recording each part of his experiment. (This was true for many of Susan's learners.) Susan gave Jason the option of going on with other writing, such as his personal journal, or working at the letter-writing center after working for ten minutes each day writing his experiment.

Young writers can find it hard to work on just one piece for a substantial period of time. They need many writing engagements to keep their interest level high. But it soon became clear that as Jason worked more and more on writing his experiment, he began to spend more time each day on this task, especially as he saw other children at his table nearly finished with their pieces. This was also true of many of Susan's early writers. Susan's reminding her students that the children in the class next door were eager to try their experiments also gave her class a strong sense of purpose for completing the write-up of their experiments. Before long, Jason wanted to spend all day writing his experiment. Susan informed me that this was true for most of her students. They became so involved in their pieces that they would beg to continue even after writer's workshop was over.

In addition to providing demonstrations on how to write experiments using an appropriate structure and language features, Susan also gave many demonstrations on spelling, grammar, handwriting, and presentation skills. Her children required much assistance with spelling, as many of them were not risk takers. Susan often made corrections for her children, especially for those who were at the early developmental stages of invented spelling. (Refer to Chapter 5 for more ideas on helping children with spelling.)

Is That a Fact?

Sharing and Reflecting

When the recording of the experiments was completed, Susan and her children celebrated the completion of their pieces and gave them to the class next door. What followed was a waiting game. Susan's children were eager to find out whether their experiments were clear enough to follow and whether the children next door would come up with the same results as they had. Each morning they would ask Susan, "Have they finished yet?" Clearly, Susan had set up an authentic purpose for her children to write, and writing fever had taken over her classroom. Finally they received word that the class from next door had finished reading and conducting the experiments, so a sharing session was arranged. It became clear in the course of this sharing session that writing fever had also taken over the class next door. Not only had they loved reading and performing the experiments, but also they were eager to begin writing their own instructions for Susan's children to follow.

Susan completed the unit by reflecting with the children on what they had learned about writing instructions and the steps writers go through when composing such texts. Here is what they said, as Susan recorded their thoughts on a chart:

What We Learned About Writing Instructions
You need to know why you are writing it up. Who is it for?
You start with what you are telling people to do.
You then write down the things you need.
You then tell people how to do it step by step.
You can use pictures to help the reader.
You make sure your writing looks good.
You do your best handwriting so the person can read it.
You try your best with your spelling.

Susan then brainstormed other possible topics of investigation with the children and wrote these ideas on cards. She also copied the information from the charts that were displayed during the investigation onto large cards and put them, with the form the children had used (Appendix F), into a box labeled "How to Write Instructions," which was kept in the writing center for children to use as future reference, should they later decide to write another instructional piece. By placing this information in one place in the writing center, Susan was giving her children guidance as writers. Too often we do wonderful units of study, make excellent charts with our children, and, when the unit is completed, throw away all the information gathered. Without any reminders to refer to, it doesn't take long for children to forget past demonstrations. By keeping a record of findings and references from previous studies we are better able to jog children's memories—and our own.

Assessing Children's Growth

Susan analyzed her students' final pieces and compared them to their first ones. She also returned these pieces to the children so that they could see their own improvement. Both Susan and the children were amazed at how much they had learned. One child, Jacky, commented, "Gee, look at this writing [referring to her first piece]. It's baby stuff! This one [referring to her last piece] is really good!" Too often we don't allow children to be involved in their own assessment. When they do get involved, they are able to recognize their growth and take pride in their achievements.

If we look at both Julia's and Danny's final pieces and compare them with their initial recordings, their growth becomes evident.

Julia's first piece
We put things in the water. I put in the wood and it floated.

Julia's final piece (using the form for an instructional text)
How to:
   Putting flour and water together
What you need:
   Some flour some water a bucket
What you do:
Step 1
   get some flour. I got flour on me.
Step 2
   get the water.
Step 3
   mix it together.
What you found:
   It made sticky stuff.

Julia had made much progress. She had realized that the purpose of an instructional text was to inform the reader about how to do something—in this case, how to repeat her experiment. She had included the materials necessary to perform the set task and three steps for the reader to follow. Even though she had not included information such as amounts and a more detailed account of the steps involved, for such an early learner Julia had shown remarkable progress from her initial piece. She had used the action verbs "get" and "mix" and had written the piece as instruction rather than personal retelling. This was a significant step in Julia's understanding of how one writes differently depending on purpose and audience.

Danny's first piece

Sink/Float

Step 1. Put a bucket of water on the table.

Step 2. Put a pencil in the bucket.

Step 3. Put in a milk cap in the bucket of water.

Step 4. Put a penny in the bucket of water.

The penny sank. The cap floated. The button sank. The pencil floated.

Danny's final piece

Name of my experiment: Ice Matter

My guess: The ice will melt fast in the hat.

Things you need: A hat. 3 cups and 3 ice cubes.

Steps:

1. People take a piece of ice and rub it in their hands.

2. People put it inside the hat.

3. People put it by the window.

4. Which one melts the first? Which one melts the last?

What you find out. The hands melted the ice fastest because the hands are hot. The window melted the ice slowest.

Like Julia, Danny had also made progress in his understanding of and ability to write an instructional piece. Danny's final piece showed that he now understood that writers need to include the materials and amounts necessary to perform a set task. He had shown that he knows that procedures are organized into distinct stages. Danny didn't need a form like Julia did to help him identify these stages. He was able to remember on his own that they were needed.

Reflection and Future Considerations

At the conclusion of the investigation Susan told me that she was amazed at how far her children had progressed in their understanding and ability to write instructional texts. She was also pleased that they wanted to write more instructional pieces. Danny informed Susan that this writing was fun and that he had lots of things to tell people how to do. The chart that the children had drawn up with Susan at the end of the unit, in which they had listed other possible investigations, had stimulated their interest and desire to work with this form of nonfiction writing.

Susan's dilemma now was whether to let the children explore this type of writing further or whether to introduce them to a whole new genre. This was a good dilemma as far as Susan was concerned, for she realized that no matter which path she took, her children were now eager to write nonfiction with a sense of both audience and purpose.

Possible Topics for Whole-Class and Independent Investigations

The unit described in this chapter is just one of many possible ways to explore instructional texts with children. (Chapter 2 describes another unit on instructional texts, using recipes as the selected form.) Listed below are suggestions of other topics that could be explored as a whole class or independently. These investigations may run for any length of time, from one week to six weeks. What is important is that they not be one-day wonders. Children need time and opportunity for immersion, demonstrations, and engagement in instructional texts if they are to become proficient writers in this form.

Here are possible topics:

How to play a specific game (soccer, basketball, volleyball, a card game, hide and seek, etc.).
How to make bread.
How to make pancakes or cookies.
How to get to school.
How to make vegetable soup.
How to make fruit salad.
How to care for a class pet.
How to clean the classroom.
How to tie your shoelaces.
How to get to the school office from the classroom.
How to make a kite.
How to make a paper plane.
How to make clothes out of paper.
Science experiments.
How to grow plants (carrots, potatoes, radishes, wheat, etc.).
How to write a story.
How to fix a flat tire on a bicycle.
Class rules.
Maps (of the classroom, school, local area, home, etc.).
A treasure map.
How to make different colors with paint using only the primary colors.
How to draw or make different shapes.
How to write different letters of the alphabet.
How to draw different animals.
How to use a computer.
Fire safety procedures.
How to find out how tall you are.
How to find out what size your foot is.
How to make a birthday card.
How to make your mom happy.

Resources

This last section lists books that may be of use in helping children locate, research, and write instructional texts. The books are listed alphabetically by title, with series title or author name (if any) and publisher. There are thousands of wonderful books that can be used as valuable resources; the list below provides only a small sample of what's available. I have grouped the books by readability, according to Reading Recovery levels and the Fountas and Pinnell levels. There are a great many different leveling systems in existence, as most publishers have their own method of categorizing texts. I have chosen the Reading Recovery and Fountas and Pinnell systems because they are the most commonly used. (For further information on how to organize classroom books and materials in your classroom, see Chapter 3.)

Instructional Writing

■ Emergent Readers

Approximate Reading Recovery levels 1–4; Fountas and Pinnell levels A–C

Before I Go to School	Storyteller series	Shortland Publications
The Bird Feeder	Storyteller series	Shortland Publications
Can You Make a Bird?		Sundance
Caring for Our Pets		Benchmark Education
Chop and Pop	Reading Safari Magazine	Mondo Publishing
City Signs	Discovery Links series	Newbridge
How to Make a Henhouse	Ready Readers series	Modern Curriculum
How to Make a Mudpie	Learn to Read series	Creative Teaching Press
How to Make a Sandwich	Visions series	Wright Group
How to Make Can Stilts	StoryBox series	Wright Group
How to Make Snack Mix	by Meredith Oppenlander	Kaeden Books
Make a Piñata	Little Celebrations series	Celebration Press
Make a Valentine	Beanbags series	Mondo Publishing
Making a Bird	PM Plus series	Rigby
Making a Dinosaur	PM Plus series	Rigby
Making a Garden	Foundations series	Wright Group
Making a Hat	Windows on Literacy series	National Geographic
Making a Mask		Sundance
Making a Rabbit	PM Plus series	Rigby
Making a Road		Sundance
Making Butter		Sundance
Making Pancakes		Sundance
Making Raisins	Windows on Literacy series	National Geographic
Play Ball		Richard C. Owen
Play Ball	Beanbags series	Mondo Publishing
A Puppet Play	Storyteller series	Shortland Publications
Rules for Pets	Joy Readers series	Dominie Press
Rules, Rules, Rules	Reading Safari series	Mondo Publishing
Signs	Literacy 2000 series	Rigby
Signs	Little Celebrations series	Celebration Press
Signs	Carousel Earlybirds series	Dominie Press
Super Duper Sandwich		Richard C. Owen
You Can Make a Pom-pom	Windows on Literacy series	National Geographic

■ Early Readers

Approximate Reading Recovery levels 5–12; Fountas and Pinnell levels D–G

Baking a Cake		Sundance
Can You Read a Map?		Creative Teaching Press

Caring for Our Lizard		Creative Teaching Press
Chopping and Popping	Reading Safari Magazine	Mondo Publishing
Class Rules	Windows on Literacy series	National Geographic
Cooking Dinner	Windows on Literacy series	National Geographic
Experiments with Water	by Ray Broekel	Children's Press
Gardens Are Great	Reading Safari Magazine	Mondo Publishing
Grow Seed Grow	Discovery Links series	Newbridge
Growing a Plant	Discovery World series	Rigby
How Do You Make a Bubble?	by William H. Hooks	Bantam Doubleday Dell
How to Clean a Dinosaur	Windmill Books series	Rigby
How to Grow a Plant	Visions series	Wright Group
How to Make an Earthworm Farm	Little Green Readers series	Sundance
How to Make a Card	by Kathleen Urmston and Karen Evans	Kaeden Books
How to Make a Sun Hat	Home Connection series	Rigby
Is It Floating?	Sunshine series	Wright Group
It's Fun to Exercise		Rosen Real Readers
Just Graph It		Creative Teaching Press
Keyboards	Reading Safari Magazine	Mondo Publishing
Let's Brush Our Teeth		Rosen Real Readers
Let's Make Something New	Discovery Links series	Newbridge
Let's Measure It		Creative Teaching Press
Make a Glider	Storyteller series	Shortland Publications
Make a Lei		Pacific Learning
Making a Car		Sundance
Making a Cat and a Mouse	PM Plus series	Rigby
Making a Caterpillar	PM Plus series	Rigby
Making a Toy House	PM Plus series	Rigby
Making Oatmeal	Interaction series	Rigby
Making Pancakes	Carousel Readers series	Dominie Press
Making Paper	Little Green Readers series	Sundance
Making Things	Foundations series	Wright Group
Maps		Creative Teaching Press
My Boat	by Kay Davies and Wendy Oldfield	Garth Stevens Publishing
Playing Games	Reading Safari Magazine	Mondo Publishing
Reading a Graph		Benchmark Education
Rules	Discovery Links series	Newbridge
Taking Care of the Dogs	Discovery Links series	Newbridge
Washing the Dog		Sundance
We Can Make Graphs		Creative Teaching Press
What Can You Measure with a Lollipop?	Benchmark Education	
What Floats? What Sinks?		Benchmark Education
Zoo Map	Windows on Literacy series	National Geographic

■ Transitional Readers

Approximate Reading Recovery levels 13–20; Fountas and Pinnell levels H–K

Charlie Needs a Cloak	by Tomie de Paola	Prentice Hall
Finger Puppets, Finger Plays	Storyteller series	Shortland Publications

Floating and Sinking	BookShop series	Mondo Publishing
Floating and Sinking	Sunshine series	Wright Group
Growing Radishes and Carrots	BookShop series	Mondo Publishing
How to Cook Scones	Bookshelf series	Scholastic
How to Make a Crocodile	Little Books series	Sadlier-Oxford
How to Make a Mud Pie	Little Readers series	Houghton Mifflin
How to Make Salsa	BookShop series	Mondo Publishing
How to Ride a Giraffe	Little Readers series	Houghton Mifflin
How to Stay Safe at Home On-Line	Rosen Real Readers series	Rosen Real Readers
The Key to Maps	Windows on Literacy series	National Geographic
Let's Bake	Discovery Links series	Newbridge
Let's Cook	Reading Safari Magazine	Mondo Publishing
Make Masks for a Play	Sunshine series	Wright Group
Make Your Own Party	Sunshine series	Wright Group
Making a Plate	Ready Readers series	Modern Curriculum
Making a Tape		Sundance
Making Caterpillars and Butterflies	Literacy 2000 series	Rigby
Making Electricity		Sundance
Making Lemonade		Sundance
Making Party Food	PM Plus series	Rigby
Making Shapes		Benchmark Education
Map My Town	Reading Safari Magazine	Mondo Publishing
Mapping North America	Windows on Literacy series	National Geographic
Measuring Tools		Benchmark Education
Off to the Shop	Storyteller series	Shortland Publications
Reading Maps	Discovery Links series	Newbridge
Roads Take Us Home	Building Block Books	Lerner Classroom
Signs	Discovery Links series	Newbridge
Ten Easy Steps for Staying Safe	Rosen Real Readers series	Rosen Real Readers
What Scientists Do	Discovery Links series	Newbridge
Who Makes All the Rules?		Benchmark Education

■ Fluent Readers

Approximate Reading Recovery levels 20+; Fountas and Pinnell levels L–S

Building a Castle		Benchmark Education
Dream Catcher	Storyteller series	Shortland
Experiments with Movement	by Bryan Murphy	Scholastic
Experiments with Water	by Bryan Murphy	Scholastic
Finding Your Way	Orbit series	Pacific Learning
How Is a Crayon Made?	by Charles Oz	Scholastic
How to Choose a Pet	Discovery World series	Rigby
How to Grow Crystals	BookShop series	Mondo Publishing
How to Make a Cake	Foundations series	Wright Group
The Magic School Bus Plants Seeds	by Joanna Cole and Bruce Degen	Scholastic

Is That a Fact?

Make a Cloud, Measure the Wind	Foundations series	Wright Group
Make a Shake and a Bakeless Cake	Foundations series	Wright Group
Making Popups	BookShop series	Mondo Publishing
The Map Book	Sunshine series	Wright Group
Maps and Codes	Wildcats series	Wright Group
Maps of the World	Explorers series	Shortland Publications
Once Upon a Time Map Book	by B. A. Hennessy	Candlewick Press
Our Book of Maps	Discovery World series	Rigby
Planning a Birthday Party	BookShop series	Mondo Publishing
Science—Just Add Salt	by Sandra Markle	Scholastic
Send a Message	Discovery Links series	Newbridge
Six Things to Make	BookShop series	Mondo Publishing
Taking Care of Trees	Discovery Links series	Newbridge
Today's Weather Is . . .	by L. J. Hopping. BookShop series	Mondo Publishing
Toy Designer	Realization series	Rigby

7

Descriptive Reports

There's a turtle. Miss La Porte has got a turtle. Let me touch it!
Vivian, kindergarten

Linda La Porte is a kindergarten teacher with a mission. The turtle she holds in her hand has been brought into her classroom for a purpose. She knows that the tiny creature will cause great excitement, much discussion, and a mountain of questions, and will serve as a springboard for her children's writing descriptive reports. When I first began working with Linda in her first year of teaching, I was impressed with her enthusiasm and hunger for learning. She is an excellent educator who constantly strives to improve her teaching. The environment she has established for her children is warm and inviting, yet challenging. Linda is just one of the many fine new teachers who enter our profession each year.

Linda and I decided to select animal reports as the form of descriptive writing to focus on with her kindergarten children. We chose this topic for several reasons. First, animals are always of high interest to young children, and their natural curiosity for living things is often at a peak during the early years of school. Second, part of Linda's course guides for science dealth with learning about living things—namely, animals. We decided that doing animal reports would be a good way to integrate our science goals with our writing goals, getting the children to understand the how and why of writing descriptive reports as they learned about animals. Third, Linda and I had noticed that during writing workshop the children constantly wrote or drew personal narratives even though we had in the past provided them with brief demonstrations of other writing forms. They had become comfortable with writing "I like TV" or "I love my cat" each day. We needed to immerse them in a comprehensive unit of study that would motivate and teach them another purpose for writing.

Before commencing the unit, Linda and I read and talked about descriptive reports and what they entailed so that we could provide appropriate demonstrations and learning engagements for the children. It was difficult to categorize descriptive reports, as they could be seen as encompassing many different kinds of writing. For example, a biography could be seen as a form of descriptive report, as it describes the life of a particular individual. Similarly, a report about a field trip could also be considered a descriptive report. For the purpose of this chapter, however, we limit our definition of descriptive reports to writing that seeks to classify and describe the way things are in the world. (Texts that retell a series of events, such as the life of a person or a historical event, are explored in Chapter 10, on nonfiction narrative.)

Overview of Descriptive Reports

Here is an overview of descriptive reports, which formed the basis of Linda's unit on animal reports.

Purpose/Social Function

According to Beverly Derewianka (1990), descriptive reports are texts that classify and describe the way things are in our world. They give details, often physical, about such things as animals, plants, weather, medicine, machines, and countries. Their purpose is to describe a thing rather than to retell a series of events.

Types or Forms

There are two major types of descriptive reports:

> General descriptions—for example, reports on animals, plants, housing, machines, space, geographical features such as mountains, and so on.
> Specific descriptions—for example, reports on a specific animal, plant, planet, mountain range, and so on.

Text Structure

Descriptive reports usually begin with a title that identifies what is being described and continue with an opening general statement or classification of the subject.

They then include facts on the subject, which may be grouped through paragraphs and/or subheadings.

They often conclude with summarizing comments.

Language Features

Descriptive reports commonly have the following features:

> Action words (examples: *run, erupt, bloom*).
> Linking verbs (*is, are, belong, to*).
> Timeless present tense (*are, exist, grow*).
> Factual descriptive, not imaginative, language.
> Pictures, labels, and diagrams.

Examples

Here is an analysis of a report that consists of a general description about an animal. Language features are highlighted in bold.

Let me tell you about Tigers by Katie, Grade 2	Title
They **are** mammals and **belong to** the **cat family**.	General classification; timeless present tense; linking verb
Tigers have **stripes** and **are yellow** and **black**. They are really strong and are big animals.	Descriptive information on appearance
Tigers like to **live in the jungle** and **at the zoo**. There are not many left in	Descriptive information on habitat

the jungle because they have been hunted.	
They like to eat **meat** and **animals**. They like to **drink water**.	Descriptive information on what it eats
The tiger likes to **chase** animals to **eat** them. They **sleep** a lot.	Descriptive information on what it does; action verbs
Tigers are lots of people's favorite animals. Some sports teams have them as their emblem. They are my favorite animal.	Concluding comments

Next is an analysis of a report that consists of a specific description of a building.

Our School	Title
by Jonathan, Kindergarten	
Our school is big.	Opening statement
It is red and it has stairs. There are lots of kids in the school.	Description of the important elements
There **are** lots of teachers.	Linking verb
Kids have fun and learn a lot. They learn to read. I love our school.	Concluding statement

A Unit in Action

Before Linda brought in the turtle, which would form the entry point for our whole-class investigation, we had immersed the children in the idea of writing animal reports by doing shared reading with several big books about animals. The children were excited by the facts about different animals that the texts presented, and all had their own stories to tell about the different animals they loved. Linda and I commented on how much they knew and asked them what other information they had about different animals. This brought us to the next step: asking them to write down and/or draw the information they had about a favorite animal. We did this so that we could assess their present understanding of writing descriptive reports. This in turn would guide us as to the types of demonstrations we would need to provide during the whole-class investigation.

Assessing the Children's Understanding

The children were given adequate time to record and draw information about their selected animal. All the children completed their entries quickly, in about

Is That a Fact?

ten minutes. This suggested to us that even though they had lots to talk about, when it came to recording their information, they were happy to write down just one thing of interest. When examining their writing pieces, we found that they had all reflected on their personal feelings toward, or encounters with, the animal they had selected. Amun wrote, "I like pandas but I like more animals." Betty wrote, "Tigers are nice." Jasmine drew a picture of a girl with a scribble underneath and told us that her writing said, "I like the princess." It was clear that Jasmine had not even understood that her piece was supposed to be about an animal. These examples are typical of what many early writers will record. They gave Linda and me a starting point for getting the children to understand both the purpose and format of writing animal reports.

We used the children's initial reports and filled out the assessment rubric to help us get an overview of what demonstrations we would need to provide for our young learners (see Figure 7.1). From our review of the children's initial pieces it became evident that we would need to demonstrate that animal reports tell the reader facts about different aspects of an animal, such as what it looks like, where it lives, and what it eats. We would also need to lead the children to the understanding that reports can also tell the reader about personal experiences and feelings the writer has about a particular animal, *if* they are used to support specific facts that have been presented. For example:

Bears have big claws. (Fact)
I saw a bear its claws were really big. I was scared. (Supporting evidence in the form of an observation)

The idea that personal information has a place in this form of writing is important. Often children are encouraged to eliminate their personal experiences when writing reports. The result is dry, nonengaging reports where the author's voice has been all but lost. (See Chapter 4, on voice, for more on this.)

A few children, such as Ivan, wrote their initial pieces with more detail and a greater understanding of how reports work.

Cats by Ivan
Cats have lots of fur. They have claws and can scratch you.
They like to eat fish.
My cat eats fish all the time.

Ivan had a basic understanding of the content of report writing. He had included different facts about cats, such as what they looked like and what they ate. He had also personalized his report by including specific details of his own cat to support his information about what cats eat. Ivan's understanding was more advanced than that of the majority of his classmates. This was an important consideration for Linda and me. It told us that even though most of

■ **Figure 7.1** Assessment rubric for descriptive reports

Assessment Rubric for Descriptive Reports

Key: N: Not in evidence   S: Showing signs of   C: Consolidating   M: Mostly   N/A: Not applicable

Name: **Grade:** **Date:** **Text Type or Title:**			
Purpose			
Understands that descriptive reports are factual texts that classify and describe the way things are			
Craft (Structure, features, voice)			
Linguistic or Text Structure			
Selects appropriate text type based on purpose			
Uses structure appropriate to subject, topic, and audience			
Aim or Goal			
Tells reader about the subject with facts grouped through paragraphing and/or under headings			
Method			
Begins descriptive reports with an opening general statement about the subject			
Continues to describe the subject with facts or opinions supported by facts			
Classifies information under headings			
Concludes with a summary statement			
Text/Language Features			
Uses action verbs (*climb, build, run*)			
Uses linking verbs (*is, are, belongs to*)			
Uses timeless present tense (*are, exist, grow*)			
Uses comparative and additive prepositions (*to, from, by, with*)			
Includes diagrams and labels to help the reader			
Voice			
Uses an enticing title and/or setting to engage the reader			
Is able to express ideas using own language as opposed to copying down what others say or information from books read			
Uses descriptive language that paints pictures for the reader			
Is able to state information in a unique or surprising manner			
Research Skills			
Is able to locate information from books			
Is able to locate information from nonbook sources			
Is able to interpret and talk about information located			
Surface Features (Mechanics)			
Handwriting neat and legible			
Shows improvement in attempts at spelling words			
Uses grammatically correct language			
Shows improvement in use of punctuation			
Uses an appropriate publishing format			
Work generally well presented			

the children required basic demonstrations in report writing, children such as Ivan would need to be extended in their thinking through more advanced scaffolding.

The Whole-Class Investigation Begins: Selecting the Topic

Linda and I had decided to select the topic of turtles as the whole-class investigation. Linda knew that when she brought the turtle in for the children to study, the excitement level would be high and it would give her many opportunities to get them to write about the turtle from direct observation. Linda was certainly right about the level of excitement. When the turtle was brought into the classroom the children were literally screaming with excitement, and they all wanted to hold it. Linda managed this situation well by allowing the turtle only to visit the tables of children who managed to stay calm and engaged in their daily writing routines. Linda told me that classroom management had never been better and that her children were calmer than they ever had been before as they wrote their daily journal entries, in the hope that the turtle would soon visit their table. She told the children that turtles don't like too much noise and movement, and that when he visited their table they would need to be calm. It certainly worked. When I entered her classroom I wondered if a new class had been assigned to her, for I had never seen her children so on task before.

We brought the children together and asked them if they would like to write a report about turtles, which we could make into a big book and place in the classroom library for visitors to read. We explained that a report was writing that told the reader true things, or facts, about an animal. The children were enthusiastic about this prospect and were eager to get started—until Gerald asked, "What about his name? What will he call him?" Linda and I realized that the research would have to wait and that the naming of the turtle was the top priority. The children came up with many names, which we listed on a chart. The children were then given the opportunity to vote for their favorite name. (See Figure 7.2.)

Collecting Information and Providing Demonstrations

After it was decided that our turtle's name was Junior, we arranged for him to spend five minutes on each table during writer's workshop so that the children could study him and write interesting facts about him. The children were told that while they were waiting for Junior to pay them a visit, they could go on with their journal entries or other personal writing and drawings of choice. When Junior arrived at a table, we encouraged the children to look closely at him and talk about what they saw. We also placed pictures of turtles on each table so that the children had a visual stimulus to help them with their writing.

■ **Figure 7.2** Names for the turtle

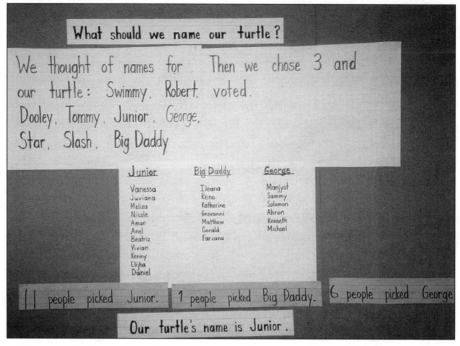

When Junior had visited each table, we brought the children together and discussed their findings. These we recorded onto strips of paper and taped them onto the chalkboard. The children had come up with many interesting observations. Many of them gave us specific information about Junior, such as "Junior is cold" or "Junior loves me." We informed the children that ours was going to be a book about all turtles, not just Junior, and that we had to find out true things about not just Junior but all turtles. We also showed them some animal reports from big books we had collected. We talked about how the authors had included lots of information about what particular animals looked like, what they ate, and how they lived, and not really about how they felt about the animal. This concept was initially difficult for some of the children to grasp, but with repeated demonstrations they finally seemed to understand. As each day passed the children began to give us more factual information, based on their observations of Junior but that applied to all turtles, and reserved more of their personal feelings about Junior for their journal entries. Engaging children in repeated demonstrations was an important lesson for Linda, and for me as well. One-off demonstrations do little to really help children internalize learning.

Besides allowing the children to observe Junior, we also provided them with pictures and books about turtles. We also encouraged them to gather information from home, from family members and friends. During this time, to

Is That a Fact?

help them as researchers, we also provided many demonstrations on researching, the author's craft, and writing mechanics, including the following.

Demonstrations in Research

How to read the pictures of turtles we had provided in order to gain information. (See Chapter 3 for more information on this topic.)

Demonstrations in Craft

Explaining how to use the words *some* or *most* if statements were not true for all turtles.

Including information about what turtles looked like, what they ate, where they lived, and what they did.

Using words such as *they, their,* and *have.*

Drawing pictures that matched their writing.

Demonstrations in Mechanics

Strategies in spelling words.

Handwriting.

Using capital letters and periods.

Linda and I soon found that even though writer's workshop was only supposed to be a 60-minute period each day, the children were so engaged in finding out about turtles that at any spare moment they would have their writer's notebooks out, busily adding new information for our whole-class report. The biggest shock came one afternoon when the children had free activity time at different play centers. A few of the children asked if they could continue looking at Junior and the books on turtles. Naturally Linda said yes, only to find that almost all of the children preferred writing to free play. Clearly, when children are engaged in writing for a purpose and the topic is of high interest, the activity can be a pleasurable one, even for five- and six-year-olds.

It wasn't long before the children had collected a lot of information about turtles in their notebooks. Linda and I transcribed their information onto strips of paper on the chalkboard as outlined below:

Turtles have shells. Junior has a very hard shell.

Turtles have claws.

Turtles have 4 feet.

The turtle's shell is hard.

They have marks on their bodies.

Turtles are reptiles.

Turtles can be slimy.

Turtles come from eggs.

Some turtles have red stripes.

Turtles hide in their shells.
Turtles wiggle their tails when they walk.
Turtles drink water.
Mommy turtles have baby turtles.
Turtles have long necks.
Turtles have eyes. Junior's eyes look scary.
The turtle's shell is bumpy.
Turtles walk. Junior walks so slow.
Turtles have mouths.
Turtles roll on their backs.

Sorting and Adding Information

Once the information about turtles had been gathered, our next step was to sort it so that it would be ready for publication. We did this by looking at examples of animal reports in big books to see how other authors of animal reports had organized their information. We came up with four main categories and wrote them on the chalkboard:

1. What turtles look like
2. What turtles eat
3. What turtles do
4. Where turtles live

Linda and I then gave out all the strips of paper to the children and asked all those who had a sentence about what turtles looked like to give it to us so that we could place it under the appropriate heading. This proved to be a more interesting experience than we had expected, as we soon found that because many of Linda's children were pre-emergent readers, they had difficulty reading the statements they had. We overcame this by letting the children assist each other with the reading of the statements. This proved to be a highly effective strategy. After the statements had been sorted, the children noticed that the heading "What turtles eat" had only one statement and that the heading "Where turtles live" had no information at all. The children decided that these topics needed more research, so for the remainder of that day's writer's workshop and for homework that evening, their task was to find information on what turtles ate and where they lived.

The children had no trouble locating additional information from a variety of sources. By the next morning the following statements had been added to the two categories:

What Turtles Eat
Turtles eat turtle food from the pet shop. Junior loves his food.
Turtles like to eat worms. They eat baby fish.

Where Turtles Live

Turtles live in a fish tank. That's when they're pets.
Turtles live in ponds. They like water.

Publishing and Sharing the Whole-Class Report

Once the information had been sorted, our next step was to publish the children's findings. Each child was given one of the statements and a piece of white paper to write and illustrate on. We stressed to the children that their writing had to be large enough for people to read it. We also encouraged them to take their time so that their writing and drawings looked fantastic. After all, this was going into our classroom library for others to read. The children were given gray lead pencils to write with so that if they made an error it could be easily erased. They could later use an assortment of colored markers, crayons, paints, and pencils to go over their recordings and complete their illustrations.

Some of the children found it difficult to copy the statement they had in front of them. Linda and I simply encouraged these children to do their best and then wrote out the statement ourselves at the bottom of their page so that readers of our report would in fact be able to read it and not have to rely only on the child's attempts (see Figure 7.3).

■ **Figure 7.3** A page of the report

Linda had prepared large green sheets of paper cut into the shape of a turtle so that when completed, each child's piece of paper could be pasted onto a cutout shape of a turtle. The children were very impressed by the concept of their report's being in the shape of a turtle, and we noticed a new sense of pride in both their writings and their illustrations. After Linda had collated all the pieces, she brought the children together to discuss a dedication for the front of the book. The discussion was quick, and the decision unanimous. The report was to be dedicated to Junior (see Figure 7.4). After all, as Frederick said, "Without him we wouldn't have found out anything." Linda then took Junior home for a much-needed rest but the children were assured that he would return, for he had now become the class mascot.

The report was then shared and quickly became the favorite book in the classroom. Each time a visitor entered the classroom the children would alert him or her to their report on turtles. One day the assistant principal entered the classroom for what he thought was going to be a brief visit. He soon found himself sitting and listening to the children read their report after Tanya told him proudly, "You probably don't know much about turtles, but we do. It's all here in our report. Can we read it to you?" Clearly, Tanya and her classmates had come to realize that the purpose of writing animal reports was to inform others about facts pertaining to a specific animal. What a wonderful understanding for such young writers to have! Linda and I also noticed that all the children were able to read their class report, even the pre-emergent readers. This confirmed that we were not only teaching our children to be competent writers but also to be able readers.

Reflecting on What Makes a Good Report and Choosing Individual Investigations

Before the children began their individual explorations, Linda and I brought them together to discuss what had made their report on turtles so wonderful. We wrote their responses on a chart:

> **What Makes a Good Report on Animals**
> The information is true.
> You tell people:
> 1. What your animal looks like.
> 2. Where your animal lives.
> 3. What your animal eats.
> 4. Where your animal lives.
> 5. Any other interesting things about your animal.
> You do your best writing and drawings when you are publishing.
> You look at pictures and books to get information.
> You ask your family and friends for information.
> You try not to use the words "I love" all the time.

We also referred them back to the big books we had used throughout the whole-class investigation to help them come up with further suggestions.

We then asked the children to decide which animal they would like to write their own report on. They had many suggestions, but finally Linda narrowed down the field to four. This number would allow the children to have choice in the content of their writing, yet it was contained enough so that they would not be overwhelmed by too many possibilities. This is an important consideration for young children, as they can become frustrated by too many options and will simply sit there chewing on a pencil, lost in a sea of thought.

This point was never demonstrated to me more clearly than the time I took my son to FAO Schwartz in New York and asked him to choose a toy. It was not long before he became frustrated by the wealth of choices available and within ten minutes he began to cry. I quickly led him to the building blocks section of the store and offered him several options to choose from. The tears soon dried up and the smile returned. I had made the selection process so much easier for him by narrowing down the enormous field of possibilities.

Another advantage of Linda's limiting the options to four was that collecting resources on only four animals meant that she could bring in more for each one, so that the children would have plenty of books, posters, and illustrations to use for their research. It would also enable the children who were researching the same animal to share and compare information with each other.

Linda displayed a sheet of paper with a picture of each of the four animals the children had voted on with space for the children to sign up for their selection. (See Figure 7.5.)

As Figure 7.5 clearly shows, giraffes and polar bears were by far the most popular choices. Linda knew that she would need to gather many books and pictures on these two animals to assist the children with their research. After selecting their animal, the children were given time to talk with each other about the animal they wanted to research and were then asked to go back to their places and begin recording what they already knew about their animal.

Collecting Information and Providing Small-Group Instruction

For the next four sessions of writer's workshop, Linda and I placed small baskets on each of the children's tables containing pictures and books about their

■ **Figure 7.5** The four choices

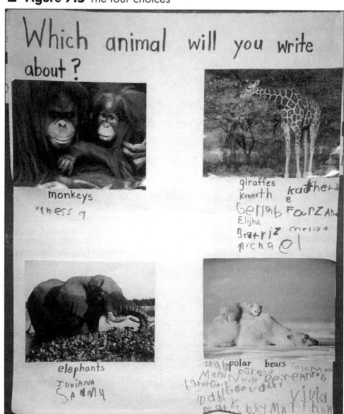

Is That a Fact?

selected animals. We also provided the children with cassette tapes of some of the books so that they could gain information through listening. (This proved a highly effective strategy.) We started each session with a demonstration into ways to read and interpret the information in the books in the baskets and constantly referred them to the chart "What Makes a Good Report on Animals."

Some of the children had a problem interpreting and processing the information from that chart, so we called these children together for small-group instruction. Linda and I had designed a form (see Appendix G) for these children to use, and we found it very beneficial as a means of focusing them into a specific aspect of the animal they were researching. We only gave these children one sheet of the form at a time to keep them on track. By the end of four sessions they had all completed a brief but effective animal report. Small-group instruction times were brief, no longer than five to ten minutes, for Linda also had the rest of the class to support.

Small-group instruction is very important for many of our young writers, as a way of giving them added support. The form sheet was another powerful aid for these young learners, yet for children such as Ivan it would not be appropriate. Ivan had little problem researching and writing information under different descriptive categories on his own. For children such as Ivan Linda and I provided demonstrations of how to gather and interpret additional information for writing reports and how to use headings as a means of sorting information.

Managing the Classroom

Classroom management became an issue during the individual explorations, as many of the children were in constant need of assistance or simply wanted to share their findings. Linda and I overcame this problem by suggesting writing activities the children could go on with while they waited for us to give them assistance. These included:

Writing or drawing a letter to a friend showing them what animal you
    were researching
Going on with journal writing
Helping someone at your table
Looking through books in the classroom library
Practicing your handwriting
Designing the cover for your report

These suggestions proved successful, and Linda and I soon found that we were able to move freely around the classroom, giving assistance where necessary to individuals and small groups. We also constructed a process chart with

the children, outlining at least four things they could write about their animal (see Figure 7.6). These points were also written on cards and put onto each table for the children to use as a reference. The illustration next to each category gave them instant visual information and was extremely helpful, especially for children who could not yet read the print.

During the individual investigations, spelling also became an issue. Many of the children who were at either a precommunicative or semiphonetic stage of development became frustrated. Linda and I simply encouraged these children to have a try and also to seek help from their peers. When it came time for publication we wrote out the correct spelling for them so that they could record it correctly onto their published pieces. (Refer to Chapter 5 for more information on helping children with spelling.)

Sharing the Investigations

The children worked diligently to complete their reports. Many of them had researched, composed, and published at home or whenever a free moment arrived during the course of the school day. They were excited by the prospect of having their reports completed and eager to share them with family members and friends.

When all the reports were completed, Linda and I arranged a sharing time, and parents and family members were invited into the classroom. It was a time of great excitement. The children were running on an adrenaline high. Having an audience with whom to share their work gave them the sense of being real authors. The session was slightly chaotic but well worth the effort, for not only were the children excited to share their reports, the parents were equally excited and proud of the wonderful work their children had produced. As one of the mothers later commented, "If we'd done things like this when I was in school I would have wanted to go every day. I always hated writing, but Nicole [her daughter] loves it. That's all she wants to do at home—write, write, write."

Linda completed the unit by again reflecting with the children on what they had learned about writing animal reports. Then she and the class brainstormed other possible topics of investigation, which Linda wrote on cards. She also copied the information from the chart "What Makes a Good Report on Animals" onto a large card. This, together with the focus cards (Figure 7.6) and the report form (Appendix G) were placed into a box labeled "How to Write Reports." The box was placed in the writing center for children to use as a future reference should they again decide to write a report.

Follow-Up Assessment

At the conclusion of the unit, Linda and I collected the children's published reports and compared them to their initial pieces. We then added our new-found information on each child to their assessment rubric. We were truly impressed with the progress they had made and were delighted by their increased understanding of how reports were written. What we were particularly pleased with was that the phrase "I love" had not been the focus of their report. Linda was delighted when she realized this, as she had been trying desperately to wean the children off these words for the past two months. When I asked her why she thought they had not used this phrase in their reports, she replied that she believed this was due to the many models of reports that we read to the children. She also believed that our constant positive feedback to the children who didn't use this phrase as they were composing was strong reinforcement. By highlighting what good writers of reports do, the children had internalized that the phrase "I love" was just not appropriate when they were writing their animal reports.

The children had not only demonstrated better word usage in their reports but had also given far more information on the selected animal than they had earlier. Linda and I attributed this to our many demonstrations on how to gather information from books, magazines, pictures, direct observations, and family members. When we compared Betty's and Amun's original pieces which we highlighted in the beginning of the chapter with their latest reports, their overall growth as writers became evident.

Betty's original report

Tigers are nice.

Betty's final report

Giraffes are animals.
They have long necks.
Giraffes live in the jungle.
I see them at the zoo. I have to look up high to see them.
Giraffes eat lots of leaves.

When comparing Betty's two pieces it became clear that she had gained an understanding that reports tell the reader many different things about the selected topic. Her inclusion of the adjective "long" displayed an understanding of how writers can give additional information to their readers. Betty also included a personal encounter with giraffes to support her information about their having long necks ("I see them at the zoo. I have to look up high to see them"). This shows that she understands that it is okay to include personal observations in a report to validate information.

Amun had also made enormous progress, as can be seen below:

Amun's original report

I like pandas but I like more animals.

Amun's final report

Polar Bears by Amun
Polar Bears are mammals.
Polar Bears have white hair and it is soft.
Polar Bears like to eat fish.
Polar bears live in the snow and ice.

In his final piece, Amun begins with a title and proceeds to give the reader lots of interesting information. He starts with a general classification of polar bears, which is what most animal reports begin with. He also includes more complex sentences, using the conjunction "and" to connect two pieces of information ("Polar bears have white hair and it is soft").

With the unit at an end, I asked Linda what she was next planning to focus on during writer's workshop. She didn't have to think long before telling me that she was going to go even deeper with report writing, only this time she would extend the topic selection to include reports about plants, objects, and places. The unit of study had truly engaged her children and they were eager to write more descriptive reports. Many of them had already begun to draft another piece. Linda's students had found a new purpose for writing and were feeling confident with the format. Betty's comments summed it up: "I like writing about animals. I know a lot and I can tell people lots."

Considerations for Older Children

Older children (grade 2 and up) are likely to demonstrate a more advanced knowledge of descriptive report writing. This will become evident from their initial pieces. Third grader Carla, for example wrote the following.

Snakes by Carla
Snakes are reptiles which mean they have cold blood.
Snakes have scales and move on their bellies.
Snakes eat small reptiles and animals. They also like eggs.
Snakes like warm weather to warm their blood. They usually sleep at night and come out in the day.
Snakes have fangs and kill you if they bite you.

Carla clearly has a more advanced understanding of report writing than, say, kindergartner Betty; but there are still many features of this form of writing that she, and other children at this stage, need to learn. Demonstrations for Carla might, for example, focus on:

Use of headings and or paragraphs.
More details about specific aspects about snakes.
Methods of researching and locating additional information.
Avoiding generalizations (such as "Snakes have fangs and kill you if they bite you").
Use of diagrams and illustrations to help the reader.

Teachers of children in older grades also need to be aware that the children may have explored descriptive reports in past years and that another form may be more suitable (for example, writing procedures or explanations). Or perhaps they may need further engagement with descriptive reports but are bored with writing animal reports. This was made clear to me one year when I was teaching third grade and had decided to explore nonfiction descriptive writing with my children. I had selected dinosaurs as the whole-class investigation, thinking it would be a highly motivating topic, and had spent many weeks gathering resources. I had even arranged a field trip to the local museum so the children could engage in a hands-on approach to gathering information. When I suggested this topic to my children, the response was unanimous. They all groaned and said, "Not dinosaurs again! We do them every year." I realized then that if I wanted these children to become engaged in writing descriptive reports for an authentic purpose, I would need to find a topic of interest to them collectively. After brainstorming topics, we decided to write a whole-class report about the planet Mars, as it was of high interest to them at the time and one they were motivated to research. I was able to teach successfully all the necessary skills in how to write reports through this topic, but I was a little depressed by the fact that I had all this wonderful information on dinosaurs and had spent countless hours gathering resources now unused. However, I realized that it would have been pointless to pursue the idea of dinosaurs, as it would have most definitely turned these children off from being writers, something I would never want to do. How delightful it was the following year when I had a grade 1–2–3 multi-age class and found that, for them, dinosaurs was a hot topic. (I was just thankful that I had kept all those resources on dinosaurs I had gathered the year before.)

Children in older grades also require more complex demonstrations in their independent investigations. Below are some ideas you may find useful.

Topic Selection

When older children select topics for independent investigation, it is not necessary to limit the number of choices to four, as Linda did with her kindergartners. Older children are usually capable of selecting their own topics from a wide range and are usually able to locate relevant information. Also, topics do not have to do only with animals; any topic of interest to individual children can be considered. Brainstorming a possible selection list with the children is a great way to start.

Report Plan

Once children have selected their topic, demonstrating how a project plan can assist them with composing their reports is a good idea. In a grade 2 classroom, for example, I did this with a modeled writing on how I plan when writing a report. I selected the topic of flowers and showed the children how a web helped me organize my information and compose my report. I wrote the word "Flowers" in the center of a piece of chart paper, then drew arrows to signify the different elements I could cover in my report—types of flowers, where different varieties are found, what flowers need to survive, how flowers are formed, and so on. I then encouraged the children to make similar plans for their own topics before commencing their investigations. German's plan for his report on dinosaurs (Figure 7.7) is an example of the children's plans for their work. We can see from German's plan that he is now ready to begin his focused investigation on dinosaurs. His headings—when they lived, where they lived, what they ate, types of dinosaurs and their sizes—have given him an excellent start to his investigation.

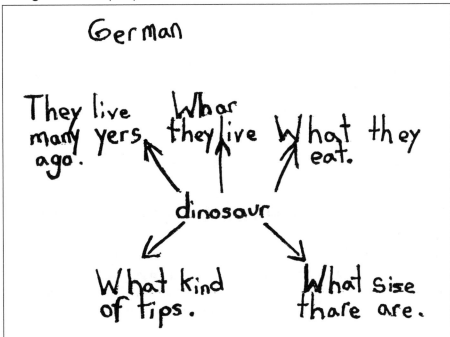

Contents Page, Glossary, and Index

Providing demonstrations in whole-class and small-group settings on how to use such key elements as contents pages, glossaries, and indexes can be extremely beneficial to children in older grades. Refer to Chapter 3 for further details on these components of reports.

Process Chart

At the beginning of individual explorations, it is a good idea to brainstorm with older children procedures for researching and composing. This session can be based on the steps the children followed when constructing their whole-class report. It is important that the children come up with this structure and that the teacher not simply present it to them, for if they are able to articulate the steps involved it shows they have internalized the process and will be more able to write their own reports. Here is one second-grade class's process chart:

Steps in Writing Nonfiction
1. Choose a topic. What interests you?
2. Write what you know or think you know.

3. Research your topic.
4. Add new information.
5. Reread—make all corrections and make sure all information is true.
6. Sort information into chapters.
7. Publish:
   write neatly
   illustrate using diagrams and labels
   table of contents
   page numbers
   glossary and index

Possible Topics for Whole-Class and Independent Investigations

The unit described in this chapter is just one of many possible ways to explore descriptive reports with children. Listed below are suggestions of other topics that could be explored as a whole class or independently. These investigations may run for any length of time, from one week to six weeks. What is important is that they not be one-day wonders. Children need time and opportunity for immersion, demonstrations, and engagement in descriptive reports if they are to become proficient writers in this form.

Here are some general topics for reports:

Chickens (hatch chickens in the classroom).
All about fish (set up a mini-aquarium).
Insects (have children collect them and place them in jars for research).
Ants (set up an ant farm).
Turtles.
Dinosaurs.
Birds.
Snakes and lizards.
Space.
The planets.
Trees.
Flowers.
Deserts.
Oceans.
Video games.
Television.
Houses.
Foods from around the world.
Clothing.
Pets.

Zoos.
Machines.
Sports.
Countries.
Mountains.

Here are some more specific topics:

A particular type of animal, plant, or thing (bull terriers, daffodils, Mars, etc.).
Missing posters.
Wanted posters.
A famous landmark (the Empire State building, the Grand Canyon, the Eiffel Tower, the Great Barrier Reef, etc.).
A country, state, or city.
A specific sport (baseball, basketball, swimming, etc.).

Resources

This last section lists books that may be of use in helping children locate, research, and write descriptive reports. The books are listed alphabetically by title, with series title or author name (if any) and publisher. There are thousands of wonderful books that can be used as valuable resources; the list below provides only a small sample of what's available. I have grouped the books by readability, according to Reading Recovery levels and the Fountas and Pinnell levels. There are a great many different leveling systems in existence, as most publishers have their own method of categorizing texts. I have chosen the Reading Recovery and Fountas and Pinnell systems because they are the most commonly used. (For further information on how to organize classroom books and materials in your classroom, see Chapter 3.)

Descriptive Reports

■ Emergent Readers

Approximate Reading Recovery levels 1–4; Fountas and Pinnell levels A–C

Animal Habitats	Ready Readers series	Modern Curriculum
Animal Homes		Benchmark Education
Animal Legs	Discovery World series	Rigby
Animals	Smart Starts series	Rigby
Animals That Work	Foundations series	Wright Group
Ants	Discovery Links series	Newbridge
Baby Animals	Reading Corner series	Dominie
The Baby Shark		National Geographic
Ball Games	PM Starters series	Rigby
Bats, Bats, Bats	Pair-It Books series	Steck-Vaughn
Bears	Storyteller Nonfiction series	Shortland Publications
Big Cats	Reading Safari Encyclofacts series	Mondo Publishing
Big Things	PM Starters series	Rigby
Blocks	Early Emergent series	Pioneer Valley
Bugs and Beetles	Reading Safari Encyclofacts series	Mondo Publishing
Cars	Pebble Books series	Capstone Press
Cars	Little Readers series	Houghton Mifflin
Cats, Cats, Cats	Pair-It Books series	Steck-Vaughn
Chinese Kites	Twig series	Wright Group
City Life	Rosen Real Readers series	Rosen Real Readers
Fall	Discovery Links series	Newbridge
Flowers	by Karen Hoenecke	Kaeden Books
Frogs	Twig series	Wright Group
Fruit	Rise and Shine series	Hampton Brown
Homes for People		Benchmark Education
In the Woods	Beanbag-BookShop series	Mondo Publishing
Keys	Ready Readers series	Modern Curriculum
Kites	Joy Readers series	Dominie
Lights at Night	Learning Media series	Pacific Learning
Living Things	Factivity series	Dominie
Nests	Wonder World series	Wright Group
Our Amazing World	Reading Safari Encyclofacts series	Mondo Publishing
Parades!	Pair-It Books series	Steck-Vaughn
People Live Here		National Geographic
Rain	Reading Corners series	Dominie
Reading Safari Magazines		Mondo Publishing
Science and Technology	Reading Safari Encyclofacts series	Mondo Publishing
Seasons	Discovery World series	Rigby
Snails	First Stories series	Pacific Learning
Tails and Claws	Wonder World series	Wright Group
Toys	Foundations series	Wright Group

Trucks	Twig series	Wright Group
Whales in the Ocean	Rosen Real Readers series	Rosen Real Readers
What Lives in a Swamp?		National Geographic
Wheels	Discovery Links series	Newbridge
Who Lives in a Tree?	Discovery Links series	Newbridge
Who Lives in the Sea?	Beanbag-BookShop series	Mondo Publishing

■ Early Readers

Approximate Reading Recovery levels 5–12; Fountas and Pinnell levels D–G

Airplanes	Pebble Books series	Capstone Press
All Kinds of Wheels	Pair-It Books series	Steck-Vaughn
Animal Coverings		Benchmark Education
Animals	Foundations series	Wright Group
Animals in the Desert	Carousel Readers series	Dominie
Ants	Pebble Books series	Capstone Press
Baby Animals	Discovery Links series	Newbridge
Bats, Bats, Bats	Pair-It Books series	Steck-Vaughn
Beaks	Discovery Links series	Newbridge
Bears	Joy Readers series	Dominie
Big Rocks, Little Rocks	Early Connections series	Benchmark Education
Bikes	Foundations series	Wright Group
Birds	Bird series	Dominie
Black Bears	Pebble Books series	Capstone Press
Boats	Twigs series	Wright Group
Cars	by Anne Rockwell	Dutton
Chickens	Books for Young Learners series	Richard C. Owen
Chickens	BookShop series	Mondo Publishing
City Buildings	Discovery Links series	Newbridge
Dinosaurs	BookShop series	Mondo Publishing
Farms	Foundations series	Wright Group
Fast Machines	Foundations series	Wright Group
Frogs	Pebble Books series	Capstone Press
Homes	Rise and Shine series	Hampton-Brown
Horses	Twig series	Wright Group
Koalas	Literacy 2000 series	Rigby
The Moon	Joy Readers series	Dominie
Mosquitoes	Pebble Books series	Capstone Press
New York Buildings	Books for Young Learners series	Richard C. Owen
Night Animals	Ready Readers series	Modern Curriculum
Noisy Toys	Home Connection series	Rigby
Oak Trees	Pebble Books series	Capstone Press
Our Amazing World	Reading Safari Encyclofacts series	Mondo Publishing
Our Earth	Discovery Links series	Newbridge
The Penguin Chick		National Gepgraphic

Quilts	Twig series	Wright Group
Reading Safari Magazines		Mondo Publishing
Rocks	Voyages series	SRA/McGraw Hill
Science and Technology	Reading Safari Encyclofacts series	Mondo Publishing
Shoes	Book Bank series	Wright Group
Signs	Twig series	Wright Group
Spiders	Discovery Links series	Newbridge
Tall Things	PM Nonfiction-Red series	Rigby
Tarantulas Are Spiders	BookShop series	Mondo Publishing
Water, Land, and Air		National Geographic
What Do You Know About Dolphins?		National Geographic
Wheels	Rise and Shine series	Hampton-Brown
Worms	Literacy 2000 series	Rigby

■ Transitional Readers

Approximate Reading Recovery levels 13–20; Fountas and Pinnell levels H–K

All Kinds of Eyes	Learning Media series	Celebration Press
Amazing Eggs	Discovery World series	Rigby
Animal Fibers	Science series	Wright Group
Animal Homes	Pair-It Books series	Steck-Vaughn
Animals Build	Discovery Links series	Newbridge
Animals' Eyes and Ears	Early Connections series	Benchmark Education
Beach Creatures	Pair-It Books series	Steck-Vaughn
Beavers	BookShop series	Mondo Publishing
Bird Beaks	Wonder World series	Wright Group
Cats	PM Animal Facts series	Rigby
Dinosaurs	BookShop series	Mondo Publishing
Dinosaurs	Sunshine series	Wright Group
Dinosaurs and Planet Earth		Rigby
Dogs	PM Animal Facts series	Rigby
Dolphins	Wonder World series	Wright Group
Elephants	PM Animals in the Wild series	Rigby
Families	Early Connections series	Benchmark Education
The Farm	Pebble Books series	Capstone Press
Fire Engines	Pebble Books series	Capstone Press
Food Trappers	Early Connections series	Benchmark Education
Foxes	PM Animal Facts series	Rigby
Friends	Early Connections series	Benchmark Education
Fur, Feathers, Scales	Discovery Links series	Newbridge
Goldfish	PM Animal Facts series	Rigby
Hello USA series		Lerner Classroom
Life in the City	Early Connections series	Benchmark Education
Machines at Work	Little Red Readers series	Sundance
Meet the Octopus	by Sylvia James. BookShop series	Mondo Publishing

Mice	PM Animal Facts series	Rigby
Monarch Butterfly	Foundations series	Wright Group
Ocean Animals	Early Connection series	Benchmark Education
Our Amazing World	Reading Safari Encyclofacts series	Mondo Publishing
Owls	Discovery Links series	Newbridge
Palm Trees	Pebble Books series	Capstone Press
Pine Trees	Pebble Books series	Capstone Press
The Planets	Wonder World series	Wright Group
Police Cars	Pebble Books series	Grolier, Capstone
Reading Safari Magazines		Mondo Publishing
Science and Technology	Reading Safari Encyclofacts series	Mondo Publishing
Sea and Land Animals		National Geographic
Sharks	Ready Readers series	Modern Curriculum
Slugs and Snails	Wonder World series	Wright Group
Snails in School	Discovery World series	Newbridge
The Rain Forest		National Geographic
A Ticket To series		Lerner Classroom
Time for Kids	Magazines series	Keith Garton
Tiny Creatures	Discovery World series	Rigby
Tunnels		National Geographic
Unusual Machines	Little Red Readers series	Sundance

■ Fluent Readers

Approximate Reading Recovery levels 20+; Fountas and Pinnell levels L–S

All About Plants	Home Connection series	Rigby
Amazing Crickets	Discovery Links series	Newbridge
Animals and Their Young	Wonders series	Hampton-Brown
Animal Shelters	BookShop series	Mondo Publishing
Animals in Danger	Pair-It Books series	Steck-Vaughn
Bats	Literacy 2000 series	Rigby
Birds of Prey	BookShop series	Mondo Publishing
Birds of the City	Sunshine series	Wright Group
Bridges	Discovery Links series	Newbridge
Caterpillars	BookShop series	Mondo Publishing
Caves	Discovery World series	Rigby
Cities Around the World	Pair-It Books series	Steck-Vaughn
Crabs	Wonder World series	Wright Group
Crocodilians	BookShop series	Mondo Publishing
Dinosaur Reports	Little Red Readers series	Sundance
Exploring Habitats	BookShop series	Mondo Publishing
Eyewitness Books series		Dorling Kindersley
Farms	Wonders series	Hampton-Brown
Flowers	Pebble Books series	Capstone Press
Frogs	BookShop series	Mondo Publishing

Geography Series	Bridgestone Books series	Capstone Press
Grizzly Bears	by M. Woolley and K. Pigdon	Mondo Publishing
Hand Tools	Wonder World series	Wright Group
Hot Air Balloons	Pair-It Books series	Steck-Vaughn
Houses	Wonder World series	Wright Group
In the Rain Forest	Wildcats series	Wright Group
In the Treetops	by M. Woolley and K. Pigdon	Mondo Publishing
Incredible Places	Wildcats series	Wright Group
Insects	BookShop series	Mondo Publishing
Inside a Rainforest	Pair-It Books series	Steck-Vaughn
Life in the Desert	Pair-It Books series	Steck-Vaughn
Lightning	Pebble Books series	Capstone, Grolier
A Look at Dogs	Pair-It Books series	Steck-Vaughn
A Look at Spiders	Pair-It Books series	Steck-Vaughn
Octopuses and Squids	Wonder World series	Wright Group
Our Amazing World	Reading Safari Encyclofacts series	Mondo Publishing
Penguins	by M. Woolley and K. Pigdon	Mondo Publishing
Platypus	BookShop series	Mondo Publishing
Rabbits	Literacy 2000 series	Rigby
Reading Safari Magazines		Mondo Publishing
Reptiles	Discovery Links series	Newbridge
Salmon	BookShop series	Mondo Publishing
Science and Technology	Reading Safari Encyclofacts series	Mondo Publishing
Seashells	Marine Life for Young Readers series	Dominie
Spiders	BookShop series	Mondo Publishing
Stems	Pebble Books series	Capstone Press
Thinking About Ants	BookShop series	Mondo Publishing
Time for Kids	Magazines series	Keith Garton
Titanic	by Judy Donnelly	Random House
Tornadoes	by Lorraine Hopping	Scholastic
Trees	Early Connections series	Benchmark Education
Watching Whales	Discovery Links series	Newbridge
Whales	BookShop series	Mondo Publishing
Wild Baby Animals	Little Celebrations series	Celebration Press

Scientific Explanations

I t is 9:15 A.M. in Maryanne Meza's grade 1–2 classroom, and she is reading Julie Viorst's classic, *Alexander and the Terrible, Horrible, No Good, Very Bad Day*. The children are enthralled, even though they have heard this story many times before, when suddenly the door flies open. Enter Bryan, huffing and puffing as if he had just completed a marathon. "I'm sorry," he says, out of breath. "I'm late, but I can explain. There was this big puddle. It wasn't a puddle yesterday, it was snow, and it just got in my way, and then I'm all wet and then I have to go home and change my clothes and then I can't find new pants because Mom is washing them so I had to get my brother's pants." "Mmm," replies Maryanne. "A puddle got in the way. Well, that explains it all."

I am struck by how well Bryan has explained his reason for being late and wondered if he had rehearsed his lines before entering the classroom. His inclusion of more than one consequence that followed his account of stepping into the puddle is certainly persuasive. What Bryan is engaging in is just one form of explanatory discourse. He is engaging in a personal narrative that is a factual explanation. Bryan's words immediately have a rippling effect on the rest of the class; the children link Bryan to Alexander. "He's having a terrible, no good day!" exclaims Stephanie. "He certainly is," replies Maryanne. The children are sympathetic to Bryan's plight. Snow in the area had been heavy in the past week, but now that the weather had warmed up the snow was rapidly melting, leaving large puddles everywhere. Then Shyheim asked, "Why does it snow?" This question was to launch us into a wonderful four-week journey into the world of scientific explanations.

Maryanne's students already were engaged in many different types of writing for various purposes. They had just completed a unit on farm animals, and their interest in report writing was high. Shyheim's question, however, had raised another purpose for writing: to explain how and why things are the way they are. Writing explanations was not something Maryanne's students were familiar with, for although they had engaged in nonfiction writing in the past, it had always been for animal reports. This is typical for most first- and second-grade classrooms across the country. Having children engage in writing explanations that deal with scientific phenomena is not something most teachers in the primary grades consider. This kind of writing is usually reserved for children in older grades, for two major reasons.

First, many teachers believe that children at such a young age are not developmentally ready for such text types. But work by Lucy Calkins (1986), Don Graves (1989), Tom Newkirk (1989), and Bobbi Fisher (1991), to name a few, has demonstrated just how able young learners can be in writing differ-ent forms of nonfiction, given the right kind of immersion, demonstration, and engagement. It can be torturous for adults to be around a child of about three years of age who has discovered the word *why*. Yet it is this very word that tells us that children at even this very young age want to know how the world around them works. They are seeking explanations, and once they are satisfied in getting one they can often use complex language to explain to an adult what it is they have learned. What we need to do is tap this natural curiosity and hunger for explanations in the early years of schooling and trans-late them not only into engagements with talk but also into writing and draw-ing. I can vividly recall an incident in my kindergarten class when a spider happened to walk across the classroom ceiling. My children instantly lost interest in the story I was reading and began talking about this spider. "How does it stay up there?" asked Alex. "It's got glue on its legs, like Spiderman," replied Peter. It was at this point when I realized that writing explanations was not only possible in the beginning years of schooling, but also appropriate.

A second reason we don't usually explore writing explanations with chil-dren at this age is that we ourselves are not well versed in how this kind of text works and how to teach it. We stick with story because it's safe. We know that

Is That a Fact?

form because we read and breathe story in our daily writing routines. When we do venture into nonfiction writing it is usually animal reports we explore because, again, we feel comfortable with this type of writing. We limit our children's research to finding out about what specific animals look like, what they eat, and where they live. We often don't consider dealing with scientific phenomena such as how birds fly or why specific animals became extinct. This was certainly true for Maryanne, who confessed, "Tony, I don't have the faintest clue how to teach the children to write explanations about a scientific phenomenon. I usually leave that to the fourth-grade teachers." Therefore, before Maryanne could teach her children how to write explanations of scientific phenomena, she first had to find out for herself more about the craft an author uses in this form of writing.

Overview of Scientific Explanations

Below is an overview of the purpose, types, structure, and language features usually associated with scientific explanations.

Purpose/Social Function

We use the word *explanation* for a variety of purposes. For instance, a recipe for a chocolate cake could be called a kind of explanation; however, what it really explains is a procedure and therefore is technically an instructional text. Bryan's explaining why he was late for school is his retelling of an event, a form of nonfictional personal narrative. For the purpose of this chapter, we will be exploring explanations that tell how and why things are the way they are and, in particular, explanations that deal with a specific scientific phenomenon.

Types or Forms

There are two major types of scientific explanations:

1. Those that describe why something happens or is as it is (for example, why wood floats).
2. Those that describe how something works or was formed (for example, how planes fly).

In addition, some explanations deal with both the how and the why (for example, how glaciers are formed and why they melt).

Text Structure

Scientific explanations generally begin with the writer's identifying or defining what is going to be explained. This often takes the form of a heading.

Writers often begin with an opening statement that may be personal ("I'm going to tell you about . . .").

The second part of the writing explains the how and/or why. Often the author mentions the cause-and-effect elements of the topic in a logical sequence.

Sometimes there is a third part, a concluding or summarizing statement.

Language Features

Scientific explanations often contain the following language features:

Linking words having to do with time (*then*, *next*, *finally*, *after*, etc.).
Diagrams, labels, pictures, and drawings to assist with the explanation.
Subject-specific terms (for example, in a discussion of water use of words such as *moisture*, *vapor*, *evaporation*, *steam*).

Example

Here is an analysis of a scientific explanation. Language features are highlighted in bold.

Why Does It Rain?	Naming of phenomenon to
by Claudia, Grade 1	be explained
First it rains and **then** the sun shines a lot.	Linking words to do with time
It heats up the water.	Explanation of process in a logical order
Tiny drops of water go into the sky and make clouds.	
My mom told me this was called **evaporation**.	Subject-specific term
Tiny drops of water keep going into the sky and the clouds get bigger.	
When drops in the clouds get too heavy and fat they fall as rain.	
That's how it rains.	Summarizing statement

A Unit in Action

Shyheim's question "Why does it snow?" led Maryanne and the class into a discussion of explanations. She and I talked with them about all the questions they had about the world around them. The children had many explanations for many different phenomena. One discussion I found particularly fascinating arose from an observation that Kevin had made. Kevin told the class that he had a book called *How the Baby Deer Got Its Spots*, which was a Lakota legend. This led Maryanne and me into a brief discussion about "pourquoi" tales, how they began a long time ago, when people came up with different stories to explain the way things were in the world. Maryanne and I both realized that myths and legends were early forms of explanations. Today myths and legends are considered fictional, yet in their time they were for the most part considered factual explanations. Even today scientific explanations are being constantly challenged, and some long-believed facts eventually move into the category of myth. (The recent discovery that Pluto could in fact be an asteroid and not a planet is a prime example.)

In Maryanne's classroom the children just couldn't stop talking about all the things they wanted explained. Maryanne and I proceeded to make a list of all the questions or wonderings the children had, which would form the basis of their explorations. We put the children's responses on a chart (see Figure 8.1).

■ **Figure 8.1** Explanations wanted

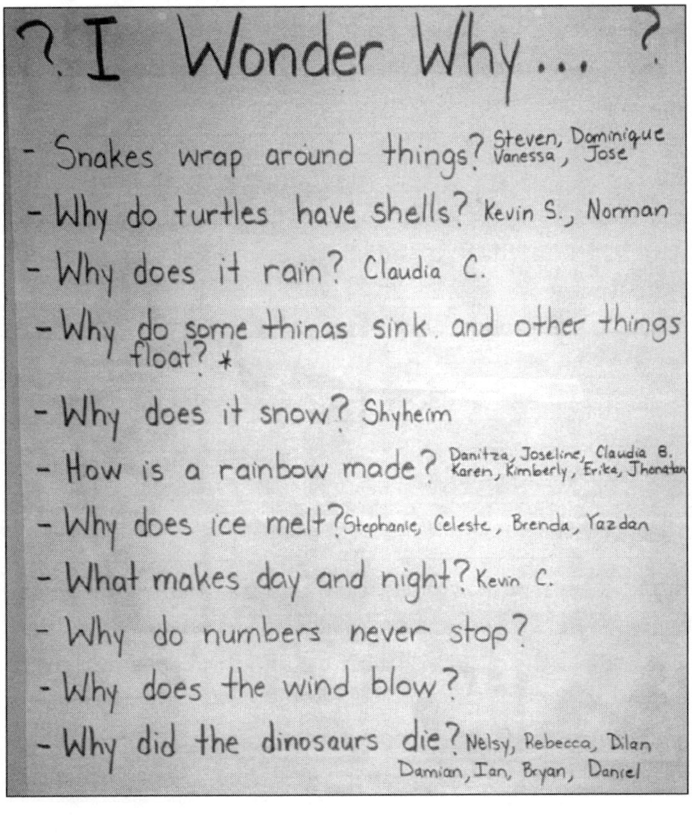

?. I Wonder Why... ?

- Snakes wrap around things? Steven, Dominique Vanessa, Jose
- Why do turtles have shells? Kevin S., Norman
- Why does it rain? Claudia C.
- Why do some things sink and other things float? *
- Why does it snow? Shyheim
- How is a rainbow made? Danitza, Joseline, Claudia B. Karen, Kimberly, Erika, Jhonatan
- Why does ice melt? Stephanie, Celeste, Brenda, Yazdan
- What makes day and night? Kevin C.
- Why do numbers never stop?
- Why does the wind blow?
- Why did the dinosaurs die? Nelsy, Rebecca, Dilan Damian, Ian, Bryan, Daniel

Assessing the Children's Understanding

We asked the children to select one of the questions raised that they thought they could answer and to then write an explanation. It was interesting to see the large number of children that selected their very own question to answer. Their written explanations were varied and extremely amusing. Maryanne and I got to see a little of how the young mind works and what the children's perceptions were about the world around them. In response to the question "Why did the dinosaurs die?" Daniel wrote, "because T-Rex was mean." Rebecca wrote, "Dinosaurs die because to save the world and for us to see the museum and to see their bones." In response to "Why does it rain?" Claudia wrote an extremely logical explanation: "It rains because water falls." Brenda decided to come up with a totally different question and explanation than those we had charted, and her writing took the form of a personal explanation. Her piece was as follows: "Why do dogs bite? Because I didn't let Sam go to the bathroom." The accompanying illustration depicted Brenda taking her dog, Sam, for a walk on a leash with a tree nearby. Poor Sam was evidently not allowed to go near that tree, even though his bodily functions were beckoning him, and therefore he nipped Brenda.

Maryanne and I could tell from the children's pieces that they already understood that explanations give a logical reason as to why something happens. These initial pieces formed the basis of our initial assessments. We used the assessment rubric (Figure 8.2) to record each child's initial understanding, then came up with a list of demonstrations the children would need in order to strengthen their skills as writers of this text type. These included:

> Commencing the piece with the title of the phenomenon that was going to be explained.
> Giving more details of how and why the phenomenon exists by actively researching the topic.
> Including explanations that other people might have as to the how and why.
> Using illustrations to help the reader understand the how and why.
> Including a conclusion.

The Whole-Class Investigation Begins

We brought the children together and invited them to share their explanations with each other. Then we drew their attention back to Shyheim's question "Why does it snow?" We asked the children how we could go about solving this mystery and came up with a list of suggestions. These included asking parents, looking at books in the classroom library, going on the Internet, and asking children in the older grades. Maryanne had already gathered a large number of

Is That a Fact?

Assessment Rubric for Scientific Explanations

Key: N: Not in evidence   S: Showing signs of   C: Consolidating   M: Mostly   N/A: Not applicable

Name: Grade: Date: Text Type or Title:			
Purpose Understands that scientific explanations are factual texts that explain how something works or why something happens			
Craft (Structure, features, voice)			
Linguistic or Text Structure Includes the title of what is going to be explained			
Begins with an opening statement, which may be personal (I'm going to tell you about . . .)			
Explains the event or phenomenon using a logical sequence			
Includes cause-and-effect elements			
Includes a concluding statement (optional)			
Text/Language Features Uses definitions having to do with time			
Is beginning to generalize			
Uses illustrations, diagrams, and labels			
Is beginning to use some subject-specific terms			
Voice Uses an enticing title and/or setting to engage the reader			
Is able to express ideas using own language as opposed to copying down what others say or information from books read			
Uses descriptive language that paints pictures for the reader			
Is able to state information in a unique or surprising manner			
Research Skills			
Is able to locate information from books			
Is able to locate information from nonbook sources			
Is able to interpret and talk about information located			
Surface Features (Mechanics)			
Handwriting neat and legible			
Shows improvement in attempts at spelling words			
Uses grammatically correct language			
Shows improvement in use of punctuation			
Uses an appropriate publishing format			
Work generally well presented			

explanation texts from the school library and her local library. She placed them into a number of baskets entitled "How and Why Books." The majority of these books were simple, as Maryanne had many children who were early emergent readers. Maryanne had made sure that there were a number of books specifically on snow, as this was the subject that would form the basis of our whole-class exploration.

The children were then given an opportunity to look at the books and pictures of snow and talk to each other in small groups. This step gave the children an opportunity to research the topic before writing about it in their writer's notebooks. At the conclusion of the small-group discussions, the children were invited to record their present thinking about why it snows. Maryanne and I then brought them together to share their recorded explanations. They had come up with many interesting ones and most were similar. The opportunity to talk with their peers prior to recording their thoughts had given them more of a uniformity in their beliefs. We then asked the children to talk with family members and friends at home that night to see if there was anything else they could find out about why it snows.

The following morning was chaotic. The children entered the classroom with much to tell, and everyone wanted to talk at once. We knew that letting each child talk about his or her findings one by one while the others waited patiently would not work, as the children were simply bursting with information to tell. This is common with children at this age. When young children have something to tell, they want to tell it immediately. Often in our classrooms, however, they have to take turns, with individual children having the chance to stand in front of the class and say their piece. But because of their classmates' inability to wait their turn to speak, the result is that the only ones who can hear what the child up front is sharing are the teacher and the children at the front. Before long the children become restless and disengaged. When finally it's Johnny's turn, he has either forgotten what he was going to say or it has already been said by a another class member. At this point the other children don't care what Johnny is going to say, as they have been sitting in the meeting area for twenty minutes and are restless and bored. Maryanne and I solved this problem by pairing the children and having them tell their partner everything they had discovered from talking to their family members the night before. The resulting noise level was high, but necessary. We needed to seize the moment.

Recording the Information

After the children had discussed their findings in pairs, we asked them to record their information into their writer's notebooks. At this point, Maryanne and I roved around the classroom, talking individually with many of the children about what they had discovered. As we talked, we wrote the chil-

144

dren's findings on chart paper so that when we brought the children together their information was already recorded and displayed:

Why Does It Snow?
We found out that:
Snow is cold, cold water just like ice blocks and popsicles.
When it gets hot, the puddles become steam, which goes up into the air.
Then the steam makes clouds.
The clouds get really full. That is why they look black and scary.
Clouds get fat and have to let the water out.
When it is cold the water looks like snow.
Then it snows.

Finding Out More

Now that our explanation had been written, it was time to find out more about the form scientific explanations take. Maryanne asked the children to go back and look at the how and why books in the classroom library to find out more about what makes a good explanation. The children worked in small groups, and Maryanne and I moved around the classroom, giving support where necessary. We then asked the children to come to the meeting area and bring their books with them so that we could discuss their findings. At this point, Maryanne's and my questioning techniques were critical in getting the children to articulate the structure and features of scientific explanations. Simply telling them would not have been sufficient. If we truly want to extend children's understanding of various nonfictional writing forms we need to lead them to discover what it is that writers do when they write to inform, or in this case explain information to, their readers. Below is a transcript of part of my discussion with the children that highlighted the features of this form of writing.

Tony: So tell me, what things did you find out about writing an explanation?
Brenda: I see these words a lot [*pointing to the words "that is why"*].
Tony: What an interesting discovery, Brenda. I think we might begin a chart called "Words We Use When We Explain," and we will write that one down.
Rebecca: The word *and* is there a lot. It's always there in everything.
Tony: That's right, Rebecca. It's a word we use a lot. Let's add it to our chart. So is there anything else you have found out?
Bryan: I found out that they tell you lots of good stuff.
Tony: So, Bryan, explanations describe how things work. That's a good thing to know. What about the beginning of explanations? Take a look at your books and see how they start.

Norman: I see! I see! It says things about what it is you're going to do—like ours [*pointing to the title, "Why Does It Snow?"*].

Tony: Wow, Norman that's a big discovery. Yes, explanations have a beginning that tells you what will be explained. That's something we need to add to our chart.

Norman: It has one like that at the end.

Vanessa: I was going to say that too. [*All the children start calling out, "Me too."*]

Tony: Incredible! What good investigators you are! Yes, explanations can sometimes end with a closing sentence. I'll write that down too. So— anything else? [*For a time there is silence, so I try a different question to focus their thinking.*] I can see lots of words in those books. Is there anything else? Or are there just words?

Karen: I see pictures. [*The children chime in with "Me too."*]

Tony: Pictures? I wonder why the authors would use pictures.

Damien [*with a puzzled look*]: You don't know, Tony? [*Laughs.*] It tells you stuff. [*All the children begin to laugh.*]

Tony: You people know more than me. That's a fantastic discovery.

Stephanie: And look—it has these things [*pointing to the labels*].

Tony: I wonder what they are called.

Damien: They are labes.

Tony: Yes, Damien, they are *labels*. I think I'd better add that to our chart as well.

After a ten-minute discussion we brought the meeting to a close, as I knew the children would have become restless if we had gone on much longer. Maryanne and I asked the children to go on with their personal writing (journals, stories, and letters) or if they preferred they could begin writing their own explanations. It is important to note that even in the middle of a unit on explanatory texts there is always time during the writer's workshop for children to engage in their personal writing. However, we soon noticed that the majority of children were selecting topics from the "I Wonder Why" chart (Figure 8.1) to write about. It was evident that they were engaged in this text type and wanted to explore it further during independent writing time.

For the next two sessions we brought the children together at the beginning of writer's workshop for brief discussions on how explanations work and words that authors often use when they write explanations. We recorded these findings on charts. (See Figures 8.3 and 8.4.) The children referred to these charts as they revised our whole-class piece on why it snows.

When completed, our final piece read as follows:

Why It Snows
An explanation by Grade 1–2
We know why it snows: Do you?

■ **Figure 8.3** Features of explanations

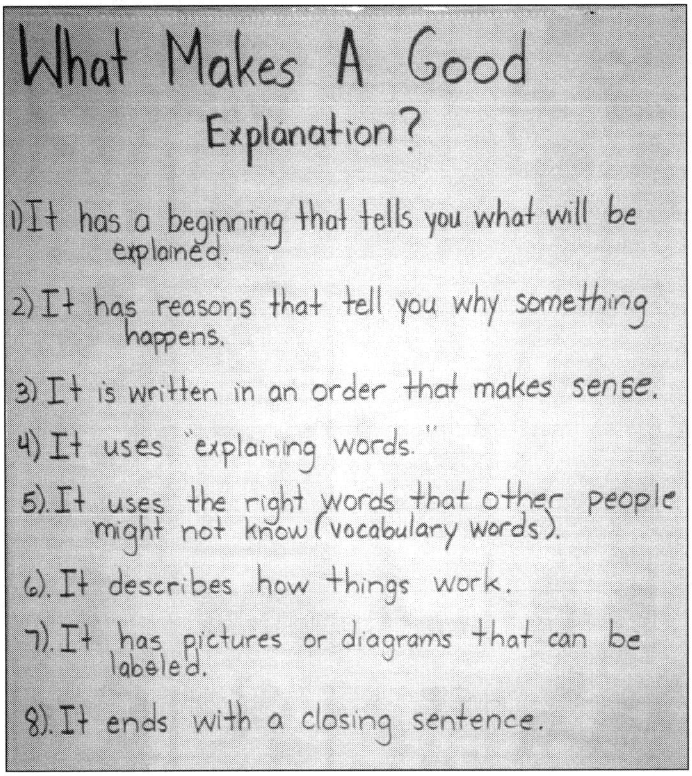
What Makes A Good
Explanation?
1) It has a beginning that tells you what will be explained.
2) It has reasons that tell you why something happens.
3) It is written in an order that makes sense.
4) It uses "explaining words."
5). It uses the right words that other people might not know (vocabulary words).
6). It describes how things work.
7). It has pictures or diagrams that can be labeled.
8). It ends with a closing sentence.

■ **Figure 8.4** Words used in explanations

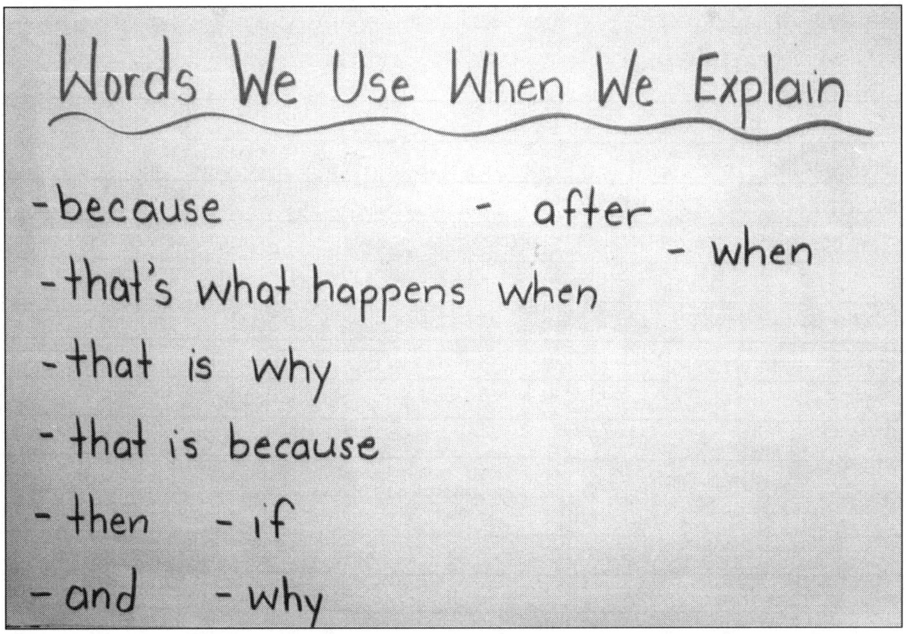
Words We Use When We Explain
-because
- after
- when
-that's what happens when
-that is why
- that is because
- then
- if
- and
- why

We found out that when it rains the water make puddles on the ground.
The puddles get hot when the sun gets hot and then puddles go in the
   air like steam.
Then the steam makes clouds. That is because there is lots of puddles
   and lots of steam.
The clouds get really big and full. They look black and scary.
The clouds get so fat and have to let the water out.
That is why it rains. But if it is very cold the water turns into snow.
So that is why it snows.
Isn't that amazing!

Included with the words were several illustrations the children had made to support the text and to help make explicit the cycle of snow.

Maryanne and I were extremely pleased with the final piece, as were the children. Together we decided to hang our explanation outside the classroom, where everyone could read it and learn more about why it snows. The children were certainly pleased with their efforts and the information they had found. One Monday morning I overheard two of Maryanne's children explaining to a fourth grader why it snows. "You see," said Dilan, proudly, "it's easy. Look here," he said, pointing to one of the pictures on the chart. "This tells you what happens even if you can't read."

Independent Investigations

Having published, shared, and celebrated the whole-class investigation of why it snows, the next step was to encourage the children to engage in independent explorations. These independent pieces would give Maryanne and me insight into what the children had learned about researching and writing explanations during the whole-class investigation. Maryanne returned to the children the original explanations they had written at the start of the unit and simply asked them to look at them in small groups. The children were then asked to come back to the meeting area. Below is a transcript of a portion of the discussion that Maryanne had with her children.

Maryanne: So what did you think about the first explanations you wrote?
Daniel: They don't really explain good.
Maryanne: So, Daniel, you think we need to give better explanations.
Rebecca: Mine's not good.
Maryanne: What don't you like about yours?
Rebecca: I don't have all that stuff [*pointing to the chart "What Makes a Good
   Explanation," Figure 8.3*].
Maryanne: And why are all these things [*pointing to the chart*] important?
Brenda: Because it helps the person.

Maryanne: Which person, Brenda?

Brenda: You know, the one that sees it.

Maryanne: Okay, now I understand. It helps the people who read your explanations. In what ways does it help?

Jose: It help my people. They know why.

At this stage I can hardly contain myself. Jose is one of the many English as a Second Language learners who rarely joins in discussions. Clearly, he is beginning to feel comfortable with expressing his ideas and opinions. His explanation of why writers write in this genre is simple, yet powerful.

Celeste: Yes, like he [*pointing to Jose*] says, when the people read they find out about why it snows.

Maryanne: So what you're telling me is that when you want to explain something in your writing to someone you need to include some of the things on this chart [*pointing to the chart*] so that your readers can understand. Wonderful! So what are we going to do about these [*pointing to the children's initial pieces*]?

Nelsy: Throw them in the rubbish!

Maryanne: Nelsy, sometimes authors do that with writing they don't like, and then sometimes they keep them so they can look back to see how much they have learned. Are there any other suggestions?

Bryan: Do 'em again. I want to put pictures in my new one.

Maryanne: That's an interesting suggestion, Bryan. I suppose we could do them again and use these charts [*Figures 8.3 and 8.4*] to help us. So, Bryan, you are going to include point number 7 in your new explanation [*pointing to the "What Makes a Good Explanation" chart*]. I have noticed that some of you have already begun new explanations during personal writing time. You may want to continue with those, using the charts to help you.
[*Nelsy gets up and throws her original piece in the trash. I retrieve the piece and say, "You know, Nelsy, sometimes authors keep their first pieces to help them write their new pieces. Can I keep this in case you need it later?" She smiles in approval.*]

We can see by the above that many of Maryanne's children were internalizing the purpose of explanations and the importance of including a relevant structure and text features as outlined in Figures 8.3 and 8.4. These were important things for the children to have learned. What we didn't want was for them to follow a predetermined set of rules for writing that had been enforced on them without their intrinsic understanding. The rules being followed were the children's own rules, which Maryanne and I had helped them discover through appropriate scaffolding and engagement.

Maryanne then referred the children back to the "I Wonder Why" chart (Figure 8.1). The children added other questions to the list and then chose one to investigate on their own. Many of the children decided to revise their initial explanations; others selected a new topic. Some had already begun individual investigations during the personal writing time they had been given during the whole-class project. These children simply continued with their research on their previously chosen topic.

Helping Children Gather Resources

To assist the children with their research, Maryanne gathered books and magazines borrowed from the school and local library. She found, however, that some of the material was at text levels way above where her children were reading. To solve this problem she came up with another way for her young researchers to collect information: she decided to ask the parents for help. She wrote a letter, which the children brought home, informing the parents about what their child was exploring and ways they could be of assistance. Maryanne stressed how important it was for parents to take an active role in talking with their children about possible explanations. She also explained that it would not be useful to send the child back with pages of information from the Internet or books the child didn't comprehend and couldn't talk about. Maryanne focused on talk. She also alerted the parents to possible resources that they would find of assistance, such as the local library or direct observation. (See Chapter 3 for more on sources of information.)

Maryanne reminded the children each day to ask their family members that night for information about their exploration. She also paired her children with students from one of the grade 5 classrooms, giving her students the opportunity to meet and work with these older children during writer's workshop. This proved effective, and Maryanne soon found that her students were able to gather a wealth of information just by talking to others. So often as teachers we fail to tap elements of the child's life, such as home and other classrooms, to assist our learners with research. We rely solely on the books we have in our classroom and ourselves as the prime source of information. The chapter in Shelley Harwayne's wonderful book *Going Public* (1999) entitled "Reaching Out to Families" gives many examples of ways teachers can tap the many resources outside the classroom walls.

Providing Demonstrations

Over the next four sessions of writer's workshop Maryanne had her students discuss and record their findings in individual and small-group settings. Maryanne and I provided many demonstrations, in whole-class, small-group, and independent settings, on ways authors research and write explanations.

Our demonstrations focused on a variety of topics—text structure, language and text features, voice, and mechanics—depending on what we saw the children needed as we roamed the classroom, giving assistance. When we noticed that most of the children were having problems with a specific aspect of their writing we would call them together for a whole-class demonstration and discussion. When we noticed that just a few were struggling with a specific aspect of writing, we would call those few together for a brief small-group demonstration. Below is a list of some of the demonstrations we provided.

Demonstrations in Text Structure

Starting with a title to highlight what is going to be explained.
Including relevant information in a logical order.
Including a concluding statement (optional) at the end of the piece.

Demonstrations in Language/Text Features

Using linking words having to do with time.
Including illustrations, diagrams, and labels.
Making sure that the illustrations match the words.

Demonstrations in Voice

Including a great beginning that captivates your audience.
Saying what you think and not just writing down what others say.
Reading your piece to someone else to see if you have said things clearly.

Demonstrations in Mechanics

Using your best handwriting.
Spelling words correctly.
Leaving spaces between your words.
Using capital letters where needed.

Publishing

Once the children's research had been collected and recorded, they were given the option of taking their pieces to publication. Maryanne began the session by engaging the children in a conversation about why authors publish and what they do when they publish. We had assumed that not all the children would want to take their pieces to publication and share them with an audience, but we soon found that all but two wanted to do so. The two children who were exceptions were given the option of going on with other personal writing (which may or may not have included drafting another explanation). We didn't want to force children to publish; instead, we presented it as an option that they could choose or not. (See Chapter 4 for more information about publishing.)

Assessing Children's Growth

When completed, the children's final pieces were wonderful. Maryanne couldn't believe the progress they had made in just four weeks. "Tony," she said, "look at these pieces—they're fabulous! I never thought these children were capable of such brilliance. I am so proud of them." Maryanne and I took some time to examine the children's initial and final pieces to discover what each had learned about writing explanations. We used the assessment rubric to help guide us in these assessments. We also called many of the children up for a brief interview to find out exactly what they had internalized.

Brenda, whose initial piece was highlighted earlier in this chapter, had made enormous progress.

Brenda's initial piece

Why do dogs bite? Because I didn't let Sam go to the bathroom.

Brenda's final piece
How Ice Melts by Brenda

Why does ice melt?

Water is made of molecules. I don't know what they are.

They are small. You can't see them.

When water is warm the molecules move and this makes the water move.
When the air is very cold the molecules go together. They get hard. They are frozen.

When the water warms up the molecules open up from each other and they move.

This is melting and that's how ice melts.

We can see that for her later investigation Brenda chose a scientific topic as opposed to the personal one she had selected for her first piece. Her inclusion of the word "molecules" with the admission that she doesn't know what these are is wonderful. It shows that Brenda is still keeping her own voice in the piece even though it is a scientific explanation. She obviously knows that molecules are important in the process of ice melting and understands that authors use technical words when writing explanations. When we talked with Brenda about this piece she told Maryanne and me that "molecules" was a grown-up word she had learned from her father and it was an important word because without molecules ice wouldn't melt. When we asked her if she had any idea what molecules were she replied, "Sure, they're little things inside the water that you can't see. You need a telescope to see them." This statement suggests that Brenda had a very good grasp of what a molecule is. We told her so and suggested that she consider including this great explanation in her piece. Brenda's piece also shows her understanding that, when writing an explanation, events need to be recorded in a logical sequence. Her inclusion of the word *when* throughout the piece helps the reader understand the elements of cause and effect.

Daniel, whose work was also highlighted at the beginning of this chapter, had also made incredible progress.

Daniel's initial piece (in answer to why dinosaurs died)

because T-Rex was mean

Daniel's final piece

Why the Dinosaurs Died. By Daniel.

Dinosaurs are big and they're strong. Some dinosaurs have teeth and some don't. Some eat meat and some don't.

A reason is that the temperature changed and the earth got cold.

The sun could not shine on the plants and the dinosaurs had nothing to eat. The meat eating dinosaurs died because their food was gone and their food was the plant eating dinosaurs.

All the water dried up and plants and dinosaurs died. They didn't have things to eat.

We don't know exactly how the dinosaurs died but we have good ideas about how it happened.

When Maryanne and I first read Daniel's final piece we thought he was going to launch into a descriptive report about what dinosaurs looked like and what they ate as opposed to an explanation of why they became extinct. We soon realized that he had included this information to give his readers background information on what dinosaurs ate, which was necessary for them to understand the effect the cold weather had on the food chain. This in turn explained why the dinosaurs died. His sequence of events, though a bit confused, is logical. His wonderful conclusion leaves his readers open to other possibilities. It almost invites them to think of other reasons the dinosaurs may have died.

What Maryanne and I were most pleased with was the way the children had researched their topics to gather information. This had ensured that they all had enough information to write about. No child had simply recorded one or two statements or just sat with a blank look, doing nothing. Giving children time to research and then talk about their topics is essential before asking them to write.

Self-Assessment and Reflection

Apart from Maryanne's and my assessments of the students' growth, we encouraged the children to review their initial and final pieces so they could also see and discuss their own improvement. Maryanne returned their pieces along with a self-assessment form (see Appendix A and Chapter 2) and asked the children to take time to reflect on what they had learned as writers. In discussions, the children confirmed that they had learned a lot about writing explanatory texts. Below is a transcript of part of the discussion Maryanne had with her children after they had had time for reflection.

Maryanne: You've just had time to look at your first and final pieces. So talk to me about what you think you've learned about writing explanations.

Rebecca [*pointing to her initial piece*]: Look at this one. It's crazy. It says nothing.

Maryanne: So, Rebecca, you've learned that when writing explanations you need to give your reader lots of information.

Vanessa: Yeah, I know that.

Maryanne: Great, Vanessa. But how did you get this information?

Steven: You know we looked at the books and we asked Mom.

Maryanne: So, Steven, that's a good thing to know when writing an explanation. I have to find information first.

Kevin C: You have to say why it happens.

Maryanne: Great, Kevin. I think you're right. It is important to let your readers know why something happens.

Daniel: Mine sounds good. I like it.

Maryanne: That's a good thing, Daniel. You need to be proud of your writing.

Nelsy [*pointing to her published piece*]: I'm proud of this one. *This* one [*pointing to her initial piece, which I had retrieved from the trash*] is yuk!

Maryanne: Nelsy, why are you so proud of this piece?

Nelsy: I do stuff like Rebecca says. This one says more. It's just better.

Maryanne: You know, it *is* better, Nelsy, because when I read it I really understood why the dinosaurs died. [*Nelsy beams with pride.*] You people have learned so much about writing explanations.

Bryan: I'm going to write another one. [*Various children agree: "Me too" echoes through the room.*]

Maryanne: Terrific! If you want to, you can certainly begin new explorations, or if you want to go on with other writing you can do so.

Daniel: I want to do what Nelsy did with the dinosaurs. I'm going to find more about why they died.

Nelsy: I'll help you because I'm the one who knows.

Maryanne: Yes, Nelsy, you are the expert. So why don't we put our explanations in the classroom library so that you can read each other's and find out more about why things happen. I'll put them into a book box and call it our "how and why books."

As the children go off to begin further independent writing and research, Maryanne looks at me and says, "Thank you. Can you believe this? My children want to write even more explanations. Look at them. Writing has never been this alive before. And look at the quality of these pieces. I never believed it possible. But where do we go from here?" I look around the room and reply, "Nowhere. You've just taken the children somewhere and they need time to explore this writing form further." Eventually Maryanne and I will move the children into another direction and help them explore a new form of writing. But for now we watch them with a sense of pride and wonder, knowing that in just four weeks we have taken them on a journey that has empowered them as writers of nonfiction explanations. To think it all started with Bryan and his terrible, horrible, no good, very bad morning when that puddle got in his way.

Possible Topics for Whole-Class and Independent Investigations

The unit described in this chapter is just one of many possible ways to explore scientific explanations with children. Listed below are suggestions of other topics that could be explored as a whole class or independently. These investigations may run for any length of time, from one week to six weeks. What is important is that they not be one-day wonders. Children need time and opportunity for immersion, demonstrations, and engagement in scientific explanations if they are to become proficient writers in these forms.

Here are possible topics:

Why there is night and day.
How planes fly.
How machines work.
What makes a tornado?
What makes a hurricane?
What makes a tidal wave?
Why kites fly.
Why some objects float and others sink.
Why we don't see the full moon each night.
Why stars shine at night.
Why people need to sleep.
Why ice blocks melt.
Why ice cream melts.
Why cookies crumble.
Why water freezes.
Why trees lose their leaves.
Where water from the tap comes from.
Where lightning comes from.
What makes a rainbow.
How airports work.

How birds fly.
Where rivers come from.
Why people have to eat.
What happens to our food after we eat it.
Why we need water to stay alive.
Why the wind blows.
Why we need the sun to stay alive.
Why spiders and flies can walk on the ceiling without falling.
What formed the Grand Canyon.
Why is it cold in winter?
Why is it not cold in Florida in winter?
Why is it hot in summer?
Why is it hot on Mercury?
Why Mars is called the Red Planet.
Why some trees turn different colors during the fall.
How skyscrapers are built.
How diamonds are made.
How stalactites are formed.
Why some animals became extinct.
Life cycles of specific animals and plants.
Where waves come from.
Where electricity comes from.
Why volcanoes erupt.
Why the sky is blue.

Resources

This last section lists books that may be of use in helping children locate, research, and write scientific explanations. The books are listed alphabetically by title, with series title or author name (if any) and publisher. There are thousands of wonderful books that can be used as valuable resources; the list below provides only a small sample of what's available. I have grouped the books by readability, according to Reading Recovery levels and the Fountas and Pinnell levels. There are a great many different leveling systems in existence, as most publishers have their own method of categorizing texts. I have chosen the Reading Recovery and Fountas and Pinnell systems because they are the most commonly used. (For further information on how to organize classroom books and materials in your classroom, see Chapter 3.)

Scientific Explanations

■ Emergent Readers

Approximate Reading Recovery levels 1–4; Fountas and Pinnell levels A–C

Across the Seasons	Early Connections series	Benchmark Education
Amazing Magnets	Twig series	Wright Group
Animals Have Babies	We Do, Too series	Dominie
Bubbles	Discovery Links series	Newbridge
Cars	Pebble Books series	Capstone Press
Changing Colors	Pair-It Books series	Steck-Vaughn
Clouds	Voyages series	SRA/McGraw Hill
Eyes	Wonder World series	Wright Group
Fall	Discovery Links series	Newbridge
Flying and Floating	Little Red Readers series	Sundance
Grow, Seed, Grow	Discovery Links series	Newbridge
Hands, Hands, Hands	BookShop series	Mondo Publishing
It's Melting	Science 1 series	Creative Teaching Press
Just Add Water	Discovery World series	Rigby
Let's Build a Tower	Literacy 2000 series	Rigby
Magnets	Early Connections series	Benchmark Education
Nighttime	Cycles of Life series	Outside the Box
Ocean Waves	Twig series	Wright Group
Our Amazing World	Reading Safari Encyclofacts series	Mondo Publishing
People Use Tools	Early Connections series	Benchmark Education
A Pond	Discovery Links series	Newbridge
Reading Safari Magazines		Mondo Publishing
Round and Round the Seasons Go	Science 2 series	Creative Teaching Press
Science and Technology	Reading Safari Encyclofacts series	Mondo Publishing
Seasons	Discovery World series	Rigby
Sending Messages	Wonder World series	Wright Group
Snow	Discovery Links series	Newbridge
Some Things Float	Windows on Literacy series	National Geographic
Toys with Wheels	Home Connection series	Rigby
Watch the Sky	Windows on Literacy series	National Geographic
Water Can Be . . .	Wonderful Water series	Outside the Box
Weather	Smart Starts series	Rigby
The Weather Chart	Sunshine series	Wright Group
What Can Float?	Windmill Books series	Rigby
What Comes First?	BookShop series	Mondo Publishing
What Do Animals See?	Read-More Books series	Dominie
What Do Insects Do?	by Susan Canizares and Pamela Chanko	Scholastic
What Goes Up High?	Windmill Books series	Rigby
What Hangs from the Tree?	Questions and Answers series	Dominie
What Is Enormous?	Windmill Books series	Rigby
What Season Is This?	Wonder World series	Wright Group

What's in This Egg?	Sunshine series	Wright Group
Wheels	Windows on Literacy series	National Geographic
Who Made These Tracks?	Literacy 2000 series	Rigby
Whose Forest Is It?	Learn to Read series	Creative Teaching Press

■ Early Readers

Approximate Reading Recovery levels 5–12; Fountas and Pinnell levels D–G

Animals and Their Babies	Early Connections series	Benchmark Education
A Bird Has Feathers	Animals from Nose to Tail series	Outside the Box
Clouds	Pebble Books series	Capstone Press
Fast Machines	Foundations series	Wright Group
Food from the Farm	Home Connections series	Rigby
From Bud to Blossom	Pebble Books series	Grolier, Capstone
How Animals Hide	Wonder World series	Wright Group
How Animals Move	Discovery Links series	Newbridge
How Are We the Same?	Teacher's Choice series	Dominie
How Do Frogs Grow?	Discovery Links series	Newbridge
How Machines Help	Sunshine series	Wright Group
I Can See My Shadow	Windows on Literacy series	National Geographic
Light and Shadow	Discovery Links series	Newbridge
Loading the Airplane	Windows on Literacy series	National Geographic
Looking at Simple Machines	Pebble Books series	Capstone Press
Melting	BookShop series	Mondo Publishing
Mud, Mud, Mud	Windows on Literacy series	National Geographic
My Skin Looks After Me	Reading Science series	Pacific Learning
Our Amazing World	Reading Safari Encyclofacts series	Mondo Publishing
Push or Pull	Windows on Literacy series	National Geographic
Reading Safari Magazines		Mondo Publishing
Science and Technology	Reading Safari Encyclofacts series	Mondo Publishing
Season to Season	Pair-It Books series	Steck-Vaughn
Sink or Float?	Science 3 series	Creative Teaching Press
The Sun	Discovery Links series	Newbridge
This Is an Island	Windows on Literacy series	National Geographic
Water as a Liquid	Pebble Books series	Capstone Press
Water as a Solid	Pebble Books series	Capstone Press
Water Changes	Discovery Links series	Newbridge
The Water Cycle	Pebble Books series	Capstone Press
Water, Land, and Air	Windows on Literacy series	National Geographic
Waves	Voyages series	SRA/McGraw Hill
The Way Things Move	Pebble Books series	Capstone Press
We Need Water	Wonderful Water series	Outside the Box
What Can Change?	Discovery Links series	Newbridge
What Color Is the Sky?	Windows on Literacy series	National Geographic
What Helps a Bird to Fly?	Bird series	Dominie

Is That a Fact?

What Makes Light?	Sunshine series	Wright Group
What's It For?	Visions series	Wright Group
Wheels	Rise and Shine series	Hampton-Brown
When It Rains	Voyages series	SRA/McGraw Hill
Where Do Bugs Live?	Pair-It Books series	Steck-Vaughn
Who Works Here?	Questions and Answers series	Dominie
Why?	Twig series	Wright Group
Winter	Discovery Links series	Newbridge
Wood	Windows on Literacy series	National Geographic

■ Transitional Readers

Approximate Reading Recovery levels 13–20; Fountas and Pinnell levels H–K

Animals Build	Discovery Links series	Newbridge
The Car Wash	Windows on Literacy series	National Geographic
Clouds	Twig series	Wright Group
Corn: From Table to Table	Discovery Link series	Newbridge
Floating and Sinking	BookShop series	Mondo Publishing
Hot Air Balloons	Pair-It Books series	Steck-Vaughn
Hot and Cold Weather	Sunshine series	Wright Group
How Birds Live	Sunshine series	Wright Group
How Does It Breathe?	Home Connection series	Rigby
How Does My Bike Work?	Windows on Literacy series	National Geographic
How Do Fish Live?	Sunshine series	Wright Group
How Do Plants Get Food	by Meish Goldish	Steck-Vaughn
Human Body Systems	Pebble Books series	Capstone Press
Lightning	Pebble Books series	Capstone Press
Machines Make Fun Rides	Windows on Literacy series	National Geographic
Magnets	Windows on Literacy series	National Geographic
Our Amazing World	Reading Safari Encyclofacts series	Mondo Publishing
Rain	Pebble Books series	Capstone Press
Reading Safari Magazines		Mondo Publishing
Science and Technology	Reading Safari Encyclofacts series	Mondo Publishing
The Senses	Pebble Books series	Capstone Press
Soil	Windows on Literacy series	National Geographic
Some Machines Are Enormous	BookShop series	Mondo Publishing
Spring	Pebble Books series	Grolier, Capstone
Stars	Discovery Links series	Newbridge
Sunshine	Pebble Books series	Capstone Press
Tides	Wonder World series	Wright Group
Tubes in My Ears: My Trip to Hospital	BookShop series	Mondo Publishing
Turn on a Faucet	Windows on Literacy series	National Geographic
Water as a Gas	Pebble Books series	Capstone Press
Water Can Change	Windows on Literacy series	National Geographic
Waves: the Changing Surface of the Sea	Wonder World series	Wright Group

What Do Scientists Do?	Discovery Links series	Newbridge
What Happens When You Recycle?	Discovery World series	Rigby
When a Storm Comes	Windows on Literacy series	National Geographic
Where Does the Water Go?	Windows on Literacy series	National Geographic
Where People Live	Early Connections series	Benchmark Education
Wind Power		Pacific Learning
Wind Power	Windows on Literacy series	National Geographic
Yellow Umbrella books	Science series	Capstone Press

■ Fluent Readers

Approximate Reading Recovery levels 20+; Fountas and Pinnell levels L–S

Build It Big	Little Blue Readers series	Sundance
Chemistry	Eyewitness Books series	Dorling Kindersley
Down on the Ice	Orbit GR 3 series	Pacific Learning
Electronics	Eyewitness Books series	Dorling Kindersley
Force and Motion	Eyewitness Books series	Dorling Kindersley
Gravity	Discovery Links series	Newbridge
How a Volcano Is Formed	Wonder World series	Wright Group
Hurricane and Tornado	Eyewitness Books series	Dorling Kindersley
Hurricanes	Extreme Weather series	Lerner Classroom
Light	Eyewitness Books series	Dorling Kindersley
Lightning	Extreme Weather series	Lerner Classroom
The Magic School Bus: At the Waterworks	by Joanna Cole and Bruce Degen	Scholastic
The Magic School Bus: Inside the Earth	by Joanna Cole and Bruce Degen	Scholastic
The Magic School Bus: Inside a Hurricane	by Joanna Cole and Bruce Degen	Scholastic
The Magic School Bus: Inside the Human Body	by Joanna Cole and Bruce Degen	Scholastic
The Magic School Bus: Lost in the Solar System	by Joanna Cole and Bruce Degen	Scholastic
The Magic School Bus: On the Ocean Floor	by Joanna Cole and Bruce Degen	Scholastic
Matter	Eyewitness Books series	Dorling Kindersley
The Moon	Discovery Links series	Newbridge
Natural Disasters series		Capstone Press
Our Amazing World	Reading Safari Encyclofacts series	Mondo Publishing
Powerful Waves	Extreme Weather series	Lerner Classroom
Reading Safari Magazines		Mondo Publishing
Science and Technology	Reading Safari Encyclofacts series	Mondo Publishing
Time and Space	Eyewitness Books series	Dorling Kindersley
Tornado	Extreme Weather series	Lerner Classroom
Twisting Up a Storm	Orbit Gr 6 series	Pacific Learning
The UFO Library		Capstone Press
The Unexplained series		Capstone Press
Up and Away! Taking a Flight	BookShop series	Mondo Publishing
Up in the Air	Wildcats series	Wright Group
Volcano and Earthquake	Eyewitness Books series	Dorling Kindersley
What Animal Lives Here	BookShop series	Mondo Publishing

Is That a Fact?

What Are Food Chains and Webs?	Science of Living Things series	Sundance
What Is a Bat?	Science of Living Things series	Sundance
What Is a Fly?	Sunshine series	Wright Group
What Is a Life Cycle?	Science of Living Things series	Sundance
What Is a Living Thing?	Science of Living Things series	Sundance
What Is a Reptile?	Now I Know series	Troll
What Makes a Bird a Bird	BookShop series	Mondo Publishing
What's Happening? A Book of Explanations	BookShop series	Mondo Publishing
Why Crocodiles Live in Rivers	Sunshine series	Wright Group

Persuasive Writing

Making kids eat vegetables is wrong. My dad can eat what he wants. He hates sprouts I hate sprouts but I have to eat them because I'm a kid. I don't understand. Mom says they're good for you. Well so are potatoes. Give me potatoes not yucky sprouts.

Katie, grade 1

hen I first read Katie's piece I was instantly impressed by her arguments for not having to eat sprouts. Hers was a typical reaction by young children to the many things they are compelled to do yet don't understand why. What Katie was writing was one of the most powerful types that writers engage in: the art of persuasion.

The first question that comes to mind about persuasive writing is: How do we label such a text? Is it simply a personal narrative that centers around personal opinions, or is it a piece of nonfiction writing? I would argue that it is both, especially when the writer researches the topic and provides supportive factual evidence to support his or her stance. Typically when most young children engage in writing persuasively they do little research and merely give their opinion with little or no justification of their point of view. They often make generalizations and at times even make up their own facts to support their beliefs. The result is a composition that does little to persuade the reader.

This point was made clear to me one year when I was teaching a grade 3 class in an inner-city suburb of Melbourne, Australia. We were exploring persuasive writing, and the children composed a letter to a publisher requesting free books for the classroom library. In their letter they simply asked for books, commenting that they liked books and needed them in the classroom. We sent the letter and one week later received a small package with five books. The children were excited, but a little disappointed in the small number of publications sent to them. We decided to redo our letter, only this time we included some facts to support our request. In the letter we told the publisher that we didn't have a lot of money and loved reading. We said that our classroom library needed many more books so that we could become better readers. We added that the books we did have from their company were some of our favorites and that if they could donate some to our classroom we would place a "Kindly donated by————" sticker in each book. The children ended with a powerful conclusion: "We know you care about us kids and want us to be good readers. Please help us. We picked your company because we know you care. Thank you from the bottom of our hearts." The following week a large box with over one hundred books arrived for our class. I can't begin to describe the children's excitement. They had realized through firsthand experience the power of the pen and that persuasive writing in particular could be very powerful.

If we want our children to become effective persuaders in their writing we need to engage them in many learning experiences that will strengthen their understanding of persuasive texts and what writers do to effectively persuade others.

Overview of Persuasive Writing

The following is a general overview of the characteristics of persuasive texts.

Purpose/Social Function

Persuasive texts are written for many purposes. Some put forward a point of view or justify a position; these types of persuasive texts are often referred to as *expositions*. Persuasive texts can also be written to encourage people to purchase something, partake in a specific type of activity (such as exercise), or think in a certain kind of way.

Types or Forms

There are literally hundreds of different types of persuasive texts. Below are a sampling of possibilities specifically relevant to grades K–3. I have included poetry, for I have found it can be one of the most powerful forms of persuasive writing. As a colleague once said to me, "If you want to get someone to think your way, write a poem and tug at the heartstrings. Make them cry. That should do the trick."

Here are some forms that persuasive writing can take:

Television advertisements.
Newspaper advertisements.
Radio advertisements.
Expositions.
Debates.
Arguments.
Signs.
Posters.
Poems.
Letters.
Book reviews.
Advertising pamphlets.
Essays giving historical perspectives on past events and happenings.

Text Structure

Persuasive texts usually begin with a title or opening statement that tells the reader what is being argued or what the topic of the discussion is about. In the case of expositions, this is often followed by the position the reader is taking on the subject being discussed. Usually the writer then provides a series of reasons or arguments to support his or her stance. Persuasive texts usually end with a conclusion or summary. This is especially true for expositions.

Language Features

The following are common language features of persuasive texts:

Use of both facts and opinions to support stance.
Use of connectives having to do with reasoning (*because of, so, therefore*, etc.).

Inclusion of diagrams, labels, pictures, and drawings to help persuade the reader.

Example

Here is an analysis of a persuasive text. Language features are highlighted in bold.

Should children be given homework?	Title
by Lisa, Grade 2	
I think kids should not be given home-work.	Statement of position
Kids have to work hard all day and they need time to play.	First argument with support-ing evidence or facts
That's what kids need to do. Play.	
My dad watches TV when he comes home from work. He doesn't have to work.	Second argument with sup-porting evidence or facts
My mum works real hard even at night. I help her **so** why should I have to do homework too.	Third argument with sup-porting evidence or facts Connective
It's not fair making kids do homework. They are individuals not slaves.	Conclusion/summary

A Unit in Action: Kindergarten

When you first walk into Jessica Mazzocco's kindergarten classroom in Queens, New York, you would never guess that she has been teaching for only three years. The classroom has all the earmarks of belonging to a veteran teacher who has attended hundreds of workshops and read countless teacher references about effective teaching practices. Jessica is a natural. She has an incredible way of engaging her children and is aware of each child's strengths and needs. It is a delight to just sit and watch her in action.

I had been working with Jessica for two years. Our latest discussions focused on writer's workshop—specifically, ways to extend her children's writing from simple personal narratives that usually dealt with what the child had done the previous evening at home. Many of her writers simply wrote "I love . . ." statements each day. Jessica was looking for ways to extend the children's understanding of different purposes authors have. We discussed the idea of having the children write animal reports or recipes, but Jessica was more intrigued by persuasive writing. As she put it, "Tony, I think this type of writing will be a journey for me and my children. I would never consider doing this in kindergarten because it's something kindergarten teachers never really do. We always stick to animal reports. I want to challenge my children and myself and see if this works. They really need to extend their writing. They can write persuasively. What they don't do is justify their beliefs with facts. Let's try this."

The children had recently been to a farm, and their daily writing entries reflected this recent experience. Jason would write "I love the horse" each day. Marion would scribe "The pig is smelly." Jessica and I saw these entries as a perfect way to launch a whole-class investigation on writing persuasive texts. We brought the children together and posed a simple two-part question: "What animal do you think is the best animal at the farm, and why do you think it is the best?" The children responded with vigor. They all had a favorite animal and were eager to shout out their responses. Jasmin said, "The pig is the best," to which Maryanne replied, "No, you're wrong, it's the horse. I'm right." Marco then turned to them and said, "No, you're both wrong. It's the sheep." Clearly the children had strong opinions—so strong that they were not even willing to listen to the arguments of their peers. Jessica had a worried look on her face. I could tell that she was thinking, "If we don't do something soon we're going to lose control here. These children are getting a little too vocal. Fights could break out." But I found the children's enthusiasm exciting. The simple question had stirred them so much that when we eventually asked them to sign their names on a poster above their favorite animal and then draw and write about this animal and justify why they thought it was the best, within two minutes every child had pencil in hand, working with vigor. I was reminded of the work by people such as Don Murray, Shelley Harwayne, Lucy Calkins, Don Graves, and Ralph Fletcher, who stress the importance of writing with passion. From what I could see, passion for writing was now raging in Jessica's classroom.

Assessing the Children's Understanding

When the children had finished their pieces, Jessica and I gave them an opportunity to share their work. We then examined the children's work to assess what each child understood about writing a persuasive piece and what demonstrations we would need to do in order to strengthen the children's existing knowledge. We completed an assessment rubric for each child (see Figure 9.1).

Typically, most of the children wrote simple statements with little or no justification as to why they thought their animal was the best. Gustavo wrote, "Cows are best. They are cool." Lia wrote, "The sheep is nice." Jasmin scribed, "Chicks are beautiful I love them." We can see by these entries that the children were certainly able to identify what animal they liked best but were not able to justify their stance with supportive factual evidence. This is natural for writers so young; they don't usually consider going into depth with what it is

Assessment Rubric for Persuasive Writing

Key: N: Not in evidence   S: Showing signs of   C: Consolidating   M: Mostly   N/A: Not applicable

Name: **Grade:** **Date:** **Text Type or Title:**		
Purpose		
Understands the purpose for writing a persuasive piece		
Craft (Structure, features, voice)		
Linguistic or Text Structure		
Begins with a title or opening statement that tells the reader what is being argued		
Provides a series of arguments or reasons to support the topic being discussed		
Organizes information in a logical order		
Includes a concluding statement or summary		
Text/Language Features		
Uses only opinions		
Uses supportive facts		
Includes illustrations and labels to help persuade the reader		
Uses persuasive words or phrases		
Voice		
Uses an enticing title and/or setting to engage the reader		
Is able to express ideas using own language as opposed to copying down what others say or information from books read		
Uses descriptive language that paints pictures for the reader		
Is able to state information in a unique or surprising manner		
Research Skills		
Is able to locate information from books		
Is able to locate information from nonbook sources		
Is able to interpret and talk about information located		
Surface Features (Mechanics)		
Handwriting neat and legible		
Shows improvement in attempts at spelling words		
Uses grammatically correct language		
Shows improvement in use of punctuation		
Uses an appropriate publishing format		
Work generally well presented		

that makes them think something. The children used words such as *cool, beautiful, nice,* and *good* to justify just about everything. It was evident from these initial pieces that Jessica and I would need to provide a range of experiences to help them become more able writers of persuasive texts and in particular to lead them to discover that writers give supportive evidence when writing such texts.

Providing Demonstrations: Modeled Writing

The following morning, Jessica decided to give the children a modeled writing experience to start them on their journey to discovering what writers do when they try to persuade. She brought the children together in the meeting area and told them that she was going to write her piece on her favorite animal, which was the horse. Here is a transcript of the modeled writing session:

Jessica: Okay, everyone, I want you to watch me as I write what my favorite animal is and why I think it's the best. I think I need to have a picture of a horse in front of me because that might give me some ideas. [*She places a picture of a horse next to the chart paper where she is going to record her piece.*] I'm going to start my writing by saying "I think the horse is the best animal for three reasons." [*She writes this on the chart paper.*] Mmm, let me think. Oh, I know, the horse is the best because you can ride it. I'm going to write that down. That's a good reason or argument. Now let me think. Yes, I know. The horse is a friendly animal. It makes a good pet. That's another good argument or reason. And my third reason is that the horse can run fast, and I like animals that can do that. I really admire them. I think I'll write that down too.

Jasmin: But they can't fly. Birds can.

Jessica: You know, Jasmin, you're right. That would be a good reason why a bird could be the best animal.

Kevin: And a cow is big. It's the biggest.

Jessica: That's right, Kevin. That would be a good argument for why the cow is the best.

Liliana: The horse is beautiful.

Jessica: It is, Liliana, and I might write that down too, but I want to tell people *why* I think it is beautiful. Can you tell me why you think the horse is beautiful?

Liliana: It is brown.

Jessica: That's a great reason, so I think I might write that the horse is beautiful because it is brown. That will give my readers more information on why I think the horse is beautiful. Okay, why don't you go back and think about some reasons why your animal is the best and go write them down or draw about them like I have. I have put pictures of all the farm animals on your tables to help you think of good reasons. And remember, if you can't think of something ask a friend to help you. That's what good writers sometimes do.

Jessica was stretching her children's thought by showing them that when writers work on persuasive texts they come up with facts to support their position. She also demonstrated how a visual stimulus—a picture—can help with the composing of a written piece.

Her use of the words "a good argument or reason" throughout her discussion was powerful, as it told the children what the word *argument* meant by simply linking it with the word *reason*. I think it is imperative that as teachers we begin to extend children's vocabulary by using and explaining words that may not be common in their everyday talk. It is only by using and discussing such words that we can begin to extend their oral language, which forms the basis of their becoming more able writers.

It was amazing to watch Jessica's children for the next ten minutes after the modeled writing encounter. There was a lot of talk going on at each table, all of it constructive. The children looked at the pictures and discussed all the attributes that made each animal so special. When Jessica brought them back together to share, some of their entries were truly remarkable and confirmed just how effective Jessica's modeled writing had been. Cesar, who had originally written that the pig was the best because it was good had now changed his mind. In his latest piece he wrote, "The bird is best because it can fly. It has nice colors and colors make you happy." Jessica asked Cesar about this change of heart, and he informed her that even though he still liked the pig, he thought that the bird had more good things about it.

Reflecting and Providing Constructive Feedback

For the next three days Jessica commenced writer's workshop with individual children sharing their persuasive pieces on their animal of choice. During the sharing, Jessica recorded each child's reasons for liking a specific animal onto a chart (see Figure 9.2). Her feedback to each child was always positive and confirming, yet at the same time she always encouraged the child to be reflective and talk about what it was that made his or her writing a good persuasive piece. An example of this was her response to Sam's piece:

Jessica: Sam, I like the way you didn't just say you like the cow because it is nice. What things did you tell us?
Sam: It is black and white.
Jessica: That's right, Sam. Why is this a reason you like the cow?
Sam: I like it.

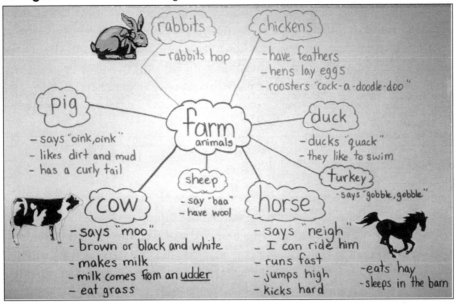

Jessica: I see. You like black and white. What a great reason or argument to include in your piece. So, Sam, Where did you get this information about the colors of the cow?

Sam: From the picture.

Jessica: Excellent. That's a great way to try and find good reasons.

At the conclusion of the share time each morning, the children would go back to their table and continue adding information to their persuasive pieces. Then they would engage in other types of personal writing, such as journals, letters, or observation sheets at the science table, or they would practice handwriting. Within three days they had all completed their persuasive pieces. They were then given the option of taking their pieces to publication. They were also given the opportunity to share. During this share time, Jessica asked the children to reflect and tell her what they thought made a good argument. She recorded the children's responses onto a chart:

What Makes a Good Argument
First you have to pick a side.
Say why you think something.
Include facts if you can.
Ask other people or look at books and pictures to help you with your facts.

The children were beginning to internalize what made a good persuasive piece. However, although Jessica and I were pleased with the way the children had begun to include supportive evidence in the persuasive pieces they had just completed, we knew that they needed more experience in writing persuasive texts and exposure to other authentic purposes for engaging in this form of writing. The big decision was whether to engage them later on in the school year with a different topic or to continue with the unit now. For Jessica it was an easy decision to make. She simply reflected on the level of engagement by her children in writer's workshop over the previous week. They were immersed in this type of writing, and it showed.

Further Explorations

Jessica continued to explore persuasive writing with her children by beginning each day by presenting them with a statement or question on a sheet of paper. These statements or questions always reflected topics of interest to the children, such as "Pokémon is better than Digimon"; "Should children sleep at school?"; or "Winter is the best season." Each morning the children would read the statement for the day and sign their names under either the Yes or No column, according to their point of view (see Figure 9.3). Then, as part of independent writing during writer's workshop, each child would write at least one reason to substantiate their belief. The children were encouraged to talk to each other first and look at the pictures Jessica placed on their tables before writing their reasons. The children were also given the option of changing their preference after looking at the pictures and talking with their peers. Jessica and I used this time to roam around the classroom, assisting the children in individual and small-group settings. The children would then come together in the meeting area, where they were encouraged to share their written or drawn opinions.

■ **Figure 9.3** Questions for persuasive writing

Is That a Fact?

Jessica would then write some of their reasons on chart paper. Each day the children's arguments grew more specific and more complex. Their skills as persuasive writers were growing with their experience in this type of writing. An example of this can be seen in the children's responses to the statement "Winter is the best season." Although many of the children still wrote arguments such as "Winter is best because it is nice," they would go on to substantiate these opinions with facts, such as "the snow looks white and fluffy."

This growth is clearly seen when we compare Gustavo's initial piece on why cows are the best farm animal with his latest piece on why he thinks summer is the best season.

Gustavo's initial piece
Cows are best. They are cool.

Gustavo's latest piece
Summer is the best. You have no school and that's cool.
I can play every day. I can swim.

Gustavo's growth as a writer is evident. In his later piece he has included supportive factual evidence to justify his position. He has continued to use the word *cool* because it is obviously a word he likes a lot and is part of his voice. However, he has not simply used this word as the sole reason for why he believes summer to be better than winter.

Jessica and I noted a great leap in the children's understanding, especially in such a short period and for children so young. It was clear to us that children need ongoing daily demonstrations and opportunities for talk and research in a specific genre if they are to become competent writers in that genre. As Jessica and I noticed new understanding in each child, we would note it on the child's assessment rubric. This not only allowed us to gauge individual progress; it also helped us decide what was needed for whole-class and small-group demonstrations each day.

Jessica brought the unit to a close by referring the children to the chart "What Makes a Good Argument," which they had constructed earlier in the unit, and reflecting with her learners on what makes a good persuasive piece. She then brainstormed with her children other possible questions or statements that they might want to write about. This list she placed with an earlier chart that the class had made at the beginning of the year entitled "Things We Like to Write About." For Jessica's students now had another purpose for writing. They could now add persuasive writing to their repertoire. When I visited Jessica's classroom two weeks later I was delighted to see just how many of her children were still writing wonderful arguments about statements of interest they had brainstormed at the conclusion of the unit. Their passion for writing was still raging.

And as for Jessica, she was delighted not only with her children's progress but also with her own deepened understanding of how persuasive texts work. She told me that when she explores persuasive texts the next time it will be a little different. She said, "Tony, I learned so much during this unit. I think I learned more than my kids. I want to do it again, maybe later in the year or maybe next year with a different group of kids. I want to get better at this. I'm going to think about immersing my children into procedural texts next, but not for a few weeks. I want them to continue with other personal writing, which for most of them will probably be persuasive texts because they have so much to argue about at the moment. It's just fantastic."

A Unit in Action: Third Grade

As I walked into the grade 3 classroom in New York City, I felt nervous. It was a typical third-grade classroom, crowded with children, desks, and general clutter. But that wasn't why I found myself a little nervous. Reading and writing persuasive texts were topics in the category of "must cover this year." Like statewide tests in numerous states across the country, the citywide test for fourth graders included persuasive writing as an element that children must show some level of competence in if they are to pass. The pressure in the fourth grade was high, but it was ever present in the third-grade classroom, where teachers were expected to get children ready for the demands of the following year.

Typically many teachers find persuasive writing difficult. They attempt to prepare their children by giving them set pieces of readings to which the children write persuasive responses. For both the children and the teacher this soon becomes a tedious ritual that dominates both reader's and writer's workshop. It is not long before children perceive reading and writing to be like medicine, something you have to take even though it leaves a bitter taste in the mouth. The passion for writing that was so evident in Jessica's kindergarten classroom has long been a thing of the past in many third-grade classrooms, when exercises in test preparation take center stage. So the question is, how do we keep this passion for writing alive amidst the pressures of children's having to pass a standardized test?

A third-grade teacher named Mary had asked me to work with her in her classroom. She wanted to explore persuasive writing and empower her students not only to understand and enjoy this kind of writing but also to be competent enough to pass the state test looming the following year. I tried to reassure myself that I had often explored persuasive writing with third-grade children with great success, and I should not let the thought of a standardized test cloud my thinking. I would not feel pressured to implement a unit of study based on a deficit model, where the children would be treated like empty vessels which I would fill them all the skills I thought they needed in order to be successful by giving them countless worksheets and test preparation exercises.

Before commencing the unit of study, I thought of the many different topics that could act as springboards to immerse the children into the world of persuasive writing. There were so many possibilities. I finally decided on an idea I got from Judy Ballister, an accomplished fourth-grade teacher whom I had worked with the year prior. We would explore advertising as a form of persuasion and specifically look at ways to entice readers to visit a place of personal interest. Advertising is probably one of the most powerful forms of persuasive writing and one that certainly dominates our present-day society. I contacted a local travel agency, told them what the third graders were studying, and inquired if they would display the children's advertisements when they were published. I did this because I was eager to have the children engage in an authentic purpose for writing a persuasive piece. The agency jumped at the chance; they thought this would be a novel way to advertise desirable destinations around the world. They also kindly gave me many travel brochures for the children to use in their research.

I commenced the unit by engaging the students in a conversation about all the different countries they came from and the different places they had visited. They were fascinated by my Australian accent and asked me many questions about both my home country and what I thought about living in New York. I told them that I loved New York but that I also loved Australia and that I loved each of these places for different reasons. I informed the children of my visit to the travel agency and asked them if they would be interested in working on writing posters that would advertise places people might like to visit. The children were so excited by this prospect that it took a few minutes to calm them down. I have found that when children are writing for an audience, especially one so public, their desire to be writers is usually at a peak. I informed the children that we would first have to draft our pieces, then spend the next few weeks working on them to make them better. I posed the questions "What country or place do you like best?" and "If you had to try and convince someone to visit this place, what would you say?"

Assessing the Children's Understanding

I gave the children pieces of paper and asked them to begin researching and writing. I intended to use these initial pieces as a form of assessment to see what skills they had as researchers and writers when engaging in a persuasive writing project. These initial pieces would guide my future whole-class, small-group, and individual demonstrations. The first thing I noticed was that many of the children went to the classroom library to locate books on specific places. I was pleased to see this, as it demonstrated that many of these children knew the importance of doing research before putting pen to paper. Mary told me that the class had recently done a unit on the ocean, and the children had been encouraged to use classroom resources when writing reports on the ocean. Some of the children, however, simply began writing. I made a note of who these children were, as it was evident that although Mary had encouraged her class to use books and magazines, not all the children had internalized the importance of this step when writing about a specific topic. These children would need further demonstrations and discussions on this part of the process.

The completed pieces showed a variety of ability levels when it came to persuasive writing, as can be seen by comparing Katherine's piece with Christopher's.

Katherine's initial piece

Come to New York. It's the best.
We have the Empire State. We have the Statue of Liberty and if you like to shop you'll find we have the best shops in the world.
If you like to play we have Central Park. It's got lots of things for kids to do. You can ride a horse. You can eat ice cream. You can play.
New York is the best. Don't miss out on all the fun.

Christopher's initial piece

I went to Disneyworld. It was fun. I went on splash mountain. I was scared. I like Disneyworld. It is fun. You will like it.

Katherine displayed a good understanding of how persuasive texts worked. Her piece invited the reader to come and explore New York. She had appealed to a range of audiences, from those who like to shop to children who like to play. Katherine's piece also reflected her use of research, as seen by her citing the Empire State building and the Statue of Liberty as important landmarks. Her concluding summary also aimed to persuade, as she told her readers that they wouldn't want to miss out on all the fun. A few other children wrote pieces as powerful as Katherine's. Mary and I knew that these children would need to be brought together at various stages of the unit to extend their already strong understanding.

Christopher, however, had simply written a personal narrative that tells of his journey to Disney World. If not for his concluding statement one would think that he had misunderstood the writing task, thinking he just had to write about a place he had visited as opposed to a persuasive piece that tried to coax the reader. Apart from his mention of Splash Mountain he provided little detail. Christopher, like others in the classroom, had not researched his topic and therefore relied exclusively on his memory of Disney World to write his piece.

Mary seemed a little shocked by the range of understanding demonstrated by these first persuasive writing pieces. She told me she had never before assessed her students prior to a unit of study, only at the end. This new experience helped her realize that without assessments prior to a unit the teacher is really just guessing at what the students need. We used the assessment rubric (see Figure 9.1) to create a profile of each child, then used these to plan some of the demonstrations we would need to provide.

The Whole-Class Investigation Begins

After the children had written their initial pieces, we brought them together to share. Many were eager to take their pieces straight to publication with no revising. We reminded them that the pieces had to be their very best, especially since they were going to be on display in a public forum. I made the suggestion that we put these first pieces aside for the present and maybe work on a piece together. We could then learn as a class how to write a wonderfully persuasive piece and use this knowledge to revise our original pieces. We then voted on a place that would be interesting to explore as a whole class. Many suggestions were put forward by the children, but Australia won in the end. The children were extremely interested in the land down under, as they had heard many tales about crocodiles, venomous spiders, and, of course, kangaroos.

Collecting Information

We divided the children into small groups and gave each group some of the travel brochures that I had been given by the travel agency. I also brainstormed with the children other possible sources of information, such as books, family members, and television documentaries. Each group was then given the task of researching Australia to find as much information as possible that would make our travel poster both inviting and persuasive. Each morning I would bring the children together to record their information onto a chart. By the end of the third session we had gathered a lot of information, as seen below:

> **Our Advertisement for Visiting Australia**
> Australia is cool. Australia is the largest island in the world. It is the smallest continent. It has a population of 18 million people. Australia is home to many animals such as the crocodile, kangaroo, koala, and platypus. Australia has more deadly snakes than anywhere else in the world. It also has lots of deadly spiders. Lots of people die from snake bites and spider bites. The crocodile can also eat people. Australia has the largest rock in the world and the biggest coral reef in the world. Australia has the Sydney Harbor bridge and the Opera House. It also has lots of beaches and rain forests. Australia is a long way away. It takes more than a day to fly there. Australia has very hot weather. Some days are over 100 degrees. Come to Australia you will love it.

The children had certainly gathered a lot of information on my home country, but whether it was persuasive was certainly questionable. If anything, I would say it was a good advertisement as to why someone would choose *not* to visit the land down under. I think this exercise was an eye-opener for Mary, as she realized that although her children may be competent collectors of information they certainly needed assistance in understanding that the purpose of the writing was to persuade and that specific information that would meet this purpose was required. Mary and I also noted that the children had included many assertions that were not backed up with facts and that many of these statements were themselves more myth than fact.

Revising the Information

The next week was eventful. Mary and I brought the children together to discuss the information they had gathered. We began by reading one of the brochures from the travel agency about Australia to the children and posing the question "How did the information in that brochure make you feel about Australia?"

The children responded that they felt Australia was a fantastic place to visit. We asked them what words in particular the author had used to make them want to visit this country. We then charted their responses. The children came up with descriptors such as "large, inviting beaches, beautiful and exotic wildlife, friendly people" and "a shopper's paradise."

Mary and I then drew the children's attention to our class piece and asked them whether we had included information that would make people want to visit Australia. The children thought hard. Finally Linda said, "I hate spiders. If I read that on a poster I wouldn't want to go." Linda's comment instantly opened up a barrage of comments on just how frightening we had made our piece to the reader who was thinking about visiting. Mary and I also asked the children to reflect on the information to see if it was even needed in the first place. Robert commented, "Just because it's got 18 million people doesn't mean it's a good place to visit." Jose supported Robert's findings by adding, "And just because it's the largest island doesn't make it the best." I could see that Mary was excited by her children's discoveries. They were really beginning to understand that the purpose of a piece of writing dictates its content.

We gave each group a number of brochures and asked them to look closely for words and phrases that they thought were persuasive. We suggested that the children use the classroom dictionaries and thesauruses to help them if they came across words they didn't understand. The thesauruses were also useful in helping the children come up with other words not mentioned in the brochure but that could be used in a persuasive piece. We recorded these words on chart paper. The children came up with almost one hundred words, including the following:

interesting	amazing	incredible
magnificent	fantastic	soothing
relaxing	breathtaking views	wonderful
panoramic views	crystal clear water	tremendous
enormous	pretty	fabulous
awesome	enjoyable	peaceful
exciting	large	delicious food
thrilling	cool	gigantic
exotic animals and plants		

Mary and I continued to provide demonstrations relevant to the identified needs of the class. Each morning, after demonstrations and discussions, the groups were given time to make revisions on the Australian advertisement. We told the groups that they could add new information if they wanted, but they could not copy the phrases from the travel brochures. Mary and I used this time to roam the classroom, giving support where necessary to specific groups. After a week the class's revised advertisement, which combined each group's information, read as follows:

Our Advertisement for Visiting Australia

Come to the land down under for an awesome experience. Australia is a large island that has so many wonderful things. Australia is home to many exotic animals such as the crocodile, kangaroo, koala, and platypus. You can see them all in Australia. Australia has the largest rock in the world and the biggest coral reef in the world. The water in Australia is crystal clear. There are thousands of interesting fish that you can see. You can go snorkeling or just swim in the warm waters. Australia has the Sydney Harbor bridge and the Opera House. They are magnificent. It also has lots of golden beaches and breathtaking rain forests. If you want an enjoyable vacation then come to Australia. You will only be sorry if you don't go.

The children were impressed with their advertisement, especially when they compared it to their first attempt. Mary and I were also amazed at how well the piece had turned out. Our discussions on using enticing words clearly had had a great effect. In Mary's words, "I've never had a desire to go to Australia, but after reading this—When does the next plane depart?" We gave each group poster paper, rulers, and markers to publish the advertisement so that we would have a number of copies for display. These were then officially handed over to the travel agency. Once the posters had gone, the children couldn't wait to visit the travel agency to see them. Maria announced, "I live near the travel agency and I'm going to look at them every day!"

Reflections

With the whole-class exploration complete, our next step was to spend time reflecting with the children on what they had learned about writing a persuasive piece and help them apply this knowledge to making revisions to their original advertisements. We gave the children time to discuss their new learning in small groups. We also gave each group more travel brochures and copies of test preparation exercises that had persuasive pieces in them. These were exercises that Mary had often used to prepare her students for the next year's test. When they saw the exercises the children instantly asked with horror, "Do we have to do these again?" I told them that Mary and I only wanted them to look at the persuasive pieces in the test to see what the author had done to try and persuade the reader. The children were relieved by my reply. Mary later told me that she had never thought of using the test preparation exercises in this way. I told her that they were a little like basal readers. I had nothing against basals per se; after all, some of the best stories I'd read were in basal anthologies. I just had a problem with the way they were usually used in classrooms, with a "one size fits all" mentality. These test preparation exercises were the same. Integrated into a purposeful unit of study and getting the children to examine them from a different stance can make them powerful learning tools.

When the children had completed their reflections we brought them together to discuss what they had found. We charted their ideas as follows:

> **What Makes a Good Persuasive Piece**
> The writer first picks a topic or a side.
> The writer researches the topic.
> Use books, magazines, television and interviews to help you.
> You need to give strong arguments that support what you are trying to say.
> Leave out things that might not support what you are trying to say.
> You can use illustrations or photographs to help you convince the reader.
> Use good persuasive words (like the ones on the chart).
> Stick to your topic.
> Make sure there is a powerful ending and a great beginning.
> Put your information in order.

The children had learned a lot about persuasive writing in a very short period of time. Interestingly some of the points that the children mentioned had come from their review of the test preparation exercises. Linda told us that she had learned to start with a great beginning because all the passages in the test preparation exercises started with beginnings that made you want to keep reading. I later suggested to Mary that she cut some of the passages out of the test preparation exercises and place them in a folder in the classroom library entitled "Persuasive Writing Pieces." In this way the children could use them for future reference or simply select them during independent reading.

Independent Investigations

With the children's notes on persuasive writing displayed on the chart, Mary and I wanted our learners to use their newfound knowledge to make revisions to the initial advertisements they had written at the beginning of the unit. The children took time to reflect on their earlier pieces; then, using the list of persuasive words and the chart "What Makes a Good Persuasive Piece" as references, they began to make revisions. Mary and I used this time each day to rove the classroom and pull small groups together based on identified needs. For learners such as Katherine, these demonstrations dealt with more complex concepts, such as the need for giving specific details and supportive evidence to some of her statements. Learners such as Christopher were given small-group demonstrations on giving at least one piece of supportive evidence in their writing.

Mary and I also brought the children together for whole-class demonstrations based on our observations of need as we roved the classroom. These included demonstrations in both craft and mechanics.

Demonstrations in Craft

Commencing the piece with an inviting beginning.
Organizing the information into a logical sequence.
Including persuasive language.
Using conjunctions to link pieces of information.
Using photographs and labels to help the reader.
Using headings.

Demonstrations in Mechanics

Spelling.
Using the word wall.
Handwriting.
Using correct grammar.
Using capital letters and periods.

One important demonstration centered around the difference between fact and opinion. Mary and I had noticed that many of the children were getting so creative with their advertisements that they were becoming a little too liberal with their claims. Robbie wrote in his advertisement about Florida, "Florida is the best place in the world. Its beaches are the best. Its food is the best and the people are awesome. They are the friendliest in the world." Now, while I would never dispute that Florida has great beaches, good food, and wonderful people, I thought Robbie may have taken this persuasive thing a little too far. We discussed the difference between fact and opinion and used the children's whole-class piece on Australia as a means of demonstrating to the children how facts and not just opinions are important to a persuasive piece. We listed all the statements from their whole-class advertisement that were facts and all those that were opinions:

Fact **Something that is true**	Opinion **Something that you think or feel**
Australia is a large island Australia is home to many exotic animals such as the crocodile, kangaroo, koala, and platypus. Australia has the largest rock in the world.	that has so many wonderful things. The water in Australia is crystal clear.
There are thousands of interesting fish you can see. Australia has the Sydney Harbor bridge and the Opera House. It also has golden beaches and breathtaking rain forests.	They are magnificent. If you want an enjoyable vacation then come to Australia. You will only be sorry if you don't go.

We asked the children what they noticed about the information on the chart and they informed us that they saw many facts and only a few opinions. They also told us that these opinions were usually about the stated facts—an important thing for the children to have realized about a persuasive piece. We asked the children to go back and reflect on their own writing to see if they had included enough facts and whether their opinions were supported by their facts. It was interesting to see how many children classified the information in their initial pieces as either fact or opinion, just as we had done with the whole-class advertisement on Australia. (See Appendix H for a form that can assist children with this task.)

Once the children had finished making revisions to their pieces, we gave them poster paper and a variety of publishing materials so that they could complete their final copy. These were then celebrated, shared, and given to the travel agency for display. There was a real sense of pride in the children as they gave their final published pieces over to the agent who had made a special visit to the school to collect them. The children were assured that the pieces would be well looked after and admired and that they would be returned whenever the children wanted.

Assessing Children's Growth

Before giving the children's final pieces to the travel agent, Mary and I took some time to compare the children's initial advertisements with their final ones to track the progress of each child. We added our latest findings to the assessment rubric we had completed at the beginning of the unit. Mary was impressed by the children's growth as writers of persuasive texts, especially in such a short period of time. A sense of this growth can be obtained by examining the initial and final advertisements of Katherine and Christopher, two students highlighted earlier.

Katherine's initial piece

Come to New York. It's the best.

We have the Empire State. We have the Statue of Liberty and if you like to shop you'll find we have the best shops in the world.

If you like to play we have Central Park. It's got lots of things for kids to do. You can ride a horse. You can eat ice cream. You can play.

New York is the best. Don't miss out on all the fun.

Katherine's final piece

Come to New York. It's the best and I'm going to tell you why.

If you like buildings we have the Empire State. It use to be the biggest building in the world. We have the Statue of Liberty. Did you know this is one of the most famous statues in the world?

If you like to shop then we have the most famous shops. We have Tiffany's, FAO Schwartz, and Macy's. Macy's is the biggest store in the world. It even says so on the building. It is gigantic.

If you like to play we have Central Park. In Central Park you can ride a horse. You can eat ice cream. You can play.

New York is the best. Don't miss out on all the fun. Book your trip now.

In comparing Katherine's two pieces it is clear that she has internalized many of the demonstrations Mary and I gave. In her later piece she has included more factual information to support her claims of New York's grandeur. She has become far more specific with the information she provides, including the names of famous stores, for example. Her information is also well organized. Finally, she has kept her strong sense of voice.

Christopher also made incredible progress.

Christopher's initial piece

I went to Disneyworld. It was fun. I went on splash mountain. I was scared. I like Disneyworld. It is fun. You will like it.

Christopher's final piece

Disneyworld is cool and awesome. You should go.
They have good rides. They have splash mountain and the Runaway Train.
They have the haunted house.
They have lots of other fantastic rides.
You can eat anything you want. The food is delicious and you will see
    Mickey Mouse and Goofey.
The weather is always good. I like Disneyworld. It is fun. You will like it.
You will Love it! You will want to go again.

Christopher in his later piece was beginning to expand on his opinions by including facts. This piece was also far more like an advertisement; he used inviting language (such as "fantastic rides" and "delicious" food) that seeks to persuade his readers, unlike his initial piece. His beginning and conclusion were strong and certainly persuasive. Christopher had also begun to link his ideas by using the conjunction "and"—the subject of one of Mary's demonstrations. Also for this later piece, Christopher had referred to brochures to assist him with his research, something he had not done when writing his first advertisement.

Self-Assessment and Reflection

In addition to Mary's and my assessments, we also had the students reflect on their initial and final pieces so they could see and discuss their own improvement. We gave the children a self-assessment questionnaire (see Appendix A and the information in Chapter 2) and asked them to take time to reflect on what they had learned as writers. This time for reflection proved to be extremely productive. The children's responses confirmed that they had learned much about writing a persuasive text.

A Time for Reflection

Just three weeks after I first walked through the doors of Mary's third-grade classroom with a feeling of apprehension, I reflected on the unit we had just completed so successfully. The children had learned a lot, but they would need many more encounters with persuasive texts to build on the knowledge they have started to acquire. Will they pass that test next year? No one can say for certain, but I am confident that with continued explorations into how different text types work, they will come closer to being successful readers and writers for a variety of purposes in a variety of situations. The fourth-grade test is to me only one such situation; it should not be viewed as the be-all and end-all of the curriculum.

I told Mary's students that I would return later in the school year, but I now had to move on to another group of school children to work with. I was

Is That a Fact?

sad to leave Mary and her group of children. It is always hard to say good-bye.

I believe I have learned as much from Mary in our three weeks together as she said she learned from me: a great deal. We have both seen the powerful effect that this unit has had on these children as they continue on their journey as lifelong writers.

Possible Topics for Whole-Class and Independent Investigations

The units described in this chapter are just two of many possible ways to explore persuasive texts with children. Listed below are suggestions of other topics that could be explored as a whole class or independently. These investigations may run for any length of time, from one week to six weeks. What is important is that they not be one-day wonders. Children need time and opportunity for immersion, demonstrations, and engagement in persuasive texts if they are to become proficient writers in these forms.

Here are possible topics:

Which is the better pet—dogs or cats?
Should children be given homework?
Should children be allowed to stay up late every night?
What is the best toy in the world?
Who is the best—girls or boys?
Which is the best place to visit?
Who is the best pop group?
What is the best picture book?
Should children be allowed to eat what they want?
What is the best program on television?
Organize a class debate on a topic of interest.
Write an advertisement.
Who should be class president?
Why should we save water?
Why should we save electricity?
Write a review on a story read to the class.
What is the best sport to play?
Which is the best baseball team?
Create a poster advertising an upcoming event.
Write a book review.
Write a music review.
Write a review of a television program.
Write a review of a sports game.
Children should be seen and not heard. Do you agree?

Should children be paid to go to school?

Should there be zoos?

Should children be able to choose what they wear to school each day?

Resources

There are literally thousands of possibilities that a teacher can utilize to help with persuasive writing, but there are very few books that are actually written as persuasive texts for the K–3 classroom. It was for this reason that I wrote a book, with the help of colleague Judy Ballister and her fourth-grade class, entitled *Should There Be Zoos? A Persuasive Text* (2000). Teachers of children in third grade may find this book a useful reference in planning an exploration of persuasive writing. Children's literature can also act as a springboard to getting children to discuss particular points of view. For example, in my K–1–2 multiage classroom one year I used Maurice Sendak's classic *Where the Wild Things Are* as the basis of a debate within the classroom. The issue in question was whether Max's adventure was dreamed or real. The children spent much time debating this issue and used the book to locate evidence to support their stance. I can still remember Martin, a first grader, stating that it was all a dream because when you look at the end of the book the plant in Max's room is the same size as it was before he left for the land of the wild things. He argued that if he had traveled for over a year to the home of the wild things and then a year back to his room that the plant would have grown. This was indeed a very convincing argument and I must admit that even though I had read this book over a hundred times in my teaching career, I had never even noticed the plant. Laura, a second grader, questioned Martin's evidence, however, when she calmly pointed out, "The plant could be plastic." Clearly, children's literature can be a powerful resource in assisting the children with persuasive talking and writing. The emphasis, in this case, at least, was not so much on who is right but rather how the children locate relevant evidence or facts to support their point of view.

I have found books by British author Anthony Browne particularly excellent as springboards into persuasive writing, as his work often deals with issues that have high relevance to young children, such as sibling rivalry, home chores, and relationships with friends and family members. Many books by Tomie dePaola are also wonderfully useful in engaging children in persuasive discussions and writing. The magazine *Time for Kids* is also a great resource for work in persuasive writing.

Nonfiction Narrative

Martin Luther King. He is a brave man. He like freedom. He like to help the people. I love him.

Joanna, kindergarten

Of all the writing forms, personal narrative is probably the one most commonly selected by children in the early years. Young children love to retell past events and write of recent happenings in their lives. They usually do this first by making a drawing of an experience or event significant to them. I noticed this when I taught kindergarten. Each day the children would happily draw about themselves and their pets, their friends, and family members. When I asked them to tell me what their drawings said, their replies always revolved around retelling a past event. I would hear an in-depth explanation by George on how the dog chewed his mom's new shoes the night before. Harry would point to his picture of a cake and proudly announce that it had been his birthday last week and he had had a party. He would then tell me that he was now six years old and that in two more weeks he would be seven and then in one more month he would be eight. And finally dear Joanna, the smallest yet chattiest member of the class, would delight me with a retelling of what happened the night before Christmas that would rival Margaret Mitchell's epic *Gone with the Wind.*

Young children seem naturally drawn to personal narrative, and this can often be a natural segue to a different kind of narrative, namely nonfiction narratives that deal with people and events outside of the personal, such as the one written by Joanna used as the epigraph of this chapter. These nonfiction narratives can often be linked with social studies units. They are also a perfect means for teaching children how to research and record information when engaging in author studies.

The unit outlined in this chapter describes a study of one type of nonfiction narrative: biography. It took place in a grade 2–3 split classroom I taught in an inner suburb of Melbourne, Australia. I selected biography because I had noticed that my students would write for hours about being famous sports stars, pop stars, astronauts, and princesses. There appeared to be no limit to the different personas they could take on and write about. Their imaginations were alive with possibilities. I had also noticed that many of them were selecting biographies (including magazines) about their favorite pop stars and sports heroes as their independent reading material. With the Olympics just over, their curiosity about different sports personalities was at a peak. Biography seemed a perfect form with which to engage these children in nonfiction narrative, given their high interest in famous personalities.

In order to best assist the children with this new writing purpose and form, I first had to find out more about nonfiction narrative and the craft an author utilizes when engaging in this type of writing.

Overview of Nonfiction Narratives

The following is an overview of the purpose, types, structure, and language features usually associated with nonfiction narrative that formed the basis of my unit of study in writing biography.

Purpose/Social Function

Nonfiction narratives retell or recount specific events and the lives of specific people for the purpose of informing and entertaining.

Types or Forms

There are a number of different types of nonfiction narratives, including the following:

> Biographies of family members, friends, famous sport stars, pop stars, movie stars, inventors, political personalities, world leaders, pioneers, authors, and so on.
>
> Retellings of famous past events, such as the first Thanksgiving, the War of Independence, natural disasters, the sinking of the *Titanic*, the origin of religious holidays, and so on.
>
> News reports about current happenings in the world.

Text Structure

Nonfiction narratives usually begin with a title followed by a setting or orientation that concentrates on details pertaining to the who, where, when, and why. This gives the reader the background information needed to understand the text. The narrative then continues with a series of events usually presented in chronological order (the what). Sometimes the narrative may include personal comments or observations by the writer. The piece may conclude with an evaluative comment or statement that reflects the writer's feelings about the events or people described.

Language Features

Nonfiction narratives often contain the following language features:

> Specific participants or subjects (my grandma, the president, our teacher, the *Titanic*, the earthquake, the Macy's parade, etc.).
> Simple past tense (she likes, he said, it was, etc.).
> Action verbs (went, climbed, saw, followed, sailed, erupted, etc.).
> Linking words dealing with time (after, later, then, before, etc.).
> Details that add interest to the narrative.
> Illustrations, such as pictures and photographs.

Example

Here is an analysis of a nonfiction narrative, specifically biography. Language features are highlighted in bold.

Babe Ruth	Title
By Carl, kindergarten	
Babe Ruth was a baseball player.	Orientation
He **was** famous. He **was** good at hitting	Series of details
the ball. He **played** lots of games.	Past tense
I wish I could play like him.	Concluding statement

A Unit in Action: Biographies

Immersing my children in biography was not difficult, for as I mentioned earlier, most of them had been selecting biographies as their independent reading material. I simply began reading short accounts about various pop stars and sports heroes as part of my daily read-aloud ritual. I asked the children if they would like to select someone to write about. The response was uniformly positive. They mentioned many notable personalities, and I noted all their suggestions on a chart; but the idea that sparked the greatest interest was Gina's suggestion that we write about someone in our class.

To ensure fairness, I asked the children to write their names on a piece of paper and then placed these into a box. Individual children then selected a name from the box as the person they would write about and vice versa—for example, Steven selected John's name, so Steven would write a biography of John and John would write one of Steven. I then asked the children to go back to their tables and commence writing their biographies. These pieces would become the basis of my initial assessment of the children's knowledge of, and skills in, writing biographies and would inform my selection of demonstrations during our whole-class investigation. As mentioned throughout this book, it is critical for the teacher to first assess children's prior knowledge of a specific writing form before launching into a series of demonstrations and learning engagements. Doing this initial assessment enables the teacher to tailor instruction to the needs of the children.

Assessing the Children's Understanding

The children completed their biographies during the next two sessions, and I collected their work to review and make decisions about what understanding they already had about this writing form. I had noticed that as they worked, none of the children had thought to go over to the person they were writing about to find out more information. Basically the children simply wrote about physical traits and personal feelings toward the person they had selected. John's biography of Steven is typical of what they wrote:

Steven by John
Steven has black hair and is tall.

Is That a Fact?

Steven has brown eyes.
He wears cool sweaters. I like his red one the best.
Steven is always kind. All the kids like him a lot.
I like playing with him.
I think he is really smart.

John confined his account to what Steven looked like and how John felt about Steven. In essence his piece about Steven was more like a personal description of Steven and his relationship with him than an account of Steven's life and interests. This was true for most of the children's pieces: they simply recorded information about physical attributes. While biographies often include this type of information, their main purpose is to inform the reader about the life of an individual, not just describe the way he or she looks.

It was evident from reading the children's biographies and filling out an assessment rubric for each child (see Figure 10.1 and the description in Chapter 2) that I would need to provide many demonstrations to help them understand both the purpose behind this writing form and what authors do when they write such texts.

The Whole-Class Investigation Begins

The children were eager to read the biographies written about themselves, so I gave them out and asked the children to reflect on the information they had in front of them. I asked them key questions: "What things did the person write about you?" and "What other things could they have included?"

The children had many responses to these two questions, and I listed them on chart paper:

What Things We Included in Our Biographies

Color of our hair
Color of our eyes
What we liked about the person

What Things We Could Include in Our Biographies

Where they live
Their favorite things (e.g., pets, color, food, hobbies, pop stars, movies, friends)
Things about their family
Interesting things that happened to them during their lives (e.g., family trips, losing their first tooth, visits to the hospital)

What struck me about the children's responses to my questions was that they could articulate some of the key features of biographies, yet none of them had included this information in their initial pieces. This told me that while

Assessment Rubric for Nonfiction Narrative

Key: N: Not in evidence   S: Showing signs of   C: Consolidating   M: Mostly   N/A: Not applicable

Name: Grade: Date: Text Type or Title:			
Purpose			
Understands that nonfiction narratives are factual texts that retell past experiences in sequential order			
Craft (Structure, features, voice)			
Linguistic or Text Structure Begins with a title			
Setting/orientation: includes background information on who was involved			
where it happened			
when it happened			
Events: includes important events			
events are in chronological order			
includes personal comments about the events in the retell			
Concluding statement (optional): includes a personal reflection or evaluative comment			
Text/Language Features Names specific participants			
Uses simple past tense			
Uses action verbs			
Uses linking words dealing with time			
Voice Uses an enticing title and/or setting to engage the reader			
Is able to express ideas using own language as opposed to copying down what others say or information from books read			
Uses descriptive language that paints pictures for the reader			
Is able to state information in a unique or surprising manner			
Research Skills			
Is able to locate information from books			
Is able to locate information from nonbook sources			
Is able to interpret and talk about information located			
Surface Features (Mechanics)			
Handwriting neat and legible			
Shows improvement in attempts at spelling words			
Uses grammatically correct language			
Shows improvement in use of punctuation			
Uses an appropriate publishing format			
Work generally well presented			

they had some of the necessary understanding of what a biography included, they didn't know how to apply this understanding when writing.

When I asked them why they hadn't included this information in their initial pieces, their responses were enlightening:

Joanne: "Because."
Steven: "Because I didn't know about all that stuff about John."
Sally: "I didn't know that's what you're supposed to write about."
Frederick: "I think I know now. I just didn't think."
Diana: "I don't know much about Ross."

The children's responses confirmed to me that they were unaware that good writers of biographies must first be good researchers. They had become used to writing simply what came to mind and calling on their imagination each day; they had not thought to include research as part of their daily writing routine. Their responses also made me realize that good writers are first good talkers, and that if I wanted my children to be competent writers for many purposes they needed first to be able to articulate their thoughts before putting pen to paper.

Selecting the Topic

I began our next session by reviewing with the children all the important ingredients in a biography. Then I read them a short article about the life of Michael Jordan, who was their favorite sports star at the time. We talked about all the important information that the author had included and discussed why readers of the article would find this information interesting. We also discussed how the author of the article had found out about Michael Jordan. I called their attention to the end of the article, where specific books and interviews were cited. I then suggested that we research and write a biography on someone of interest together as a whole class.

The children came up with many suggestions, but ultimately it was Sally's suggestion that won the popular vote. Sally had suggested that we write a biography of me so that the children who would have me as their teacher in coming years could find out all about me. Frederick commented that the class really only knew some things about me and that it would be interesting to find out more. To be honest, I was not thrilled at this prospect. I suggested that maybe we could do a biography on the principal or even the custodian, but the children had made up their minds: I was to be the subject of their biography. In the end, although I was somewhat apprehensive, a part of me felt proud that my students were more interested in writing a biography of me than of their favorite pop stars and sports heroes.

Planning the Biography

For the remainder of the session, I gave the children copies of various biographies I had collected and asked them to work in pairs and list some of the important elements that the biography of me would need to include. I then brought the children together, and we discussed their ideas and organized them in a logical sequence. We came up with the following:

Our Biography on Tony
1. Introduction
2. Where and when he was born
3. His family
4. His school days as a child
5. His school days as a teacher
6. His favorite things
7. What he is good at and why people like him

Locating Information

With the structure of our biography in place, our next step was to locate the information needed. I organized the children into groups of four and asked each group to be responsible for one of the seven identified areas. In organizing the groups I took into account many elements about the class. I wanted a good academic and social mix, and I ensured that every group had a strong leader and that each group member had someone in the group he or she worked well with. For the most part the class functioned efficiently, but there were a few children who did not work well together, so I made sure they were not placed in the same group. I also tried to have a mix of girls and boys. Often by second and third grade, boys and girls do not freely choose to work with each other, not necessarily because they don't like each other but because the peer pressure against doing so is strong. This reluctance was something I was constantly trying to break down.

When the groups were formed, I told the children that they were now reporters and needed to organize their groups. I would circulate around the classroom, talking with different groups, but only with groups that had specific questions to ask me and a means of recording the information. Jody, a second grader, came up with a wonderful idea. She suggested that we use a tape recorder so that each group could record their interview with me. She also proposed that while one group was interviewing me the other groups could watch. The children became very excited by this prospect, and for the next few sessions the groups were consumed by the desire to come up with relevant questions to ask me.

Providing Demonstrations

During these sessions, I circulated around the classroom, giving assistance to each group where needed. As I roved, I noticed that many of the groups were coming up with questions that required only one-word answers, as seen below by the questions Betty's group had written pertaining to the category "His favorite things":

Do you like chocolate?
Do you like dogs?
Do you like cats?
Do you like the color blue?
Do you like spaghetti?

I decided that I needed to bring the children together and discuss the importance of asking open-ended questions, which would enable them to gather a considerable amount of information without having to go through a series of yes or no answers. I used the questions Betty's group had brainstormed as an example and discussed with the children better ways of finding out what I liked. Mark came up with an idea for a question: "What are your favorite foods?" The children soon realized that this was a far more powerful question as it would give them all the information they required about my culinary preferences with a single question. We talked about how yes and no answers don't give researchers a lot of information. I then asked the children to return to their groups and review their questions to see if changes needed to be made. I then resumed roving the classroom, giving assistance where needed and making suggestions when children encountered difficulties.

Recording the Information

After the children had finished writing their questions we began the interviews. I used a different cassette tape for each group so that when the interview was completed each group would have its own tape to listen to and use in writing my responses. We had a lot of fun during the interviews, and the children were eager to hear my answers to the questions they asked.

At the conclusion of the interviews I gave each group of children their tape and borrowed cassette players from other classrooms so that the children could listen to their group's interview with me and complete their section of the biography. During this time I constantly roamed around the classroom, giving assistance to each group as needed. Spelling became a big issue at this point, so I provided the children with many whole-class demonstrations on what to do if they didn't know how to spell specific words. In one demonstration, we brainstormed words that biographers sometimes use in their pieces:

Words We Might Need to Use as Biographers

favorite	amazing	sometimes
beloved	younger	older
school	dislikes	owned
always	never	wanted
Williamstown	Victoria	exactly
middle	taught	different
was (when talking about the past)	forever	swimming

When brainstorming these words with the children, I too added words to the list that I knew I had used in the interviews and that I knew the children would have difficulty in spelling. One word that I intentionally added was the word *was*, and not because the children had difficulty spelling the word. I had noticed as I roved the classroom that many of the groups were writing about past incidents in the present tense, so I brought the children together to discuss the grammatically correct way to record past happenings. I displayed the word chart in the classroom for the children to use a reference, and we added words to the chart as needed. (For further ideas on helping children with spelling, see Chapter 5.)

I also called the children together to discuss how writers of biographies used illustrations to help their readers. The children had noticed that biographies often contained photographs, so they asked me if I could bring some in for them to use in their biography.

Several of my whole-class demonstrations focused on the idea of an author's voice and the different ways writers engage their audience with interesting language. I alerted the children to the way some authors begin their biographies by using such openings as

So you want to learn about . . .

or

Finding out about the interesting life of . . .

We also discussed how many authors use similes and imaginative language to engage their readers.

At the time I gave the children these demonstrations I was not always convinced that they had really understood the information I was attempting to impart. When I examined their finished biography, however, I realized that many of my demonstrations on text structure, voice, and language features had indeed had an impact. Their piece read as follows:

A Biography on the Interesting Life of Tony Stead
by Class 2–3, Room 8

Introduction by James and Gina.

So you want to know about Tony Stead. This will tell you all the things our class think are interesting and there's a lot to tell.

Part one: Where he was born. By Sally, John, and Susan.

Tony Stead was born on March 8 in Williamstown in Victoria Australia. He was born in the middle of the night.

Part two: His family. By Frederick, Steven, Mark, and Toula.

Tony Stead has a mother called Patricia and a father called Tom. He has one brother called Bill who is exactly five years younger. Bill was also born on March 8. Tony's mum came from England and his dad came from Italy.

Part three: His school days as a child. By Diana, Jody, Franco, and Peter.

Tony Stead liked school a lot. He was good at math but did not do good at English. When he was in High school, he was very good at Biology. The teachers told him that he talked too much.

Part four: His school days as a teacher. By Betty, Petra, Jason, and Danny.

Tony Stead has taught in three different schools. He has taught lots of different grades but he likes this grade the best. Tony never wanted to be a teacher but he loves teaching now. Tony likes to teach reading and writing the best.

Part five: His favorite things. By Betty, Gary, Damien, Christian, and Kate.

Tony Stead likes spaghetti, cheese, and Chinese food. His favorite drink is cola. He loves to watch football and tennis. He loves to read books and he loves to listen to music. His best animal is a bear.

Part six: What he is good at and why people like him. By Maryanne, Justin, Elisa, and Warren.

Tony is good at swimming. He swims as good as a fish. He is very good at teaching. The kids all reckon he is great because he cares about you. We hope he will teach forever and that he will teach us next year. He is our best teacher ever. The End.

I was extremely happy with the children's biography, as they had used the text structure and language features common to the way biographers write. I must admit I was also relieved that the last group viewed me in such a positive light. I was amused by the way Maryanne, Justin, Elisa, and Warren had included a simile to explain how good they thought I was at swimming. This showed that the whole-class discussion on similes had made an impression.

The demonstration and discussions on the need to use an interesting introduction had also had an effect on James and Gina.

Now that the children had completed the whole-class biography the next step was to see whether they had internalized the process of writing such texts and could construct one on their own.

Individual Investigations

We began the next session by reflecting on what had made the whole-class biography so wonderful and the steps the children had gone through as both researchers and writers. I noted their thoughts on a chart:

> **When Writing a Good Biography, You Need to:**
> Include information on the where the person was born and the person's family and friends.
> Talk about important things that happened to the person growing up.
> Try to put things in the right order.
> Include a good introduction to get the readers interested.
> Find out about the person by reading books and watching television programs about him or her or by interviewing the person.
> Use the word *was* when talking about things that happened in the past.
> Use your best handwriting when publishing.
> Use correct spelling.
> Include photographs and pictures if you can.

Constructing this chart with the children was an essential step in getting them to reflect on and internalize the ingredients of a good biography. It was an essential precursor to their independently creating their own biographies. I believe that as teachers we need to take more time to reflect with our children and get them to articulate the strategies that competent writers use. So often we put ourselves, and our students, on a roller-coaster ride of countless demonstrations without giving the children time to reflect on, question, and internalize the demonstrations we provide.

After constructing and talking about the process chart, the next step was for the children to select a person to write a biography about. The children had many suggestions, but we finally agreed that it would be beneficial for them to rewrite the biography on the person they had initially written about on their own, the piece that had formed the basis of my initial assessment. This decision pleased me, as often when children write they never go back to do revisions on content. Having the children reconstruct their original biographies would give them and me an opportunity to compare the initial pieces and the revised ones, to assess and celebrate their growth as writers of biographies.

Collecting and Recording Information

For the next five sessions the children worked in pairs, collecting information about the person they were researching and recording it in their writer's notebooks. As I walked around the classroom I constantly reminded them of the charts we had constructed during the whole-class investigation to give them guidance with their research. The pairs worked well together, and I was delighted at how the children helped each other in both their researching and their recording of ideas. One such pair was Mark and Toula. Mark was a struggling writer, whereas Toula was extremely confident. I listened as they worked together on finding out each other's favorite things:

Toula: We need to write about stuff we like. So you ask me what I like and I'll tell you.

Mark: I like soccer.

Toula: No. You're doing a biography on me. You have to ask me what I like and then write it down.

Mark: Oh, yeah. I get it. What do you like?

Toula: That's a good question, Mark. I like Barbie dolls. Here, write it down.

Mark: But I can't spell "Barbie dolls."

Toula: That don't matter. I'll show you. Now what does it start with?

Mark: "B."

Toula: Then write it down. Now listen for other sounds you hear—you know, like Tony shows us. Then I'll fix it up for you.

Wouldn't we all love to have a classroom full of Toulas! I was so impressed with the way she helped Mark that I made sure during our sharing session at the end of writer's workshop that I congratulated them for being such good helpers and researchers. This positive feedback had a profound impact on the rest of the class, and I soon found that all the pairs began working very cooperatively together. I believe it is extremely important to give children constant positive feedback when they work cooperatively. It is one of Brian Cambourne's (1988) conditions of learning that is an essential for building a community of learners.

Providing Support in Small-Group and Whole-Class Settings

A number of children found collecting and recording their information a little overwhelming; after all, not every pair had a Toula to show them how to organize and manage the collection and recording of their information. I brought these children together in small groups and gave them a form that I hoped would help them as researchers. (See Appendix I.)

This form proved to be a valuable resource in helping the children break down their biographies into manageable chunks. Each day I would bring these children together for a brief five-minute discussion on the information that needed to be included on a specific page of the form and encourage them to research and record the relevant information. In this way I was able to give the children in the group the necessary scaffolding for just one section of the biography at a time, which helped ensure success for each member of the group.

I also provided discussion time and demonstrations in both small-group and whole-class settings in other elements of writing. These demonstrations were based on my ongoing observations of the needs of my children as I roved the classroom during writer's workshop and on my assessment of each child's initial biography. These included demonstrations in voice, structure, language features, research and mechanics, as outlined below.

Demonstrations in Voice

Coming up with a great title.
Using an enticing introduction.
Using great descriptions to keep the reader engaged.

Demonstrations in Structure

Breaking down the biography into sections that deal with specific information.
Organizing the information within each section.

Demonstrations in Language Features

Using vocabulary that is common to biographies.
Using linking words dealing with time.
Using headings.
Using photographs to help the reader.

Demonstrations in Research

How to conduct an interview.

Demonstrations in Mechanics

Spelling.
Using the word wall.
Handwriting.
Grammar.
Capitalization and periods.

Publishing

After the children had completed their research they began to write and publish their biographies, using a variety of different methods. Most of the children wrote their biographies either in book form or by completing the form I had provided. Some, however, chose a different format: recording their biographies onto a cassette tape.

Jody, who had first suggested the idea of using cassette tapes when collecting the information for the whole-class investigation, asked if she could publish her research by recording it onto a tape. This thought had never occurred to me, and I thought it was a brilliant idea. So often as teachers we think of published pieces as being only in the form of books and posters or charts. Jody had reminded me that authors utilize a variety of methods to share information with an audience. (Refer to Chapter 4 for more information about different publishing formats.)

During the publishing process I ensured that the children had many different colored markers, pencils, and paper. Petra suggested that we bring in photographs to add to our biographies. This suggestion was met with enthusiasm, and soon many of the children were swapping photographs to add to their biographies. I also made sure that I had taken photographs of each child so that children who were unable to bring in photographs would not be left out. Jody, who was recording her information onto a cassette tape, now faced a dilemma. How was she going to include photographs on a cassette tape? I suggested she include the photographs on a sheet of cardboard, number them, then alert her listeners to the relevant photograph by mentioning its number on the tape. Jody and the other children who were publishing their information using this medium thought this was a great idea.

I gave the children four sessions to publish their biographies and informed them that they needed to be completed by the end of the week so that we could then share them. Many of the children took their biographies home each night as part of homework, while others used every spare moment in the day to get them completed. The children were constantly asking me if they could work on their biographies. It seemed that all they wanted to do each day was write. The children who completed their biography early were given the option of continuing with other writing of interest or assisting others. These early finishers chose to begin new biographies. This demonstrated to me that they were truly engaged in, and motivated by, this new form of writing.

Sharing and Celebrating

Having completed them, the children shared their biographies with each other. This was an exciting time for me. I had never seen my children so engaged. One of my learners, Danny, a struggling reader, sat for over thirty minutes reading and rereading his biography, beaming with pride. He was delighted when I asked him to read the biography to me, and when he did I noticed that he read material way above his independent level. This confirmed to me the power of the reading-writing connection and that young learners are capable of just about anything when they are truly engaged in their learning and see a real purpose for reading and writing.

Naturally the children were eager to take the biography that was written about them home to share with friends and family members. When the pieces were returned, they were placed into a tub in the classroom library for the children to borrow and read during independent reading time. For some time after the conclusion of the unit these biographies became the children's favorite selections during independent reading time.

Assessing Children's Growth

At the end of the unit, I collected the children's published pieces and compared them to their initial biographies, using the assessment rubric. I was impressed with the progress they had all made in deepening their understanding of biography as a writing form. If we examine John's initial piece, which we highlighted at the beginning of this chapter, with his final piece, his growth as a writer of biography becomes evident.

John's initial piece

Steven by John

Steven has black hair and is tall.

Steven has brown eyes.

He wears cool sweaters. I like his red one the best.

Steven is always kind. All the kids like him a lot.

I like playing with him.

I think he is really smart.

John's final piece

A Biography on the Life of Steven by John

So you want to know about Steven. I will tell you. He is an interesting person.

He was born in Melbourne. His mum and dad were born in Italy.

When Steven was a little boy he never ate anything but spaghetti. He loves spaghetti. Then he found out that he likes to eat hamburgers. He can eat three just for lunch.

Steven likes to play soccer. He is really good at soccer. He likes being the goalie.

Steven likes school. He is really good at reading. He reads lots of books. He likes Charlotte's Web the best.

When Steven grows up he is going to be a soccer player.

All the kids like Steven. He is famous.

And that's the life of Steven.

When we compare the two pieces we can see that John has taken on many of the demonstrations from this unit of study into his own writing. John used an interesting introduction to entice his readers. He also used many of the text structures and language features normally associated with a biography. In addition, he obtained his information through an interview with his subject, rather than simply writing from the top of his head, as he had done in his initial piece. He has learned that good writers of biographies are first good researchers.

Self-Assessment and Reflection

After I analyzed my children's final biographies and compared them to their initial pieces, I gave the pieces back to them so that they could see their improvement for themselves. My young authors were amazed at how much they had learned during the unit and were proud of their achievements. Mark commented, "This is the best writing I've ever done." To which Toula proudly announced, "That's because I helped you." Mark confidently replied, "Yeah, you were a good help, but I can do it without you now."

I asked the children key questions to help them reflect on their achievements:

> What have you learned about writing a biography?
> Look at your first piece. Now look at your latest piece. Tell me: How has your writing improved?
> If you had to write another biography, what is one thing you would try to do better?
> Is there someone's biography that you have read that you really like? What is it that the writer has done to make it one of your favorites? Is this something you could do if you wrote another biography?

These questions were critical, for they allowed my students to be active participants in the assessment process and helped them both recognize their own personal growth as writers and reflect on ways to improve future pieces.

With the unit at an end, I asked the children what they would like to write about next. They informed me that they wanted to continue writing biographies. Some of them wanted to write a piece on a famous person; others selected family members and friends. Their response told me that I had planted a seed that was now growing. I was happy to let them engage further in this form of writing, as their interest in it was at a peak. My next step would be to think about, plan, and immerse them in a brand-new writing genre to help them discover a new purpose for writing and empower them as I had done with this unit.

Possible Topics for Whole-Class and Independent Investigations

The unit on biographies described in this chapter is just one of many possible ways to explore nonfiction narrative with children. Listed below are suggestions of other topics that could be explored as a whole class or independently. These investigations may run for any length of time, from one week to six weeks. What is important is that they not be one-day wonders. Children need time and opportunity for immersion, demonstrations, and engagement in nonfiction narrative if they are to become proficient writers in this form.

Here are possible topics.

Biographies on:
a pop star
an inventor
a pioneer
an author
an artist
a sports hero
a politician
an actor
your mother or father
a friend
your brother or sister
the principal
a teacher

Retellings of past events, such as:
the first Thanksgiving
the Civil War
the War of Independence
the origin and/or customs of holidays, such as Christmas, Hanukkah, Kwanza, Chinese New Year, and Halloween
Disasters, such as the sinking of the *Titanic*, fires, floods, and earthquakes
Famous parades and events, such as Macy's Thanksgiving Day parade

Resources

This last section lists some books that may be of use in helping children locate, research, and write nonfiction narrative. The books are listed alphabetically by title, with series title or author name (if any) and publisher. There are thousands of wonderful books that can be used as valuable resources; the list below provides only a small sample of what's available. I have grouped the books by readability, according to Reading Recovery levels and the Fountas and Pinnell levels. There are a great many different leveling systems in existence, as most publishers have their own method of categorizing texts. I have chosen the Reading Recovery and Fountas and Pinnell systems because they are the most commonly used. (For further information on how to organize classroom books and materials in your classroom, see Chapter 3.) Note: A few of the titles below (such as *The Car Accident*) are fictional narratives. Though fiction rather than nonfiction, they are still valuable resources in showing children the language structures and text features that authors utilize when writing nonfiction narratives.

Nonfiction Narrative

■ Emergent Readers

Approximate Reading Recovery levels 1–4; Fountas and Pinnell levels A–C

Champions	Twig series	Wright Group
The Fourth of July	Windows on Literacy series	National Geographic
Hannah's Halloween	Little Books for Early Readers series	University of Maine
Life on a Farm	Early Connections series	Benchmark Education
My Life in a Town	Rosen Real Readers series	Rosen Real Readers
My Life on an Island	Rosen Real Readers series	Rosen Real Readers
Pilgrim Children Had Many Chores	Creative Teaching Press series	Abrams and Co.
The Royal Family	by J. Stewart and Lynn Salem	Seedling
Thanksgiving	First Stories series	Pacific Learning

■ Early Readers

Approximate Reading Recovery levels 5–12; Fountas and Pinnell levels D–G

Biographies series	Reading Power	Rosen Publishing Group
The Car Accident	Foundations series	Wright Group
Celebrations	Storyteller-Moon Rising series	Shortland
Chinese New Year		Pacific Learning
Cinco de Mayo	Fiesta Holiday series	Dominie
Easter	Fiesta Holiday series	Dominie
Fall Harvest	Pebble Books series	Capstone Press
Fourth of July	Emergent Social Studies series	Newbridge
March for Freedom	Twig series	Wright Group
My Friend Alan	Carousel Readers series	Dominie
My Little Brother Ben	Books for Young Learners series	Richard C. Owen
Now and Then	Windows on Literacy series	National Geographic
Our Heroes	Social Studies series	Newbridge
Pinata Time	Teacher's Choice series	Dominie
School Today and Long Ago	Windows on Literacy series	National Geographic
When Lincoln Was a Boy	Twig series	Wright Group

■ Transitional Readers

Approximate Reading Recovery levels 13–20; Fountas and Pinnell levels H–K

Abraham Lincoln	Pebble Books series	Capstone Press
African American History series		Lerner Classroom
America Goes to War series		Capstone Press

Biographies series		Lerner Classroom
Cesar Chavez	Pebble Books series	Capstone Press
The Dancing Dragon	BookShop series	Mondo Publishing
First Flight	by George Shea	HarperTrophy
The Flood	Wonder World series	Wright Group
George Washington	Pebble Books series	Capstone Press
Kids Rule	BookShop series	Mondo Publishing
Martin Luther King, Jr.	Pebble Books series	Capstone Press
Meet the Astronauts	Social Studies series	Newbridge
Meet Joe Paxton	Little Celebrations series	Celebration Press
Meet William Joyce	Little Celebrations series	Celebration Press
The Pilgrims	Social Studies series	Newbridge
Remember George	Social Studies series	Newbridge
Who Was Paul Revere?	Rosen Real Readers series	Rosen Real Readers

■ Fluent Readers

Approximate Reading Recovery levels 20+; Fountas and Pinnell levels L–S

Abraham Lincoln: President of a Country Divided	Rookie Biographies series	Children's Press
All-Pro Biographies series		Children's Press
The Baseball Heroes	by Irene Schultz	Wright Group
Biographies series	Bridgestone Books series	Capstone Press
Creative Mind Biographies series		Lerner Classroom
Diego Rivera	Pair-It Books series	Steck-Vaughn
Explorer	Eyewitness Books series	Dorling Kindersley
Explorers: Searching for Adventure	Pair-It Books series	Steck-Vaughn
Finding Providence: the Story of Roger Williams	by Avi	HarperTrophy
First Start Biography series		Troll
Gail Devers: A Runners Dream	Pair-It Books series	Steck-Vaughn
If You Lived in the Time of the Civil War	by Kay Moore	Scholastic
If You Lived in Colonial Times	by Ann McGovern	Scholastic
If You Sailed on the Mayflower in 1620	by Ann McGovern	Scholastic
If Your Name Was Changed at Ellis Island	by Ellen Levine	Scholastic
The Inventor's Diary	Reading Science series	Pacific Learning
Ivy's Journal	BookShop series	Mondo Publishing
Jackie Robinson and the Story of All-Black Baseball	by Jim O'Connor	Random House
Jane Goodall and the Wild Chimpanzee	by Bette Birnbaum	Steck-Vaughn
Jesse Owens: Olympic Hero	by Francene Sabin	Troll
Journey to a New Land: An Oral History	BookShop series	Mondo Publishing
Laura Ingalls Wilder	Pair-It Books series	Steck-Vaughn
Mae Jemison	BookShop series	Mondo Publishing
Martin Luther King, Jr.	Pebble Books series	Capstone Press

Your Questions Answered

D uring the past five years as I have worked with both individual teachers in their classrooms and groups of educators in conference and workshop settings, I am constantly asked a number of questions about teaching nonfiction writing. While most of these have been answered throughout the body of this book, it is worthwhile to consider some of these key questions in this last chapter. Below are teachers' and administrators' most commonly asked questions about nonfiction writing for grades K–3.

How long should a nonfiction exploration or genre study last?

The length of a unit of study depends on many factors, but in any case they must not be just one-day wonders. I believe one of the biggest problems for teachers today is attempting to get through a dense curriculum, which often results in the teacher's bombarding the children with a sea of knowledge in order to cover identified content. What we end up doing is what I call "surfing the curriculum." We do this in order to achieve as much as we can in the shortest period of time. Consequently our children end up with only surface understanding. Keith Pigdon and Marilyn Woolley (1992) refer to this as the "stop, start curriculum." If we want children to become able writers for many different purposes, we must dive deep and give our students comprehensive learning engagements so that they can develop deep understanding about how different text types work. An exploration of anything less than a week will do little to truly deepen understanding. Most of the teachers I have worked with have found that genre studies in their classrooms usually average three to five weeks.

In many kindergarten classrooms, especially at the beginning of the school year, young learners can easily become bored by drawn-out investigations. In Jessica Mazzocco's classroom, highlighted in Chapter 9, many of her learners completed tasks rapidly and were eager for the next learning engagement. For this reason Jessica found it beneficial and engaging for her learners to implement either shorter genre studies or have her longer explorations allow the children to engage in many different writing experiences within the unit of study. In the example on persuasive texts in Chapter 9, the unit of study lasted for three weeks. During that time Jessica engaged her children in many different writing experiences centered around writing persuasive pieces. The children were not expected to work just on one piece during this three-week time span.

Jessica found that as the year progressed her children were able to work on a specific piece of writing for longer periods. They had built up what a colleague of mine, Isobel Marcus, calls a stamina for writing. Jessica at that point found it was not necessary to have the children work on numerous pieces within a unit of study; they could concentrate on one or two pieces. Some kindergarteners from the outset may be able to work on a single piece for lengthy periods of time. Such children usually have had many opportunities to write and draw at home or in pre–K. The teacher should always be aware of who these children are and give them ample time to work on a specific piece.

By third grade most children have built up a stamina for writing. They are able to work for lengthy periods of time on one piece if they are suitably engaged. The words of importance here are "suitably engaged." Genre studies give children an opportunity to learn how and why writers engage in different types of texts for a variety of purposes. If an authentic purpose has been established, children will happily work on one piece over an extended time frame. Even children in grade 1 can and will want to spend large periods of time on one piece when a suitable and engaging purpose has been established. This was certainly true in both Susan Mustac's first-grade classroom, which was highlighted in Chapter 6, and Maryanne Meza's first-grade classroom, highlighted in Chapter 8. In both scenarios, the units ran for approximately four weeks.

Is That a Fact?

I have so much to cover in a school year. I see the importance of engaging my children in genre studies, but how can I do it all?

As mentioned above, teachers are faced with a barrage of content to cover over a given year. We need to streamline and integrate some of our content into focused units of study. An example of this was in Linda La Porte's kindergarten class, highlighted in Chapter 7. Although Linda had selected writing reports on animals as her major writing focus during writer's workshop, she was also aware that her children were engaged in learning about animal habitats, life cycles, and food chains, so she integrated her science and writing goals into one unit of study. Linda also ensured that during shared reading in reader's workshop the children engaged with many big books about animals, thereby integrating both her reading and her writing goals.

I have found it far more beneficial to have fewer units of study with more depth than many different, shorter, units of study.

My children have a city/statewide test in third grade. How will these explorations in specific nonfiction writing purposes and forms assist them?

Let me begin to answer this question by telling a story about one school district and its quest to have the children succeed at passing the citywide test. A large portion of the writing test was made up of the children's composing a personal narrative. The district therefore put much time and effort into having children work with narrative texts, and teachers were asked to ensure that much of writer's workshop was devoted to personal narrative. It was not long before the children in the district became masters of personal narrative, and their test scores were high. The district celebrated, as did the city.

One year, given the increased awareness of the importance of children's being competent writers of nonfiction, the city decided that a persuasive piece would be included in the test. The district and the teachers had little time to immerse children into this new writing form. Consequently the children did poorly on the test, and the district moved swiftly to mandate the study of persuasive writing in classrooms across the city. The impact was sudden and dramatic: personal narrative was gone, and soon the children had become masters of persuasive pieces and had all but lost the skills and understanding of personal narrative.

The point of my story is clear. We need to ensure that our young learners become competent at writing many forms and for many purposes, so that no matter what is on a test they will be successful. I believe if we give our children a balanced curriculum that examines many different writing purposes, we will be empowering them as able and competent writers. If a statewide test requires a piece of persuasive writing, then of course the teacher should engage the children in this type of writing. But it should be just one of many investigations that the children would explore over the course of the school year and not become the epicenter of the children's writing experiences.

After completing a nonfiction genre study, should I immediately begin a new study in a different genre?

Often when children have been immersed into a specific text type they want to pursue it further. In Susan Mustac's classroom (Chapter 6), this was certainly the case. Many of the children wanted to write more instructions, while others were happy to write in their journals or engage in personal narrative. There was certainly no immediate need for Susan to launch into another genre; the decision was up to Susan and her students. What was imperative was that sometime in the near future Susan would launch into a new study to extend her children's skills at being writers for a variety of purposes.

Susan may in fact decide to revisit instructional texts later in the year. Just because she had completed one study doesn't mean that instructional texts are over for the year. As highlighted in Chapter 1, there are many different forms of instructional texts, and Susan and her children may decide to explore one of these later. Just as in reader's workshop, when we revisit books in read-aloud and shared reading encounters, so should we revisit the different purposes for writing and their various forms. These revisits do not necessarily need to be another three- or four-week unit of study. Susan for instance may decide to revisit instructional texts throughout the school year in other curriculum contexts, such as mathematics, science, and social studies.

Are there are a set number of nonfiction writing genres that children need to explore?

Attempting to list the different purposes for writing nonfiction is not an easy task, as can be seen in Chapter 1. There is no magical list, but there are a number of key purposes for writing nonfiction that we need to be aware of and need to introduce to children during their life as writers within the primary grades. Forms such as instructional and persuasive texts, to name just two, are important, and children should be given the chance to explore them during their primary years. (See Chapter 1 for further information on this subject.)

Is there a specific order in which nonfiction genres should be explored?

Many schools I am familiar with both in the United States and Australia have found it beneficial to have a set curriculum that explored specific writing genres in a sequential order in each grade area. In kindergarten, for example, the teacher may be required to explore personal narratives, animal reports, and instructional texts. In the first grade the teacher would be required to revisit personal narrative and animal reports and introduce biographies. The rationale for this approach is that it ensures a comprehensive writing curriculum so that by the end of elementary school children have had adequate immersion, demonstration, and engagement into the different types of nonfiction writing. This approach provides a certain comfort level for the teacher, for he or she doesn't need to make any decisions on what will be explored over the year and need not feel guilty about not covering a specific genre. The teacher can relax with the knowledge that she or he will only have to cover the assigned genres because the teacher in the prior and succeeding grades will fill in the missing pieces. In addition, there will presumably be a balance so that the children don't, for example, engage in personal narratives and animal reports every year (which happens in many schools).

While I commend these schools for addressing the issue of genre and specifically nonfiction genres, I believe that such an approach also carries with it many risks. The biggest risk is having an overstructured approach to teaching and learning that dictates what children in each of the grade areas should explore in their writing. It is interesting to see that many of the schools that have a set curriculum for nonfiction writing put persuasive texts and explanatory texts dealing with scientific phenomena in grades 3, 4, and 5. This is usually due to city- and statewide test requirements, which often contain examples of these text types. Thus, children in these schools are often confronted with these types of texts for the first time when they reach grade 3 and are expected to "put it all together" in a short period of time in order to pass the test. This doesn't make sense to me. It's like telling children that they can learn to swim only in grade 3 or learn to play basketball only in grade 4. Just as children learn to become able swimmers by engaging in the activity from an early age on a regular basis, so do they learn to write for many purposes by engaging in these various forms of writing throughout their elementary schooling. We have already seen just how powerful Jessica Mazzocco's exploration of persuasive texts was with her kindergarten children (Chapter 9). We can only begin to imagine how capable these children will be if their teachers in grades 1, 2, and 3 continue to provide them with engagement in persuasive texts in the coming years.

The question remains, however: How do we ensure a sense of balance for our learners in writing for different purposes over the years of their elementary schooling? I believe the answer lies in ongoing monitoring and assessment. If we keep adequate records, such as assessment rubrics similar to the ones already highlighted in this book, then teachers will record and be able to keep track of the genres that children engage in over the school year. To ensure continuity and consistency these rubrics need to follow the children through their schooling so that teachers can know and build on children's past learning.

Are there specific types of nonfiction writing that are more important for children to be competent in than others?

Each of the forms of nonfiction writing takes center stage when the child sees an authentic purpose for that form. It is difficult even to attempt to create a hierarchy when talking about nonfiction. How can we say that being able to write a set of instructions to explain to someone how to reach a specific destination should take precedence over being able to convince some friends that they should donate money to a charity in desperate need? All the purposes of nonfiction writing are important. This of course creates a dilemma for the teacher, who therefore must wonder, "How can I cover them all in one year?" The answer is quite simple: you can't. Teachers need to select types based on factors such as children's experience, interests, and prior engagement in nonfiction writing.

What if a child doesn't want to write in an identified genre?

When children are suitably immersed into a unit of study and given choice in their independent investigations, rarely will they resist writing in a given genre. There are times, however, when a particular child will not want to write. When this happens, the one thing I would never do is force the child to take pencil in hand. This will only lead to negative feelings about writing. Often the problem is not so much that the child doesn't want to engage in a specific genre, but rather the child simply doesn't enjoy writing in general. I can remember one such child in my first-grade classroom who despite suitable immersion into a variety of authentic writing purposes simply refused to write. I grew extremely frustrated and finally decided to take the pressure off both him and me. I asked him if there was anyone in the classroom whom he liked working with. He mentioned a class peer with whom he played outside of school. I asked him if he would be interested in working with this friend during writer's workshop. He didn't have to compose his own piece; all he had to do was help his friend. Almost immediately there was a change in attitude by my reluctant learner. With the pressure off, he happily helped his friend in the planning, composing, editing, and publishing processes. When his friend's piece was completed he happily announced that they had decided to put both their names on the cover because it was a joint effort. Within three weeks this child started to compose his own pieces and soon became an avid writer. All he needed was to take slow steps without pressure to discover the many joys of being a writer.

Is there time for personal writing during a genre study?

It needs to be made clear that when children engage in writing a specific form of nonfiction, this is part of their personal writing. In individual investigations the children need to be given choice with respect to the content of their exploration. For example, in Maryanne Meza's classroom (Chapter 8), the children made individual decisions on what they wished to investigate with regard to explanatory writing. Apart from their engaging in personal writing encounters with the identified genre, children always need to be given an opportunity to pursue other writing interests if they wish to. In Maryanne's classroom, for example, if a particular child was writing an explanation of why it rains but also wanted to write a birthday card for a member of the class, the child should have the time and the opportunity to do both. From the beginning of the school year Maryanne had established writing journals and a letter-writing center so that her students were always able to pursue many types of writing during writer's workshop. At the same time, the focus of writer's workshop was the specific type of nonfiction writing Maryanne was exploring with her students.

Writer's workshop, like reader's workshop, is not a time when a child is expected to engage exclusively in one task. However, I have found that when children are suitably engaged in a specific study with a strong sense of purpose, they often choose to work almost exclusively in their independent writing in the genre being explored.

How do I help struggling writers during whole-class and independent investigations?

What we always need to be aware of is that writers only struggle if the task before them is too complex or if they are unsure why they are engaging in a specific form of nonfiction writing. I believe the child who sits there chewing on the end of a pencil is often drowning in writer's workshop. This point was clearly demonstrated to me recently as I watched a second-grade teacher give her children the task of writing a letter to a friend. She had appropriately modeled her own letter to a friend prior to having the children compose their own but had not really established a purpose for why these children would want to write to each other in the first place. She had also forgotten to brainstorm with the children possible items that could be included in the letter. Consequently when the children went to write their letters only a handful of children took pen to paper, and these were the most able writers in the class. As I walked around the room I asked many of the struggling writers whom they were writing their letter to. Most of them seemed not to have a clue. Those that did have a specific audience in mind had no idea what they were going to communicate in the letter.

I believe it is essential in a case such as this to call these children together for small-group instruction and break down the writing task into manageable chunks. First, these children need to see a real purpose for writing a letter with an identified audience in mind. Second, they need to talk about and plan the different things they would like to include in their letters. These children would also benefit from working with more able writers who can act as mentors. During writer's workshop children should work in heterogeneous groups at their tables. It is only when the teacher pulls a group together for instruction based on identified needs that homogeneous groupings should occur.

Forms similar to those provided in the appendixes can also be a valuable resource in assisting struggling writers. However, these forms are only meant to be used as a way of breaking down a form of nonfiction writing into specific elements when children are overwhelmed by the enormousness of all the components that need to be included in the piece of writing. They are best used in a small-group setting for struggling writers and should not be used as whole-class activities. In Linda La Porte's classroom (Chapter 7), not all the children required forms to help them write their animal report. Many of Linda's children were able to organize their information on their own, in ways that made sense to them, based on the discoveries they had made about this text type during the whole-class investigation.

I am a kindergarten teacher and most of my children can't write; they only draw. I really want to engage them in nonfiction writing investigations. But what do I do if they can't yet write?

This is a question I am asked often, and is of particular concern to teachers at the beginning of the kindergarten year. This was certainly the case in both Linda and Jessica's classrooms. In both of their classrooms almost all of the children were at the drawing stage of development at the beginning of the school year. These children didn't know the names of the letters of the alphabet and the sounds that each letter made. This, however, did not mean that they were unable to talk about and record their thoughts and ideas; they recorded their thoughts through pictures.

Drawing is children's earliest attempt at representing thought and therefore is also the way they represent their findings during an investigation. Far too often we assume that just because children are unable to use the conventions of print they are unable to engage in nonfiction writing explorations. We need to accept their drawings as their documents. As young learners become immersed in a print-rich environment and engage in shared reading and writing encounters they will begin to use print as well as pictures to represent thought. Until then we need to encourage them to make attempts at writing and also act as scribe to record their thoughts. (Refer to Chapter 5 for further information.)

I have a large number of children in my class. How do I help them all during independent investigations?

The teacher can easily become overwhelmed when thirty children are all engaged in independent investigations; chaos can quickly set in. I have always found that when I am in a state of chaos so are my students and at that point I should stop and rethink my management routines. Many of the teachers of young children that I have worked with found it useful to divide their children into small groups for individual investigations and work with one group at a time while the rest of the children engage in other personal writing encounters or activities in literacy centers. When one group is comfortable with the task at hand, the teacher moves on to work with another group until all the children are actively involved with researching and composing their independent investigations. We also need to consider the value of having children work with each other and not think of ourselves as the only human resource in the classroom. Parent helpers are also helpful, especially when children are engaged in independent investigations and need assistance with research. Teaching children to become independent learners is an ongoing challenge but an essential component of every classroom.

What is important is that management routines be established at the beginning of the school year and that the teacher maintain these routines. My students were so used to our daily writing routines that I never feared when a substitute teacher took the class for the day. My young learners would inform the substitute exactly what our writer's workshop looked like and the routines that needed to be followed. Sharon Taberski (see Chapter 1) is a teacher who is a master of management. Her children spend most of their time engaged in learning, not listening to a barrage of new instructions and routines each day that are completely different from those of the day before.

When my children are engaged in individual investigations the noise level is too high. What can I do about this?

Noise, noise, noise! It is an everyday occurrence and part of our lives as teachers. It is natural that children will become loud, especially during investigations, because their excitement level then is at a peak. I have used noise as an important indicator for me as a teacher, for when the noise level rises it confirms that my children are truly immersed in their learning and want to talk to each other about what they are doing and what they are learning. I never want to discourage my students from talking; still, the fact remains that even though a lot of noise may be constructive, we need to find ways to keep it under control and at an acceptable level.

One suggestion I have shared with many teachers that has proved effective in keeping noise levels at an acceptable level is a what I call a noise clock. Children usually don't realize just how loud they are when they are talking, and what I believe is needed is to give them a visual for the noise level within the classroom. The noise clock is simply a large circle made from oak tag that has a movable dial. The clock is divided into five sections with each section having a number and a visual that shows the children the gradient of noise occurring at any given time (see Figure 11.1).

In the first section of the clock is the number 1 and with it is a picture of the pin. This signifies that it is so quiet that we could hear a pin drop. I ask the children when we need to be this quiet during writer's workshop. I lead them to the understanding that when something is being read to the class or someone is sharing with the whole class, this is how quiet we need to be.

Section 2 carries a picture of a hummingbird. This signifies that there is a hum in the air. This would occur when we are all at our tables writing.

■ **Figure 11.1** A noise clock

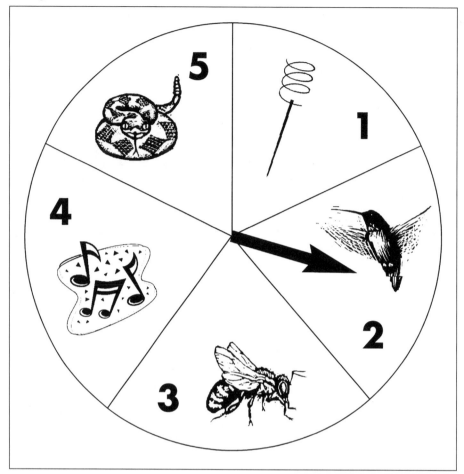

Section 3 has a picture of a bee. This signifies that there is a buzz in the air. This would occur when we are researching and sharing information with each other.

Section 4 carries with it some musical notes. This signifies the noise at a level where we are all singing or chanting.

Section 5 shows a snake. This signifies that a snake has just slithered into the classroom and we are all shouting or screaming. This is always an unacceptable level of noise in our classroom (except of course if there really is a snake at our feet).

I usually color each section of the noise clock a different color to signify its gradient. For example, section 1 may be sky blue to signify peace and calm, whereas section 5 may be red to suggest extreme noise.

During the course of writer's workshop I periodically change the dial and alert the children to what is the acceptable noise level depending on what we

Is That a Fact?

are doing. If the noise level goes higher than acceptable, I change the dial, stop the class, and show them the clock. This strategy is very effective. It gives children visual information about the noise being made and when it is unacceptably loud. It also leads them to understand that noise is okay, but that it needs to vary at different times during writer's workshop.

Another beneficial way of utilizing the noise clock is to make a smaller version and attach a piece of ribbon so that it can hang on a child's neck (see Appendix J for a form that can be used for this). Each day I appoint a noise monitor who wears the clock and has the job of monitoring the noise level and ensuring that we are all operating at an acceptable level of noise. This strategy works well and gives responsibility to the children. I am always amused to watch the loudest members of the class when they wear the noise clock. They quickly become masters of peace and serenity.

The noise clock is only used when needed. Usually after a few weeks, the children keep the noise level at acceptable levels on their own, and at that point I can set it aside. If I find that noise later becomes a problem, I bring back the clock.

We lack the resources necessary to help our children do adequate research. What can we do?

Without adequate resources, the teacher is at a huge disadvantage when attempting to engage children in nonfiction explorations. Providing schools with adequate resources is a long process. Schools first need to identify existing resources before purchasing additional materials. It is amazing just how many wonderful resources are so often locked away in some part of the school, collecting dust. The school librarian can be very helpful in locating existing resources.

Once an inventory of existing supplies is complete, schools need to consider ways of organizing these resources, whether in the form of classroom libraries or a resource area for the entire school to utilize. When all this is done the school will then be able to make informed decisions as to what further resources need to be purchased. These decisions must be based on the requirements that there be an adequate range of materials that deal with different nonfiction genres and that there be a range of readability levels within each genre. (See Chapter 3 as well as the resource sections at the end of Chapters 6 through 10 for further information.)

Schools also need to consider that resources do not take the form only of books, but that cassette tapes, posters, charts, videos, science equipment, and big books are also essential components of a comprehensive resource library. If we want to provide our children with good models of nonfiction writing, classrooms need to be adequately equipped with a variety of resources that both teachers and students can use. In addition, many schools include money for field trips as part of each teacher's budget allocation for nonfiction explorations. These schools have wisely identified the importance of direct observation as an essential ingredient of children's becoming able researchers and writers of nonfiction.

Appendixes

A. Self-Assessment Questionnaire

B. Letter to Parents

C. Forms for a Book of Maps

D. Letter for Author's Box

E. Sharetime Record Sheet

F. Forms for an Instructional Text

G. Forms for an Animal Report

H. Fact Versus Opinion

I. Forms for a Biography

J. Noise Clock

Appendix A: Self-Assessment Questionnaire

Name:

1. What was the reason you wrote this piece?

2. What have you learned about writing _____?
   (Fill in relevant text type—e.g., recipes, scientific explanations, persuasions)

Is That a Fact? Teaching Nonfiction Writing K–3 by Tony Stead. Copyright © 2001. Stenhouse Publishers

3. Where did you find your information?

4. If you had to write another _____ what would you do
   differently?

Is That a Fact? Teaching Nonfiction Writing K–3 by Tony Stead. Copyright © 2001. Stenhouse Publishers

Appendix B: Letter to Parents

Dear Parents,

Over the coming weeks your child will be involved in a nonfiction investigation about _____. The children will have lots of questions they want answered, and you can be of assistance to them. Below are some ways to help.

1. Talk to your child about the topic. Ask what he or she already knows and tell what you know. Write or draw this information together, and have your child bring it to school.

2. Join your child as a member of the local library and see if you can find books about the topic for you to read together.

3. If you have an Internet connection, see what you can find out. You will probably discover a lot of information and much of it may use language unfamiliar to your child, so don't overload him or her with facts. Just put into your own words some interesting information. *We don't want the children to come into the classroom with pages of information that you have simply printed from the Internet.* It is far more valuable for them to come into the classroom with a few facts they can talk about in their own words.

Thank you so much for your help.

Yours sincerely,

Is That a Fact? Teaching Nonfiction Writing K–3 by Tony Stead. Copyright © 2001. Stenhouse Publishers

My Book of Maps

Written by

Is That a Fact? Teaching Nonfiction Writing K–3 by Tony Stead. Copyright © 2001. Stenhouse Publishers

Can you draw a map of your classroom? Remember to include the key.

A map of my classroom	Key

Is That a Fact? Teaching Nonfiction Writing K–3 by Tony Stead. Copyright © 2001. Stenhouse Publishers

Can you draw a map of your school? Remember to include the key.

A map of my school	Key

Can you draw a map of your room? Remember to include the key.

A map of my room at home	Key

Is That a Fact? Teaching Nonfiction Writing K–3 by Tony Stead. Copyright © 2001. Stenhouse Publishers

Can you draw a map of your neighborhood? Remember to include the key.

A map of my neighborhood	Key

Appendix D: Letter for Author's Box

How to Use the Author's Box

Dear Parents,

Congratulations! Your child has the author's box tonight and together you can help your child experience the joys of being a writer. Below are some tips on how you can achieve this.

- Talk to your child about what he or she is writing at school and work together on it at home.

- Discuss and write about things together that interest you—for example, a funny thing that happened, your favorite animal, a book of favorite recipes, a biography on your favorite TV or music celebrity.

- Your child may be taking home this author's box to finish publishing an investigation he or she has been researching. If this is the case, encourage and assist your child. We want our children to do their very best and to be proud of what they do.

Ways to Care for Our Author's Box

- Please make sure that everything is put back where it belongs.

- If anything breaks, try to replace it or put something new in the box as a substitute.

- Make sure the author's box comes back with your child tomorrow. We have many writers in our class who are all eager to take home this box.

- If you would like to donate materials to the author's box, please do so. We greatly appreciate anything you have to spare, such as extra erasers, markers, pencils, paper, oak tag, stickers, letter stencils, and the like.

Enjoy!

Is That a Fact? Teaching Nonfiction Writing K–3 by Tony Stead. Copyright © 2001. Stenhouse Publishers

Appendix E: Sharetime Record Sheet

Name

How to

Written by

What you need:

What you do:

What you found in the experiment:

My Animal Report

About

Written by

What my animal looks like

What my animal eats

Is That a Fact? Teaching Nonfiction Writing K–3 by Tony Stead. Copyright © 2001. Stenhouse Publishers

What my animal does

Other interesting facts

Appendix H: Fact Versus Opinion

Name:

Look at your information to see what are facts and what are opinions.

These are my facts	These are my opinions

A Biography of

Written by

Where the person was born

About the person's family

Is That a Fact? Teaching Nonfiction Writing K–3 by Tony Stead. Copyright © 2001. Stenhouse Publishers

The person's favorite things

Other interesting things about this person

Is That a Fact? Teaching Nonfiction Writing K–3 by Tony Stead. Copyright © 2001. Stenhouse Publishers

What people like about this person

Note: Cut out this arrow and use it on the clock.

Bibliography

Children's Books Cited

Chan, H. 2001. *The Key to Maps*. Washington, DC: National Geographic Society.

Cullen, E. 1996. *Spiders*. New York: Mondo Publishing.

Drew, D. 1997. *From Egg to Butterfly*. Crystal Lake, IL: Rigby.

Harwayne, S. 1996. *What's Cooking?* New York: Mondo Publishing.

Hopping, L. J. 2000. *Today's Weather Is . . .: A Book of Experiments*. New York: Mondo Publishing.

James, S. M. 1996. *Meet the Octopus*. New York: Mondo Publishing.

Lehn, B. 1988. *What Is a Scientist?* Brookfield, CT: Millbrook Press.

Sendak, M. 1963. *Where the Wild Things Are*. New York: Harper Trophy.

Snowball, D. 1995. *Chickens*. New York: Mondo Publishing.

Stead, T. 2000. *Should There Be Zoos? A Persuasive Text*. New York: Mondo Publishing.

Viorst, J. 1972. *Alexander and the Terrible, Horrible, No Good, Very Bad Day*. New York: Macmillan.

Professional References

Ashton-Warner, S. 1963. *Teacher*. New York: Simon and Schuster.

Baker, D., C. Semple, and T. Stead. 1990. *How Big Is the Moon? Whole Math in Action*. Portsmouth, NH: Heinemann.

Beaver, J. 2001. *Developmental Reading Assessment*. Parsippany, NJ: Celebration Press.

Bolton, F., and D. Snowball. 1993. *Ideas for Spelling*. Portsmouth, NH: Heinemann.

Bolton, F., C. Montgomery, D. Snowball, and T. Stead. 1997. *Bookshop Teacher's Resource Book*. Stage 3. New York: Mondo Publishing.

———. 1998. *Bookshop Teacher's Resource Book*. Beanbag Books. New York: Mondo Publishing.

Britton, J., T. Burgess, N. Martin, A. Mcleod, and H. Rosen. 1975. *The Development of Writing Abilities*. London: Macmillian.

Brown, H., and B. Cambourne. 1987. *Read and Retell*. Portsmouth, NH: Heinemann.

Bruner, J. 1986. *Actual Minds, Possible Worlds*. Cambridge: Harvard University Press.

Bull, G., and M. Anstey. 1991. "Achieving Independent Learning: Drawing Process and Genre Together." In F. Mckay, ed., *Public and Private Lessons: The Language of Teaching and Learning*. Carlton, Australia: Australian Reading Association.

Calkins, L. M. 1994. *The Art of Teaching Writing*, new edition. Portsmouth, NH: Heinemann.

————. 1991. *Living Between the Lines*. Portsmouth, NH: Heinemann.

Cambourne, B. 1988. *The Whole Story: Natural Learning and the Acquisition of Literacy in the Classroom*. New York: Scholastic.

Cazden, C. 1988. *Classroom Discourse: The Language of Teaching and Learning*. Portsmouth, NH: Heinemann.

Chandler, K., and the Mapleton Teacher-Research Group. 1999. *Spelling Inquiry: How One Elementary School Caught the Mnemonic Plague*. Portland, ME: Stenhouse.

Christie, F. 1992. Genre-Based Approaches to Teaching English Literacy. Paper presented at the Second National Language Education Seminar. University Utara. Kedah, Malaysia.

————, ed. 1984. *Children Writing: Study Guide*. Geelong, Australia: Deakin University Press.

Clay, M. 1991. *Becoming Literate: The Construction of Inner Control*. Portsmouth, NH: Heinemann.

————. 1992. *The Early Detection of Reading Difficulties*. Portsmouth, NH: Heinemann.

————. 1993. *An Observation Survey of Early Literacy Achievement*. Portsmouth, NH: Heinemann.

Cullum, A. 1971. *The Geranium on the Window Sill Just Died, but Teacher You Went Right On*. London: Harlin Quist.

Derewianka, B. 1990. *Exploring How Texts Work*. Rozelle, New South Wales, Australia: Primary English Teaching Association.

Duthie, C. 1996. *True Stories: Nonfiction Literacy in the Primary Classroom*. Portland, ME: Stenhouse.

Education Department of Western Australia. 1997. *First Steps*. Writing Developmental Continuum. Portsmouth, NH: Heinemann.

Elliott, M. 1991. "What Is This Thing Called 'Genre'?" *Journal of Australian Council of TESOL Associations*, 1, 2: 5–7.

Fisher, B. 1991. *Joyful Learning: A Whole Language Kindergarten*. Portsmouth, NH: Heinemann.

Fletcher, R. 1993. *What a Writer Needs*. Portsmouth, NH: Heinemann.

Fountas, I., and G. S. Pinnell. 1996. *Guided Reading: Good First Teaching for All Children*. Portsmouth, NH: Heinemann.

————. 1999. *Matching Books to Readers: Using Leveled Books in Guided Reading, K–3*. Portsmouth, NH: Heinemann.

Gentry, J. R. 1987. *Spel . . . Is a Four-Letter Word*. Portsmouth, NH: Heinemann.

————. 2000. *The Literacy Map: Guiding Children to Where They Need to Be (K–3)*. New York: Mondo Publishing.

Gentry, J. R., and J. W. Gillet. 1993. *Teaching Kids to Spell*. Portsmouth, NH: Heinemann.

Goodman, K. 1986. *What's Whole About Whole Language?* Portsmouth, NH: Heinemann.

Goodman, Y. 1982. "Kidwatching: Evaluating Written Language Development." *Australian Journal of Reading,* 5, 3.

Graves, D. 1981. *Donald Graves in Australia: "Children Want to Write."* Rozelle, New South Wales, Australia: Primary English Teaching Association.

———. 1983. *Writing: Teachers and Children at Work.* Portsmouth, NH: Heinemann.

———. 1989. *Investigate Nonfiction.* Portsmouth, NH: Heinemann.

———. 1994. *A Fresh Look at Writing.* Portsmouth, NH: Heinemann.

Gray, B. 1987. "How Natural Is 'Natural' Language Teaching: Employing Wholistic Methodology in the Classroom." *Australian Journal of Early Childhood,* 12, 4.

Halliday, M. 1985. *An Introduction to Functional Grammar.* London: Edward Arnold.

Harrison, A., and M. R. McEvedy. 1987. *From Speech to Writing: Modelling, Evaluating, and Negotiating Genres.* Malvern, Australia: Robert Andersen and Associates.

Harste, J., V. Woodward, and C. Burke. 1984. *Language Stories and Literacy Lessons.* Portsmouth, NH: Heinemann.

Harvey, S. 1998. *Nonfiction Matters: Reading, Writing, and Research in Grades 3–8.* Portland, ME: Stenhouse.

Harwayne, S. 1999. *Going Public: Priorities and Practice at the Manhattan New School.* Portsmouth, NH: Heinemann.

———. 2000. *Lifetime Guarantees: Towards Ambitious Literacy Teaching.* Portsmouth, NH: Heinemann.

Holdaway, D. 1979. *The Foundations of Literacy.* Portsmouth, NH: Heinemann.

Kress, G. 1982. *Learning to Write.* London: Routledge and Kegan Paul.

Martin, J. 1985. *Factual Writing: Exploring and Challenging Social Reality.* Geelong, Australia: Deakin University Press.

Metropolitan East Disadvantaged Schools Program. 1989. *A Brief Introduction to Genre.* Sydney, Australia: Language and Social Power Project.

Moline, S. 1995. *I See What You Mean: Children at Work with Visual Information.* Portland, ME: Stenhouse.

Mooney, M. 1990. *Reading To, With, and By Children.* New York: Richard C. Owen.

Murray, D. M. 1982. *Learning by Teaching: Selected Articles on Writing and Teaching.* Portsmouth, NH: Heinemann.

———. 1984. *Write to Learn.* New York: Holt, Rinehart. OP.

Newkirk, T. 1989. *More Than Stories: The Range of Children's Writing.* Portsmouth, NH: Heinemann.

Painter, C. 1986. "The Role of Learning to Speak and Learning to Write." In C. Painter and J. R. Martin, eds., *Writing to Mean: Teaching Genres Across the Curriculum.* Queensland, Australia: Applied Linguistic Association of Australia. Occasional Papers no. 9.

Parkes, B. 2000. *Read It Again! Revisiting Shared Reading.* Portland, ME: Stenhouse.

Pigdon, K., and M. Woolley. 1992. *The Big Picture: Integrating Children's Learning.* Armadale, Australia: Eleanor Curtain Publishing.

Pinnell, G. S., and I. C. Fountas. 1998. *Word Matters.* Portsmouth, NH: Heinemann.

———. 1999. *Interactive Writing.* Portsmouth, NH: Heinemann.

Semple, C., and T. Stead. 1991. "Children as Maths Researchers: Learning Language and Maths Together." In E. Furniss and P. Green, eds., *The Literacy Connection: Language and Learning Across the Curriculum*. South Yarra, Australia: Eleanor Curtain Publishing.

Smith, F. 1982. *Writing and the Writer*. New York: Holt, Rinehart, and Winston.

———. 1986. *Insult to Intelligence: The Bureaucratic Invasion of Our Classrooms*. Portsmouth, NH: Heinemann.

———. 1988. *Joining the Literacy Club: Further Essays into Education*. Portsmouth, NH: Heinemann.

Snowball, D., and F. Bolton. 1999. *Spelling K–8: Planning and Teaching*. Portland, ME: Stenhouse.

State of Victoria Department of Education. 1998. *Early Years Teaching Writers in the Classroom*. South Melbourne, Australia: Addison Wesley Longman. Distributed in the United States by Mondo Publishing, New York.

Stead, T. 1992. "Setting the Scene as Head of the Family." *Teaching Pre-K–8*. September issue.

Taberski, S. 2000. *On Solid Ground: Strategies for Teaching Reading K–3*. Portsmouth, NH: Heinemann.

Warner, Sylvia Ashton. 1963. *Teacher*. New York: Simon and Schuster.

Vygotsky, L. S. 1978. *Mind in Society: The Development of Higher Psychological Processes*, ed. M. Cole, V. John-Steiner, S. Scribner, and E. Souberman. Cambridge: Harvard University Press.

Wing Jan, L. 1991. *Write Ways: Modelling Writing Forms*. Melbourne, Australia: Oxford University Press.